Multimodal Studies

Routledge Studies in Multimodality

EDITED BY KAY L. O'HALLORAN, *National University of Singapore*

**1. New Perspectives on Narrative
and Multimodality**
Edited by Ruth Page

2. Multimodal Studies
Exploring Issues and Domains
Edited by Kay L. O'Halloran and
Bradley A. Smith

Multimodal Studies

Exploring Issues and Domains

Edited by Kay L. O'Halloran and Bradley A. Smith

Routledge
Taylor & Francis Group
New York   London

First published 2011
by Routledge
711 Third Avenue, New York, NY 10017

Simultaneously published in the UK
by Routledge
2 Park Square, Milton Park, Abingdon, Oxfordshire OX14 4RN

First issued in paperback 2014

Routledge is an imprint of the Taylor and Francis Group, an informa company

Typeset in Sabon by IBT Global.

Library of Congress Cataloging-in-Publication Data
Multimodal studies : exploring issues and domains / edited by Kay L. O'Halloran and Bradley A. Smith.
   p. cm. — (Routledge studies in multimodality ; 2)
   Includes bibliographical references and index.
1. Modality (Linguistics)   2. Semiotics.   I. O'Halloran, Kay L.   II. Smith, Bradley A.
   P99.4.M6M85 2011
   302.2'2—dc22
   2010039339

ISBN13: 978-0-415-88822-6 (hbk)
ISBN13: 978-0-415-75441-5 (pbk)

Dedicated to
Michael O'Toole and Theo van Leeuwen
who have inspired as well as laid the foundations
for much of the subsequent and ongoing work
in multimodal studies

Contents

Figures

Tables

Copyright Permissions Acknowledgments

The authors are grateful to the following organisations for the right to reproduce the images which appear in this book.

CHAPTER 2

Figure 2.5, 2.6   Reprinted with kind permission from Dorling Kindersley Limited

CHAPTER 4

Figure 4.3 (Image 1)   Reprinted with kind permission from Alison Ho, Tan Chong Motor Sales Pte Ltd

Figure 4.3 (Image 2)   Reprinted with kind permission from Junn Chia, Cycle and Carriage Industries Pte Ltd, Mercedes—Benz Marketing

Figure 4.3 (Image 3)   Reprinted with kind permission from Tina Sutinah, Borneo motors

Figure 4.3 (Image 4)   Reprinted with kind permission from David Tay, Euroautomobile Pte Ltd

CHAPTER 5

Figure 5.1a   Copyright owner: Staatsbibliothek zu Berlin—Preussischer Kulturbesitz Musikabteilung mit Mendelssohn-Archiv, shelf mark: Mus.ms.autogr. Beethoven Mendelssohn-Stiftg.

Figure 5.1b   Source: Wikimedia Commons User: Carloferrari
http://commons.wikimedia.org/wiki/File:Extrait_toccata_
kapsberger.png
License: Public domain

Figure 5.2a   Source: Wikimedia Commons Photo: Daniel Williams
Retrieved from: http://commons.wikimedia.org/wiki/
File:Reactable_Multitouch.jpg
License: Creative Commons Attribution/Share-Alike License

Figure 5.2b   Photo: Marcos Alonso used by direct permission from
image author

CHAPTER 7

Figure 7.1   Reprinted with kind permission from Marc Burton

Figure 7.2   M. C. Escher's "Day and Night" © 2009 The M.C. Escher
Company-Holland. All rights reserved. www.mcescher.com

Figure 7.3   Reprinted with kind permission from University of
Technology, Sydney

CHAPTER 8

Figure 8.3a, 8.3   Reprinted with kind permission from Jasmin Sydow

Figure 8.3c   Reprinted with kind permission from Stephan Bethauser

Figure 8.3d   Reprinted with kind permission from Jenny Arendholz

Figure 8.5a, 8.7   Reprinted with kind permission from Jorg Junige

Figure 8.5b   Reprinted with kind permission from Steve Crombie

Figure 8.6b   Reprinted with kind permission from Mark M. Lambert

CHAPTER 12

Figure 12.1a   Promotional Figure for *Baby Touch Cot Book* (Land,
2007)

Figure 12.1b   *Bouncy Lamb*, two panels (Church, 1999)

Figure 12.2a   Double page spread from *At Home with Maisy*, (Cousins, 2002)
Cousins, L (2002). *At Home with Maisy*. London. Walker Books
first published in Cousins, L (1999). *Maisy Makes Gingerbread*. Somerville, MA: Candlewick Press

Figure 12.3b   Double-page spread from *Rascal the Dragon* (Jennings, 2004. Lea, illus)
Jennings, P (2004). *Rascal the Dragon*. Camberwell. Puffin.

Figure 12.5a   Double-page spread from *Are We There Yet?* (Lester, 2005)
Lester, A (2005). *Are We There Yet?* London. Penguin.

Figure 12.5b   Double-page spread from *The Giraffe and the Pelly and Me*. (Dahl, 2003)

Dahl, R (2003). *The Giraffe and Pelly and Me*. London. Johnathan Cape.

Acknowledgments

This research was supported by the National Research Foundation (NRF) in Singapore through the Interactive Digital Media Research and Development Program Office (IDMPO), under Research Grant NRF2007IDM-IDM002–066.

The editors would like to extend their sincere gratitude to Melany Baring Legaspi for the excellent work done in preparing the manuscript for publication. Sincere thanks to Hanizah Ali who has assisted in more ways than one. Both of you are competent, efficient, helpful and good-humoured in everything you do.

1 Multimodal Studies

Kay L. O'Halloran and Bradley A. Smith

The phenomenon of multimodality has, as Jewitt (2009: 3) observes, generated interest 'across many disciplines . . . against the backdrop of considerable social change'. Contemporary societies are grappling with the social implications of the rapid increase in sophistication and range of multimodal practices, particularly within interactive digital media, so that the study of multimodality also becomes essential within an increasing range of practical domains. As a result of this increasing interest in multimodality, scholars, teachers and practitioners are on the one hand uncovering many different issues arising from its study, such as those of theory and methodology, while also exploring multimodality within an increasing range of domains, for example, corporate advertising, cartoons, museums etc (e.g. Bednarek and Martin 2010; Jewitt 2009; Ventola and Moya 2009).

Such an increase in interest in multimodality heralds the emergence of a distinct field of study within which a diverse range of scholars and practitioners converge to discuss phenomena and issues specific to multimodal study and develop theories and methodologies appropriate to such a field. Yet at the present state, as Jewitt suggests (2009: 2), '[m]ultimodality, it could be argued, strictly speaking, refers to a field of application rather than a theory'. Kress (2009: 54) similarly observes that 'multimodality as such is not a theory even though it is often used as if it were. The term maps a domain of enquiry'. Nevertheless, it is a field that requires the (Jewitt 2009: 2) 'ongoing development of theories that account for the multimodal'. Thus, as Jewitt argues (2009: 12), 'multimodality can be understood as a theory, a perspective or a field of enquiry or a methodological application'.

While the term multimodality, as such, does 'map a domain of enquiry' (Kress 2009), we would like to draw an important distinction here between studies of multimodality, which focus on particular domains of enquiry (multimodal phenomena within specific contexts, media, etc), and multimodal studies as a field of expertise, distinct from linguistics or any other field of expertise. The reason for this distinction is that while multimodality has tended to be explored within specific sites and for specific disciplinary purposes, any study of multimodal phenomena inevitably raises issues that have wider relevance to the study of multimodality in general, while proposals for solutions to such issues have relevance and application to any particular study of multimodality. In this sense, although there can be no (single) theory of multimodality, certainly there can, should be and indeed are already emerging theories and descriptions of and methodologies for studying multimodal phenomena (semiotic resources, modes and their interactions in multimodal discourse)—in the same way as there are theories (not a theory) of language within the field of linguistics potentially applicable to any study (within or outside of linguistics) involving a consideration of language. The recognition of the need to develop and apply theories of multimodality is in fact a prerequisite for the emergence of a distinct field of multimodal studies, as a site for the development of such theories.

Although most scholars working within this emerging field do come from established disciplines (as identified in Kress 2009), with their own theoretical and descriptive orientations, styles and concerns, there has been a clear movement towards the development of generalisations applicable beyond the particular concerns of those studying within particular domains of reference or with particular academic backgrounds and with application to the study of multimodal phenomena in general. Scholars such as O'Toole (1994/2010), Kress and van Leeuwen (2006), O'Halloran (2005), Bateman (2008), Lemke (2009) and Baldry and Thibault (2006) have, for quite some time, devoted energy to developing theoretical, descriptive and methodological resources particularly adapted to and for the study of multimodality, in general, and in facing issues arising from such developments. Jewitt's comprehensive (2009) volume is an exemplar of the diversity of interests and issues in and approaches to contemporary multimodal studies and offers itself a persuasive argument that while there is no single theory of multimodality as such, there are certainly distinct theoretical concepts and frameworks emerging from the study of multimodality as a field. Martin's (2010: 1) contribution also is explicitly 'concerned with developing the general theoretical framework informing' research into the variety of semiotic resources used by humans to communicate meaning within that volume. The development of such theories, methodologies etc to account for multimodal phenomena across multiple domains of application is therefore evidence that such a field is emerging to take its place alongside other established fields such as linguistics.

Thus it is in two senses that we refer to the emergence of a distinct multimodal studies field: as both the mapping of a domain of enquiry and as a site for the development of theories, descriptions and methodologies specific to and adapted for the study of multimodality (although potentially applicable, at certain levels of generality, to other distinct fields of study, including linguistics). In the first sense, multimodal studies applies existing generalisations (of theory, description, methodology) to the exploration of specific multimodal phenomena, sets of texts or contexts in order to cast new light on those domains. Such domains might be more broadly defined areas of multimodality; e.g. 'language of displayed art' (O'Toole 1994), 'grammar of visual design' (Kress and van Leeuwen 2006), 'speech, music, sound' (van Leeuwen 1999), 'mathematics discourse' (O'Halloran 2005); particular (sets of) semiotic resources in interaction; e.g. images and text (e.g. Martinec 2005; Unsworth and Cleirigh 2009) and gesture and phonology (e.g. Zappavigna, Cleirigh, Dwyer and Martin, 2010); or sites where multimodal discourse is at issue, such as classroom discourse (e.g. Clarke 2001; Jewitt 2006), corporate advertising, video and interactive digital media such as games and the Internet, mobile media etc (e.g. Jewitt 2009; Ventola and Moya 2009).

In the second sense multimodal studies, such as those listed above, use texts or types of text to explore, illustrate, problematise or apply general issues in multimodal studies, such as those arising from the development of theoretical frameworks specific to the study of multimodal phenomena (e.g. modeling semiotic resources other than language, inter-semiosis and the integration of semiotic resources and resemiotisation of multimodal artefacts and events) or methodological issues (including challenges in transcription, analysis and representation within publications). In any particular work, of course, one may always find a complementarity of attention, to the specifics of a particular corpus or area of research, practice or teaching, and to the more general issues that inevitably arise when considering particular domains of research. Both O'Toole's (1994) and Kress and van Leeuwen's (2006) pioneering works, while extending the study of 'language' and 'grammar' into new domains, were also clearly foundation texts exploring issues of theory and methodology of general significance to multimodal studies.

This categorisation is therefore perhaps better seen as a continuum, the two different orientations—focus on general theoretical and methodological issues, or on specific domains of study—representing poles along which individual works range in terms of their major concerns. This approach acknowledges that most, if not all studies, no matter how focused on an issue of general relevance or a specific domain of application, contribute both to the development of our understanding of multimodality in general as well as to the application of that understanding to the study of specific domains of multimodality. The main point to be made here is that the specific demands of multimodal phenomena motivate ways of approaching, conceptualising or *doing* multimodal studies distinct from those which have been standard practice within the study of language or other (particularly monomodal) semiotic phenomena, but that such demands only appear when analysts are confronted with specific multimodal phenomena in actual texts. Such considerations appear relevant if we are to begin considering multimodal studies as a field, not only of application but also as the site of emerging theories, descriptions and methodologies.

EXPLORING ISSUES AND DOMAINS

In this volume our aim is to present new explorations within the emerging field of multimodal studies by bringing together fourteen chapters that both discuss issues arising from the study of multimodality and explore the scope of this emerging field within specific domains of multimodal phenomena, to map out an exemplar of current multimodal studies work. The chapters in this volume are thus organised into these two broad categories according to the main focus within each: either on exploring general issues arising from multimodal studies or on extending multimodal studies into or focusing on specific domains of multimodality.

However, as discussed in the previous section, there is always a complementarity of attention within any work on multimodality, to the specifics of a particular corpus or area of research, practice or teaching, and to the more general issues that inevitably arise when exploring these domains. Generalities tend towards obscurity or irrelevance if developed without reference to the specifics of actual discourse, while insights obtained into specific texts or types of texts remain trivial or barren, or are indeed impossible, if uninformed by the consideration of more general perspectives on theory and methodology. We wish therefore to present the various studies in this volume as representing a dialectic and complementarity, between the exploration of issues of general significance to multimodal studies and the exploration of specific domains of multimodality, while, however, also acknowledging that some works do tend towards one or other of these main areas of focus.

We propose, therefore, following our observations in the previous section, to present this categorisation as a continuum, the two different orientations—focus on general issues, or on specific domains of study—representing poles of a cline, along which individual works range in terms of their major concerns. The aim of this approach is to characterise the works in terms of their main focuses, while at the same time highlighting the productiveness of this complementarity of focus both within individual chapters and across the volume as a whole.

The terms 'issues' and 'domains' are used here in a very general sense, in the present volume. First, issues may be those involving theoretical or methodological apparatus, the comparison of or application of different theoretical or analytical approaches or models to account for the integration of different semiotic modes. Thus Bateman's Chapter 2 is concerned with the theory of semiotic mode, with the aim of developing a definition of a semiotic mode that supports the identification of more fine-grained semiotic modes than has hitherto been the case, and which has greater applicability and responsiveness to the needs of multimodal texts. Drawing on social semiotic approaches to multimodality, but also upon work within other fields such as cognitive science, computer science and film studies, the chapter begins by problematising the tendency within multimodal studies towards the application of a priori assumptions with respect to this important aspect of multimodal theory: in particular the assumptions that such categorisations are self-evident and/or aligned with sensory modalities (visual, auditory modalities etc). Bateman is very much focused on theory in his discussion, but he demonstrates through consideration of empirical analysis how such a characterisation of semiotic modes can be of assistance in analytical tasks.

In Chapter 3 Smith considers the consequences of taking different approaches to the study of multimodal phenomena, finding analogies in the history of intonation study. Exploring bottom-up (anatomistic) and top-down (functional) approaches to intonation description, he shows how two different theoretical approaches to the study of intonation can yield different results in terms of analysis and in terms of what gets analysed and argues that each approach thus has its own affordances and constraints in terms of its capacity for making statements of meaning about semiotic phenomena. He also explores variation in the interpretation of a written transcript into speech, the implications of this potential variation for literate cultures in general and concludes with some observations of relevance to theory and practice in multimodal studies.

Feng explores the calibration of a cognitivist perspective with aspects of social semiotic theory in Chapter 4: in particular, in relation to the construction and viewer interpretation of spatial orientations and page layout and the construction of persuasive ideology through such resources. The comparison of different theoretical perspectives is however firmly grounded in the analysis of a corpus of 100 static visual car advertisements from newspapers, magazines and the Internet.

Berry and Wyse discuss issues arising from the design of tangible interfaces for music composition in Chapter 5, in particular, the relations of the abstract and material planes in music and in computational interfaces. The discussion combines perspectives from the study of music, including discussions of the composition process, inspiration and execution with respect to instruments in their relations to and representations of musical abstraction, from computing, in particular the development of graphical user interfaces, and also from Piaget's observations of child development of formal thinking through concrete operations. They observe that tangible interfaces generally offer advantages in terms of their physical accessibility and nature, features that are of benefit to adults as well as children, but are limited in what they can offer in terms of the large-scale abstractions that motivate and constitute a significant aspect of music composition.

Goebel draws upon ethnomethodology, linguistic anthropology and studies of embodied interaction to present an exploration of the concept of 'enregisterment' in Chapter 6. Via the analysis of an episode taken from a corpus of shows from an Indonesian television serial, Goebel explores how multimodal signs become emblems of identity leading to the formation of a 'semiotic register', by which interactants orient to one another with respect to characteristic signs of their personhood. Goebel teases out the distinctive affordances of the televisual medium within this genre for representing personhood in relation to ethnicity and social relations and discusses how the persistence of particular semiotic encounters over time, across a variety of multimodal signs such as facial expressions, gestures, prosodies and the like, creates an emergent semiotic register which then forms the context for interpretation of such emblematic signs. The chapter thus contains important suggestions towards the theory and analysis of multimodal signs, particularly the integrative analysis of multiple signs within multimodal communicative acts.

In Chapter 7, the final chapter in the 'Issues' section of the volume, Van Leeuwen is ostensibly concerned with an argument for and suggestions towards the study of a new domain, urging a new 'semiotics of decoration'. But for van Leeuwen, this domain of application is very abstractly identified, 'decoration' representing here a particular philosophical approach to design within different modes, materials and eras—in dress, architecture, PowerPoint, language, music, typography etc in the nineteenth and twentieth centuries—which is contrasted with the bare functionalism of the Bauhaus and other similar approaches to design. However, in extending and thus defining the domain of multimodal studies this way, van Leeuwen in fact models an approach to multimodality, one which has important consequences for the way in which the emerging field of multimodal studies might develop. He shows that, as semioticians, we need attend to meaning-making activities beyond those traditionally thought of or attended to as such. Not for the first time, van Leeuwen may have sketched here not only a whole sub-field for multimodal studies but also an approach to doing multimodal semiotics.

In the same way that the term 'issues' in this volume encompasses a broad range of theoretical and methodological concerns, 'domains' of multimodal phenomena may be defined in a variety of ways, as evidenced in van Leeuwen's chapter. Like van Leeuwen, Eisenlauer, although interested in a particular domain, 'personal publishing texts', in fact explores a broader domain of study in Chapter 8: social networking as a category, distinct from the old and new media through which such social action has historically been mediated. However, here the domain itself is clearly the primary concern, with the discussion being based upon the analysis of an interesting and valuable corpus of data: examples of the German Posiealbum or 'poetry album', a site for social networking since the mid-sixteenth century, persisting into the twentieth century primarily amongst school pupils. Eisenlauer applies a diachronic perspective on a new media form, Web 2.0 social network sites, showing the continuities and also the differences between new and old forms of media (again, similar to van Leeuwen who explores decoration across different modes and media and thus shows the semiotic continuities between them). Nevertheless, in relating the analysis of higher-level social contexts and communicative structures to their expression in lower-level media resources, Eisenlauer thus models a useful approach to multimodal analysis.

Maier explores the domain of marketing discourse in Chapter 9, specifically the multimodal communication of knowledge within eco-business contexts. While clearly focused on this domain as an area of sustained interest, Maier seeks 'to identify how the meaning-making potentials of language and images are integrated, and how this multimodal integration influences the persuasive communication of knowledge types', with a 'central focus on the model of analysis'. Maier explores the issue of interdependencies between different semiotic modes, with the verbal and visual modes of discourse being shown to subvert rather than complement one another, thereby identifying an important change in advertising discourse from persuasion to presenting eco-friendly credentials. The chapter also orientates to practitioners within this domain by offering recommendations for those engaged in producing marketing discourse with respect to discrepancies between what such discourse is ostensibly aiming to convey and what it actually (multimodally) communicates.

The focus in Lim, Nekmat and Nahar's Chapter 10 is on new media literacy, broadening the study of new media to address a range of issues with respect to the changing demands made of consumers of contemporary media and multimodal communication. The critical link is made between consumption and production—their integration within an understanding of the new media landscape; and the need for a multimodally literate media consumer is identified, a range of key literacies discussed and continuities observed between the critical literacies of contemporary and traditional media practices and also contemporary refinements of these literacies. While the authors point to the changing responsibilities of producers and consumers of new media, with a greater pressure on consumers' critical media literacy, greater transparency on the part of media producers is nevertheless also urged.

Jewitt has a similar focus on multimodal literacy in Chapter 11, specifically the consequences for pedagogic practice within UK schools of the use of interactive digital technology—the interactive whiteboard (IWB)—this as part of a more general focus on 'School English through a multimodal lens'. A key perspective is the diachronic one: the changes since year 2000 in the technological landscape of typical UK classrooms and the use of various multimodal resources and practices. However, pointing to the relations of multimodal communicative practices and competencies and the evolving critical social contexts within which such practices occur, Jewitt poses several questions regarding the types of modes available and their uses, the changing positions of teachers and students in the classroom and the kinds of texts entering and being produced in the English classroom, questions that will resonate beyond this particular domain of study. A general theme for multimodal studies articulated here is that changes in technologies and modalities do not come with their own immanent meanings, uses and significances but are conditioned and constructed within the wider contexts of prevailing and emerging social practices and conventions.

Multimodal literacy again figures as a focus in Chapter 12, with Wignell's specific domain of interest being children's picture books. Wignell presents an ontogenetic study of the changes that occur to the relationships between images and written text in picture books for children of increasing ages. The discussion is based on large-scale and detailed small-scale analytical treatments of a large corpus of picture books: sorted into a continuum according to amount of written text and relative prominence of images and writing and then mapped onto age groups, with a detailed metafunctional analysis following of a sample of texts from each category. The findings show that the amounts and relations of image and text change over increasing age groups, with the study revealing a shift from foregrounding of the interpersonal metafunction in books for younger infants to a less interpersonal prominence in books for older children (an increasing focus on ideational and textual aspect of literate discourse), corresponding with other changes along the same timeline. Wignell identifies other key tendencies in the move along the ontogenetic timeline, for example, the move from a tendency for words to depend on images to the reverse, where images depend on the words for interpretation—that is, representing an apprenticeship into reading written text.

Ventola's Chapter 13 explores the domain of home styling. Her choice of text upon which the analysis and discussion are based—her own home, before and after a professional home 'makeover'—allows her to foreground different approaches to the semioticisation of home living space, in particular the differing ways in which inhabitants and professional home decorators interpret and design the same living space within the context/s of the discourses and functions of/within those spaces, as interpreted through the lens of social semiotic theory and description. Ventola points to the professional separation of, for example, architecture and building, and with these understandings of how people inhabit and construe their living spaces and conduct their semiotic social activities within them, advocates a holistic approach that takes into account all of these aspects, both in terms of multimodal studies and its application to interior design tasks.

In Chapter 14 O'Toole presents a diachronic study of the popular satirical cartoon television series, 'South Park' from its pre-digital to digital phases of production. O'Toole shows how the semiotic affordances available to and exploited by the producers have changed over time and the consequences of this multimodal evolution: what has and hasn't changed in the multimodal discourse and ideology of the series. A hallmark of O'Toole's pioneering application of systemic functional theory to the analysis of visual art is his emphasis on enjoying works of art and on attending closely to actual texts as the basis of developing descriptive, methodological and theoretical generalisations, making his work, and the issues it raises, clearly presented and very accessible. O'Toole importantly identifies the difficulties inherent in presenting a discussion of an audiovisual text where much of the discussion relies upon some form of annotated representation of the audiovisual (multimodal) aspects of the text under examination. His detailed textual annotations thus form the main basis for the discussion, allowing the reader to reference the aspects of the source text of essence to the analysis and argument.

The basic principle for the categorisation of chapters into the two sections above is, 'does the study and its conclusions orientate more to the study of multimodality in general or to the study of a specific domain of multimodality?'. Yet, as discussed, the various chapters can be thought of as being arrayed along a continuum in terms of focus, rather than simply belonging to a category. Bateman's Chapter 2 and O'Toole's Chapter 14 are thus construed as standing the 'closest' to each of the 'poles' of this cline. While Bateman's chapter does draw on empirical analysis from specific domains (but from secondary texts), and O'Toole's chapter clearly raises issues of significance to multimodal studies in general, in both these chapters there is a clear case for categorisation within the sections within which we have located them: Bateman's focus is on the theoretical apparatus of multimodal study (towards a finer differentiation of semiotic mode), O'Toole is very much orientated towards discussing a particular set of texts (stop-motion and digital forms of animation video, in terms of changes in the deployment of particular semiotic resources).

However, other chapters, in particular those 'in the middle' of this continuum, do not fit so neatly into this categorical distinction. For example, van Leeuwen's 'the semiotics of decoration' in Chapter 7 has a distinct focus on a particular domain of application of social semiotic theory, yet in defining a domain in such abstract terms (i.e. 'decoration' across different types of text, semiotic modes and eras), van Leeuwen's chapter in fact serves to model a new approach to multimodal classification and description, one that operates across modes and media: a generalisation of genuine significance to multimodal studies. By comparison, Eisenlauer's focus on social networking in old and new media does clearly orientate in aim to this particular domain but nevertheless draws on an understanding of multimodality that transcends this domain thus having more general relevance for multimodal studies. The categorisation into 'issues' and 'domains' in fact, for these chapters, cannot be said to be anywhere near as useful as for the chapters by Bateman and O'Toole. Hence, by making the principle of organisation that of location along a continuum rather than a categorical classification, we aim to draw attention both to the complementarity of focus within all the chapters, and to the degree to which any individual chapter, in our estimation, can be located within one or the other category.

Such a characterisation of works—as being ranged along a continuum rather than separated into discrete categorisations—seems appropriate to this emerging field of study, in which the concept of parametric gradience as an appropriate form of description has been so important (cf. for example van Leeuwen 1999, 2009), challenging traditional linguistic notions of sets of categorical distinctions. However, the concept of a cline of differentiation may also in fact be related to Halliday's (1992) deployment of the concept of a 'cline' in relating systemic potential and actual choice in text, the 'cline of instantiation', and also to other work on the modeling of linguistic theory in terms of gradience (e.g. Pike 1959) and indeterminacy, in particular topological as contrasted with typological systems (e.g. Lemke 1999; Martin and Matthiessen 1991). While such an approach has several important applications within linguistics, it is clearly particularly relevant to the study of parametric systems so characteristic of multimodal semiotic resources.

MULTIMODAL STUDIES AS AN EMERGING FIELD

As can be seen in the many contemporary publications dealing with multimodality, there is a diversity of viewpoints and approaches that seems inherent in multimodal studies. This diversity can perhaps be related to the range of resources humans have developed for communication and the many sites and social contexts in which multimodal communication is found so that there is potentially a large range of disciplinary, theoretical and practical traditions implicated in the study of multimodality.

For example, although there are in this volume, as in many other works addressing multimodality, several authors working from within the perspectives afforded by social semiotic theory (a tradition that has been a major contributor to contemporary developments in multimodal studies), the different issues and domains addressed across the volume represent a variety of viewpoints and concerns, in terms of disciplinary origin, theoretical approach, methodology and domain of research. Several of the chapters presented in this volume specifically deal with or apply multi-disciplinary or multi-theoretical perspectives, although of course usually from the standpoint of one established tradition. Meanwhile, even within one tradition such as social semiotics, we can see such a contrast in methodology, framework and even academic discourse style as are evident between, for example, the chapters by van Leeuwen and O'Toole and Bateman and Ventola, that it is difficult to talk of a unified approach across these chapters.

The diversity of approaches to and concerns within multimodal study is perhaps one of the reasons why there may be something of a reluctance to classify multimodal studies as an academic discipline, with its own distinct theories etc. Issues of access to the multimodal signal, methodological issues in terms of analytical resources and techniques, theoretical challenges, as well as the institutional landscape also, have all no doubt also contributed to the difficulties of construing and enacting a distinct multimodal studies discipline, alongside the study of language, media, psychology, etc. The study of dynamic video has only been practically feasible within recent decades; and these and more contemporary interactive digital media present many problems to the multimodal analyst and publisher that are yet to be solved, including the immense complexities and difficulties of analysing and relating multiple semiotic resources within multimodal discourse. As yet most working within this field are, institutionally, allied within other established disciplines; and although funding is increasing for multimodal studies, this is distributed in general across those existing disciplines rather than being for multimodal study as such.

Yet part of the challenge of developing a field of multimodal studies may be confronting the problem of characterising and finding ways to classify the broad range of contemporary work dealing with multimodality: that is, identifying and categorising the challenges, concerns and scope of works belonging to such a field. The range of scholars bringing new areas and perspectives to the study of multimodal phenomena means that such a discipline cannot simply be classified along the lines of dominant theoretical orientations or disciplinary origins of those working within the field, nor according to any specific domain of interest.

Halliday (1991: 39) has remarked that the twentieth century was the 'age of disciplines, when knowledge was organised into subjects each having its own domain, its own concept of theory, and its own body of method'. Identifying this trend as an increasing constraint, he predicted that the twenty-first century would find emerging (1991: 39) 'structures of another kind, this time not disciplinary but thematic', organised according to the 'kinds of questions that are being asked'. It certainly appears that disciplinary boundaries are increasingly being crossed in the early twenty-first century, with inter-disciplinary collaboration becoming increasingly valued in the pursuit of particular research questions and social challenges. The emerging field of multimodal studies stands in an interesting historical relationship with such changes.

If by its very nature, the study of multimodality calls upon scholars to address issues within a wide range of domains—different modes, semiotic resources and practices, media, etc—of relevant to a wide range of disciplines, then the development of 'theory' begs the question, 'whose theory?' as much as 'what theory?'. Just as cultures at large have developed registers and genres of discourse, specialised ways of communicating requiring initiation, so too academic cultures have their registers and genres requiring initiation. To venture into another's academic and intellectual domain (for example, phonology, grammatics, musicology, theatrical and literary studies, art theory, anthropology, ethnography, psychology, architecture) is still, in the present socio-academic environment, daunting to say the least. Each domain has its own expertise, varieties of registerial conventions, both in researching and discoursing about (including publishing) one's research. Each scholar cannot be expected to learn the specialised knowledge and discourse conventions of every domain, field or tradition potentially relevant and of use to any multimodal study. Inter-disciplinarity may be, in this sense, more of an aspiration than an actuality, at least in terms of the genuine integration of theories, methods and practices of different disciplines.

Yet the challenge to multimodal studies in the present century is to incorporate contributions from physical, biological and social sciences, the humanities and arts, and from academic researchers, teachers and practitioners. No one discipline, theoretical tradition or academic style can claim ownership of this enterprise, either in terms of their discursive and analytical conventions, or institutionally. In the present volume we provide a forum for various interpretations of multimodal phenomena and practices of multimodal study, presented as a complementarity of focus between issues within and domains of multimodal study. We thus wish to present the works within this single volume as a discourse within this shared space, of different issues, approaches and concerns, between a variety of scholars and practitioners interested in multimodal study. Here we are advocating not so much inter-disciplinarity as multi-disciplinarity: a 'shared space' within which scholars may discourse according to the styles and conventions appropriate to their backgrounds and aims. Such a forum does not necessarily provide the means for quick and easy solutions to the (explicit or implicit) questions raised therein; but is an essential step along the path.

The wealth of new work from an increasingly wide variety of disciplinary and theoretical positions, and the challenges being faced, makes the development of a field of multimodal studies increasingly important. The ways in which we study multimodality should and no doubt will reflect in some way and be appropriate to the nature of the phenomena we study. Increasing interest in developing and applying theories and descriptions of multimodal discourse and its phenomena suggest that scholars are taking stock and considering what such a field might look like, what makes multimodal theories distinctive from, what makes them alike to theories of language or other monomodal domains of study. The range of publications in recent years dealing with issues in and domains of multimodal studies suggests that such a process is well and truly underway. Multimodal studies will thus inevitably develop its own distinctive flavours, its own styles as well as theories and methodologies. We think of the contributions within this volume as part of an ongoing collaborative effort which addresses and finds solutions to the vexing problems confronted in contemporary academia and social practice by the increasing proliferation of multimodal texts and their manifold semiotic and material complexities and challenges.

REFERENCES

Baldry, A. P., and Thibault, P. J. (2006) *Multimodal Transcription and Text Analysis*, London: Equinox.

Bateman, J. (2008) *Multimodality and Genre: A Foundation for the Systematic Analysis of Multimodal Documents*, Hampshire: Palgrave Macmillan.

Bednarek, M., and Martin, J. R., eds. (2010) *New Discourse on Language: Functional Perspectives on Multimodality, Identity, and Affiliation*, London and New York: Continuum.

Clarke, D., ed. (2001) *Perspectives on Practice and Meaning in Mathematics and Science Classrooms*, Dordrecht and Boston: Kluwer Academic Publishers.

Halliday, M. A. K. (1991) 'The notion of context in language education.' In Le, T. and McCausland, M. eds. *Language education: Interaction and development. Proceedings of the International Conference on Language Education.* Launceston, Tasmania: University of Tasmania: pp. 1–26.

Jewitt, C. (2006) *Technology, Literacy and Learning: A Multimodal Approach,* London: Routledge.

Jewitt, C., ed. (2009) *Handbook of Multimodal Analysis,* London: Routledge.

Kress, G. (2009) 'What is Mode?.' In Jewitt, C., ed. *Handbook of Multimodal Analysis,* London: Routledge: pp. 54–66.

Kress, G., and van Leeuwen, T. (2006) *Reading Images: The Grammar of Visual Design,* 2nd ed, London: Routledge.

Lemke, J. L. (2009) 'Multimodal Genres and Transmedia Traversals: Social Semiotics and the Political Economy of the sign.' *Semiotica* 177:(1–4), 1–27.

―――― (1999) 'Typological and Topological Meaning in Diagnostic Discourse.' *Discourse Processes* (2): 173–185.

Martin, J. R. (2010) 'Semantic Variation—Modelling Realisation, Instantiation and Individuation in Social Semiosis.' In Bednarek M. and Martin J. R. eds. *New Discourse on Language: Functional Perspectives on Multimodality, Identity, and Affiliation,* London and New York: Continuum: pp. 1–34.

Martin, J.R. and Matthiessen, Christian M.I.M. (1991) 'Systemic Typology and Topology.' In Christie, F. ed. *Literacy in Social Processes: Papers from the Inaugural Australian Systemic Functional Linguistics Conference, Deakin University, January 1990.* Darwin: Centre for Studies of Language in Education, Northern Territory University: pp. 345–383.

Martinec, R. (2005) 'A System for image-Text Relations in New (and Old) Media.' *Visual Communication* 4(3): 337–371.

O'Halloran, K. L. (2005) *Mathematical Discourse: Language, Symbolism and Visual Images,* London and New York: Continuum.

O'Toole, M. (1994) *The Language of Displayed Art,* 1st ed, London: Leicester University Press.

―――― (2010) *The Language of Displayed Art,* 2nd ed, London and New York: Routledge.

Pike, K. L. (1959) 'Language as particle, wave and field.' *Texas Quarterly* 2(2): 37–54.

Unsworth, L., and Cleirigh, C. (2009) 'Multimodality and Reading: The Construction of Meaning through Image-Text Interaction.' In Jewitt C. eds. *The Routledge Handbook of Multimodal Analysis,* London and New York: Routledge: pp. 151–163.

Van Leeuwen, T. (2009) 'Parametric Systems: The Case of Voice Quality'. In *The Routledge Handbook of Multimodal Analysis,* ed. C. Jewitt. London and New York: Routledge: pp. 68–77.

―――― (1999) *Speech, Music, Sound,* London: Macmillan.

Ventola, E., and Moya, J., eds. (2009) *The World Told and the World Shown: Multisemiotic Issues,* Hampshire: Palgrave Macmillan.

Zappavigna, M., Cleirigh, C., Dwyer, P., and Martin, J. R. (2010) 'The Coupling of Gesture and Phonology.' In Bednarek M. and Martin J. R. eds. *New Discourse on Language: Functional Perspectives on Multimodality, Identity, and Affiliation,* London and New York: Continuum: pp. 219–236.

Part I
Issues in Multimodal Studies

2 The Decomposability of Semiotic Modes

John A. Bateman

INTRODUCTION

With a few notable exceptions to which I will return below, most discussions of multimodal analyses and multimodal meaning-making still proceed without an explicit consideration of just what the 'mode' of multimodality is referring to. Two common assumptions contribute to this. First, it may be assumed that the modalities under investigation are unproblematic and self-evident: e.g. 'language', 'graphics', 'music' are clearly distinct modalities, and so there is little need to labour the division; second, it may be assumed that semiotic modalities naturally align with sensory modalities and so visual, auditory, tactile, etc, information are clearly distinct. These assumptions can be both held separately or combined in various ways and are prevalent in both technological (e.g. theory and design of human-computer interfaces: Bordegoni et al. 1997; Oviatt 1999; Wahlster 2006) and non-technological (linguistic, cognitive, semiotic, etc) approaches to multimodality.

Although appealing, the assumptions of self-evident modalities and of channel dependence give rise to a syndrome of interwoven research problems. Moreover, particular difficulties emerge for one, perhaps the, central task of multimodal research, that of showing how a combination of modes expands what it is possible to express beyond that possible within individual modes. As Stöckl writes

> multimodal refers to communicative artefacts and processes which combine various sign systems (modes) and whose production and reception calls upon the communicators to semantically and formally interrelate all sign repertoires present. (Stöckl 2004: 9)

Just how this interrelation is to be achieved 'semantically and formally' remains an unsolved problem. If modalities are maintained distinct from one another, then accounts of meaning 'multiplication' (cf. Lemke 1998) have to explain how it is that there is anything to combine; if modes reflect more a choice of output modality (e.g. spoken vs. written vs. graphic) for some 'content' area, then modes are made to appear more similar than they actually are. Adhering to these assumptions also raises the following methodological problem: it becomes difficult to reveal just what semiotic modes are operating in an artefact because it has already been taken for granted just what those semiotic modes are. Below I will suggest several rather more fine-grained semiotic modes that have arisen out of our recent empirical research.

The assumption of particular modes holding even prior to empirical investigation is one major reason why the vast majority of multimodal 'analyses' still go little beyond detailed description—indeed, Forceville's recent criticism of one particular example of such analyses is entirely relevant here and unfortunately applies to a considerably broader body of current work than his original target:

> . . . these descriptions seldom result in non-trivial explanations why the texts convey what they supposedly do convey, let alone in the formulation of—however tentative—patterns or generalizations. By and by these long descriptions become a real chore to read, and often do not exceed the level of truisms . . . Bluntly speaking, the authorial descriptions procure insufficient insights that a moderately attentive viewer-reader of the case-study under discussion had not already grasped himself. (Forceville 2007: 1236)

When the analysis of a multimodal artefact already assumes that the semiotic modes operative in that artefact are known, there is little left to do than 'read off' the artefact the distinctions being drawn. In the future this may become possible and even desirable, but for the present it presumes a far more mature state of multimodal analysis than is currently the case. As I have written elsewhere:

> applying rich interpretative schemes from other areas of study—including multimodal linguistics—may all too easily swamp the rather weak signal that we are currently capable of receiving from the multimodal artefacts themselves. (Bateman 2008: 13)

To improve our ability to 'hear' what multimodal artefacts are saying and how they are doing so, this article argues that it will be necessary to develop a more discriminating notion of semiotic mode. This is the case equally for approaches to multimodal analyses where the construct has been taken for granted and for those approaches where the construct has been problematised (e.g. Stöckl 2004; Forceville 2006).

The main goal of this article is therefore to pursue a tenable definition of semiotic mode that is particularly supportive of both the composition and the decomposition of semiotic modes within single artefacts. This will allow the multimodal analyst to adopt a much finer granularity when considering semiotic modes, one which is responsive to empirical results without prejudging what is occurring. A useful analogy can be drawn here with Biber's (1988) corpus-based study of the distinction between 'written' and 'spoken' language. Whereas prior to Biber's study, it was commonly assumed that spoken and written language were two distinguishable 'modes' of language use, Biber demonstrated that the division was not empirically motivated—instead the spoken-written dimension has to be seen as co-variation along a range of distinct dimensions, such as 'narrative vs. non-narrative', 'overt expression of persuasion', 'online informational elaboration' and others. These dimensions provide a far closer representation of the variation observed in distinct text genres than the simple spoken-written distinction. The same is true, I will now suggest, for semiotic modes. Any notion of a semiotic mode such as 'visual', 'image', 'verbal', etc, is under-differentiating in *much the same way* as 'spoken'/'written' is now known to be. Our task will be to set out how we can discover more appropriate descriptions.

The structure of the article is as follows. First, I will provide the basis of a new definition of semiotic mode, showing how this draws on previous work. Second, I will show how this definition is applied to distinguish more finely some of the semiotic work performed within static multimodal artefacts; these examples will move us particularly towards issues of mode composition. And third, I sketch a formal framework for capturing inter-semiotic relations, followed by a brief example of its use for supporting analysis.

REBUILDING THE NOTION OF SEMIOTIC MODE

The Basic Strata of a Semiotic Mode

Rather than assuming a range of semiotic modes or sensory channels in advance, the starting point for the definition of semiotic mode pursued here is the following observation from Kress and colleagues:

> . . . the question of whether X is a mode or not is a question specific to a particular community. As laypersons we may regard visual image to be a mode, while a professional photographer will say that photography has rules and practices, elements and materiality quite different from that of painting and that the two are distinct modes. (Kress et al. 2000: 43)

That is, essentially, a semiotic mode is developed by virtue of the work that a group of users puts into using some material substrate as a tool for constructing meaning. The materials that can be put to this kind of use are extremely varied but require minimally that they are sufficiently 'controllable' as to admit of purposeful articulations. No further constraint should be provided at this foundational level of definition for what is or is not a semiotic mode. The articulations made serve as the physical record of semiotic 'decisions' and can be used accordingly by any member of the relevant community of users as evidence of those decisions. Thus, for example, marks made with burnt sticks on cave walls are one controllable material substrate ideally suited to leaving records of various kinds; similarly, variations in the sound produced by the vocal chords via manipulations of the shape of the mouth are also an excellently controllable physical substrate. Both have had considerable effort invested in them as purposeful articulations for meaning-making; the latter to such an extent that it has had, arguably, evolutionary consequences.

The fixing of a material substrate is one essential component for any semiotic mode but is an insufficient 'starting' point for definition. The bare possibility of drawing distinctions in a substrate material by itself only allows for semiotic resources that are rather too simple for sophisticated meaning-making. They might, for example, consist of a collection of distinguishable marks with particular meanings-in-context (e.g. traffic lights, patterns of sticks left at decision points to indicate which path to follow, etc)—these all make up 'sign repertoires' and so meet minimal conditions for a semiotic resource. This does not yet distinguish 'semiotic resources' in general, i.e. semiotically charged organisations of material that can be employed for sign-construction, from the particular bundle of properties that I will suggest to be necessary for a fully fledged semiotic mode. For this, several further properties are required.

First, following in the tradition of de Saussure, Hjelmslev and Halliday, I propose that we characterise any non-material semiotic contribution in terms of the paradigmatic and syntagmatic axes of organisation: i.e. paradigmatic systems of choice together with a syntagmatic organisation for re-expressing paradigmatic choices in structural configurations. It is then the structural configurations that have to leave traces in distinctions drawn in material form. This provides a rich organisation for the 'space' of semiotic decisions available within any semiotic resource. We can then describe a topology over such spaces in terms of Kress and van Leeuwen's (2001) distinction between 'lexically-organised' semiotic resources and 'grammatically-organised' semiotic resources. Lexically-organised semiotic resources consist of collections of signs in the simple style mentioned above: the sign repertoire constitutes a 'lexicon' with little internal organisation. In contrast to this, grammatically-organised semiotic resources organise their signs into a productive system of meaning potential. This provides the power to compose simpler signs into complex signs employing mechanisms analogous to those of grammar. And, again, this distinction is not 'absolute' but is itself anchored to particular communities of users; as Kress and van Leeuwen (2001: 113) explain: 'No semiotic resource is by "nature" either "lexically" or "grammatically" organised'.

Semiotic resources may differ considerably concerning how complex their non-material component may become: verbal language, for example, is richly stratified (cf. e.g. Halliday, 1978 for a 'tri-stratal' view) while other codes may be simpler. Traditionally a distinction is drawn here going back to Hjelmslev between the content and the expression planes of a semiotic resource. The expression plane for language is typically taken to include graphology and phonology (cf. O'Halloran 2008: 449), while that for visual images has been suggested to include colour, framing and perspective (cf. O'Halloran 2008: 451). Discussions often consider the material substrate for a semiotic resource as already included within the (substance component of the) expression plane. This is one reason why materiality has generally been undervalued in the semiotic traditions of de Saussure and Hjelmslev. However this is no longer tenable for several reasons, two of which are particularly relevant here.

First, properties of the substrate influence the range and kind of syntagmatic organisations that can be carried—that is, differing physical substrates will support different possible articulations; this is of considerable semiotic interest because multimodal analyses now address an increasingly diverse range of substrates. Second, we will be concerned below precisely with what happens when semiotic modes migrate *across* differing physical substrates and so need this aspect to be explicitly represented. Thus, within the account being developed here, a semiotic 'code' is defined to include a non-material component taking in *both* the content and expression planes and, *in addition* to these, a material component. The material substrate provides for the physical possibility of any systems of choice within an expression plane but is itself distinct from such systems.

One further step is necessary to reach what will be considered here a full-blown semiotic mode. So far the model has simply assumed that the articulations imposed on the physical substrate are somehow 'interpretable' in context. To provide mechanisms by which this can proceed, we must also consider the notion of *discourse*. The paradigmatic choices lying behind any particular physical articulation need also to be organised so as to support contextualised interpretation and, for this, it is useful to place the entire semiotic organisation uncovered so far within a further 'semiotic stratum' of *discourse semantics*: that is, the semiotic code only becomes interpretable in context by virtue of being embedded within an unfolding discourse. This is taken to apply across all semiotic modes, and, indeed, I propose here that the presence of a discourse stratum be adopted as a defining property of a semiotic mode as such. Without a discourse semantics, a semiotic mode would only be effective when used within very particular contexts with little possibility of extension; we might speak in such cases of 'semiotic proto-modes'. However, the additional stratification of a discourse semantics allows the semiotic resources involved to generalise across different specific contexts of use by providing guiding schemes of contextual interpretation.

We can find evidence of the discourse semantic stratum at work whenever the interpretation of a particular configuration of physical articulations depends on context. Consider, for example, the distinct interpretations of textual 'paragraphs' in a phone book and textual 'paragraphs' in a novel. In terms of the visual semiotics of typography, we are concerned in both cases with a particular kind of segmentation: the paragraphing has the typographical 'meaning' of dividing up the message into recognisable units. Removed from context, however, we do not know what kind of interpretation is to be given to the relations between these units: we can guess, but we might well be wrong. This 'defeasible' inference is the hallmark of discourse interpretation: the semiotic code has provided particular information, i.e. division into units, and the discourse semantics then must provide candidate interpretations of that information.

A similar example can be taken from film if we consider the distinct interpretations that are possible for a shot sequence punctuated by a black screen. The most common interpretation is that a boundary in the unfolding story has been reached—a change of scene, time or place. But this is an interpretation that can also turn out to be false (cf. Kieslowski's *Three colours blue*, 1993), and so the interpretation is a discourse interpretation and not a property of filmic 'grammar'. Many of the 'rules' of film design and interpretation (e.g. camera angle reflects power, maintenance of the 180° rule, etc) are of this kind, emphasising the importance of incorporating a proper discourse semantics within accounts of filmic semiotic modes (cf e.g. Möller 1978; Branigan 1984: 29).

Much of the meaning assigned to semiotic organisations is of this kind: i.e. they are *situated discourse interpretations*. This means that they are subject to defeasible mechanisms of discourse interpretation as set out in considerable detail for verbal language by Asher and Lascarides (2003) and in more exploratory form by Moriarty (1996) for visual semiotics and by myself for film (Bateman 2007). It is also the embedding within a discourse semantics that makes available varieties of rhetorical organisation, tropes and 'metaphor' for *all* semiotic modes—a possibility also suggested in Forceville's (2006) discussion of 'multimodal metaphor'.

This then gives a 'three-stratal' organisation for semiotic modes, placing the semiotic code presented above within a stratum of discourse semantics. The discourse semantics provides defeasible rules of interpretation that are typically applied to show how interpretations can be uncovered dynamically while at the same time also sensibly constraining the range of interpretations that are relevant. In short, discourse semantic rules control when and how world knowledge is considered in the interpretation process and offer a useful treatment of the process of logogenesis.

MULTIPLE SEMIOTIC MODES

The account of semiotic modes presented so far will now be developed further in two directions. First, I briefly consider what happens when the material substrate of a mode is changed; second, I consider how single-material substrates can support multiple modes. Both situations give rise to considerable discussion in the multimodality literature and are examples where an insufficiently grounded or refined notion of semiotic mode leads to problems.

The classical example of a semiotic mode with a changed physical substrate is that observed in the progression from spoken language to written language. Here it is important to be clear that the written variety is not a straightforward mechanical re-rendering of the properties of the spoken physical substrate. Instead it is a re-rendering of the properties of the *syntagmatic organisation* of the originating semiotic mode. This appears to be a very general capability, one which no doubt contributed de Saussure's and Hjelmslev's lack of consideration for the physical substrate altogether. A semiotic mode *may select any physical substrate* that is capable of being shaped and moulded in ways that capture the regularities necessary for coding its syntagmatic organisation. If the physical substrate can 'do the job', then a community of users may put the effort into making it do so. In the shift from spoken to written language, there is then rather more at stake than a simple swapping of physical substrate within a single semiotic mode would suggest. Not only are further submodes (cf. Stöckl 2004: 14) made possible by the new materiality, it is also commonly argued that the shift from spoken to written language has had considerable consequences for just what can be done with language as such (e.g. Ong 1982). This is, however, largely predictable from a consideration of the physical substrate as an essential component of a semiotic mode.

In Figure 2.1, we can see this development in action. We begin upper left, with the originating spoken language semiotic mode. Subsequently, a visual

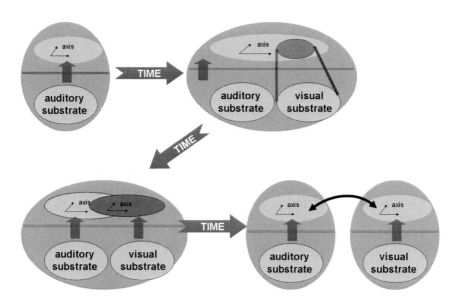

Figure 2.1   The development of a semiotic mode across distinct materialities.

materiality was co-opted by the semiotic mode by articulating a selected subset of its semiotic distinctions within the visual physical medium. At this stage, the visual materiality necessarily makes available a range of further semiotic modes—we will return to this in a moment when I take up the second line of development mentioned above. Here there is no requirement that any of these 'extra' modes have anything explicitly to do with the semiotic mode of language. They might, for example, express particular social standing by virtue of the kind of material used, and so on. In the next stage, however, shown lower left, distinct language-relevant semiotic codes can begin to develop supported by the affordances of the new materiality. Examples would be the extended use of thematic development and large-scale patterns of given-newness that appear to have grown with the use of written language, particularly in scientific discourse (cf. Halliday 1993), or the use of punctuation for certain kinds of intonational meaning. The overlap between distinct semiotic codes shown in Figure 2.1 might also be characterised more finely using O'Halloran's (2008: 453) classification of intersemiotic relations in terms of semiotic adoption, semiotic mixing, semiotic cohesion, etc. The final stage of development is when distinct semiotic modes develop that may be *related* with the originating semiotic mode of language but which are not themselves *part* of the same semiotic mode.

The situation that a visual substrate may carry distinct semiotic modes, for example, when a given piece of written language includes both extensions of the language semiotic mode (e.g. punctuation) and non-linguistic semiotic modes (e.g. layout), turns out to be very common. This is because material substrates are typically sufficiently 'dense' that they offer a rich potential for carrying simultaneous patterning; that is, their materiality can be articulated simultaneously in a variety of ways independently of one another. Sound can be made to carry a variety of frequencies at a variety of volumes and, if we add in both ears, in a variety of locations. Similarly, a visual image can be made to carry distinct shapes, colours, textures, brightness and so on. Multiple modes can then develop on the basis of single substrates by selecting to manipulate only a subset of the physically variable dimensions on offer. We can see this again in spoken language: whereas in the acoustic signal the first two formants carry information about vowel quality, the fundamental frequency (predominantly) carries simultaneous information about intonation and the third and higher formants carry information about emotional and physical state of the speaker. These are independently variable and so are available for independent co-option by distinct semiotic modes.

The ability to construct distinct semiotic modes on the 'same' material foundation is very powerful. Something of this has been considered in graphic design but without the semiotic underpinnings that bring out just how powerful the possibility is. Tufte, for example, proposes that for good design

> The same ink should often serve more than one graphical purpose. A graphical element may carry data information and also perform a design function usually left to non-data-ink. Or it might show several different pieces of data. Such *multifunctioning graphical elements*, if designed with care and subtlety, can effectively display complex, multi-variate data. (Tufte 1983: 139)

But the possibilities here go far beyond Tufte's characterisation of the phenomenon as visual *confections* (Tufte 1983: 121). We have instead a basic property of semiosis: the use of multiple semiotic modes simultaneously, even with respect to single physical substrates.

UNCOVERING DISTINCT SEMIOTIC MODES ACCORDING TO THEIR RESPECTIVE DISCOURSE SEMANTICS

We saw in the previous section that it makes sense to consider spoken language as clearly being a 'complex' semiotic mode, since it has evolved as a combination of theoretically distinct modal contributions involving various features of the sound stream. Due to this 'co-evolution', it is in many cases difficult to pull the contributing modes apart again. It is also not self-evident where the boundaries of the mode are best drawn: for example, spoken face-to-face language has also co-evolved in the presence of gesture, and so it is also possible to posit gestural components as parts of the intrinsic whole (cf. Bavelas and Chovil 2000). For present purposes, however, we are focusing on one aspect of this complexity—the ability of single physical substrates to carry multiple modes. And in this respect, written language has moved in a precisely analogous direction. Just as the sound stream carries simultaneous patterns, so can the visual material substrate also carry simultaneous patterns of visuality. The support of the visual substrate for a diverse range of simultaneous semiotic modes is, however, still underappreciated. In this section, I turn briefly to using the account of semiotic modes developed so far in order to isolate some more fine-grained semiotic modes at work in visual multimodal artefacts. I will then use this as a starting point for the final issue to be addressed in this article, the description and formalisation of mode combination.

Three Visual Semiotic Modes Active on the Page

The first area is drawn from static two-dimensional documents as investigated in depth in Bateman (2008). In that work it was proposed that in addition to established visual semiotic modes, such as diagrams and pictures, there were additional modes waiting to be teased out by detailed empirical investigation. In particular, three distinct semiotic modes were found to be co-present on many pages. These were termed *text-flow*, static *image-flow* and *page-flow*.

Text-flow refers to the one-dimensional unfolding of a written text; it is closely related to Twyman's (1979) notion of 'linear interrupted' artefacts in which a text unfolds subject to constraints, such as the size of the page and typography, but without making any additional use of the intrinsic two dimensionality of the enclosing page. Pictures and graphics may also appear in the text, but their positioning is generally not significant apart from being 'at' a particular point in the one-dimensional extent of the text. It is this mode that is being employed within this article: there is segmentation into sections, subsections and paragraphs as well as diagrammatic figures, but the two dimensionality of the page is not being used to construct further meanings. The relation between consecutive units within this semiotic mode is simply one of textual progression or textual cross-reference.

The second semiotic mode, static image-flow, is in many respects a parallel organisation but already moves out of the language semiotic mode *per se*. Within static image-flow we typically find pictures or diagrams arranged in a perceptible sequence. This is then made decisively into a distinct semiotic mode by the fact that its *discourse semantics* is of a completely different nature to that of text-flow. Although also using spatial sequence, here this property of the physical substrate expresses a completely different set of possible semantic relations. These relations are essentially those set out for comics by McCloud (1994) and closely resemble (but differ from) Martin's conjunctive relations (Martin 1992; Martin and Rose 2003).

The third semiotic mode, page-flow, takes a further step away from linearity, and the semiotics of page layout come into their own. This semiotic mode relies upon the complete two-dimensional space of the 'canvas' provided by the physical substrate and uses proximity, grouping of elements, framing and other visual perceptual resources in order to construct patterns of connections, similarity and difference. In Bateman (2008) it is argued following previous work in the area that a suitable discourse semantics for the relational configurations set up among the elements inhabiting the canvas is provided by a multimodally extended version of Mann and Thompson's (1988) *rhetorical structure theory* (RST). Thus, here again, I take as evidence of a distinct semiotic mode the fact that a completely distinct discourse semantics is in operation.

Something of this range of semiotic modes acting in combination in multimodal artefacts is suggested in the partial decomposition of a page from a book on wildlife used as data within the study reported in Bateman (2008), reproduced in Figure 2.2 along with some of the contributing modes. Here, the entire page is constructed using the resources of the page-flow semiotic mode in order to relate the various contributions within both the genre established for this type of books from this publisher and within the 'virtual canvas' constructed for the series. Within this predominantly hierarchical page-flow, we find both traditionally recognised elements, such as

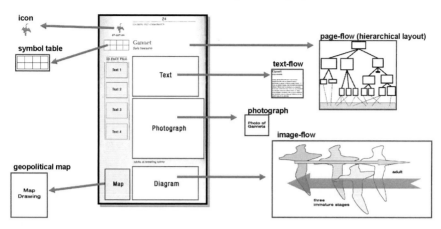

Figure 2.2   Semiotic modes contributing to the Gannet page used by permission within the corpus of the GeM project (Holden, P. *Collins Wild Guide: Birds of Britain and Ireland*, HarperCollins, 1996: 24).

maps, photographs and tables, as well as an image-flow element, depicting the maturation of the animal at issue here: the gannet. As is typically the case within image-flow elements, we find spatial extent coding temporal relationships: here time runs from left to right (while the birds, for some reason, fly from right to left).

The dense co-existence of distinct semiotic modes presents significant challenges for multimodal literacy. Not only must readers learn how to combine elements on a page, but they must also be able to interpret the various semiotic modes with their respective semantics in order to find their contributions. Current approaches to multimodal literacy have not, however, decomposed the component semiotic modes in the artefacts they are studying to anywhere near the granularity necessary to do them justice. This complicates the tasks both of providing analyses and of teaching the use of such artefacts since the contributions of the individual semantic components remain hidden.

Discourse Semantics and 'Multiplying' Semiotic Modes

With several semiotic modes now introduced, along with sketches of the discourse semantics that they draw upon, we can now proceed to the final topic of the article: semiotic mode combination. Providing a formalised account of the kinds of semantics that applies for each semiotic mode, together with a close mapping between properties of the articulated material and those semantics, is the first step towards a well-founded account of the semantics of modes both individually and in combination. In all cases, we can begin formalisation by drawing out a connection between the syntagmatic relational configurations deployed within the physical substrate and the relations from the discourse semantics that apply. This will be expressed in the form of 'back-and-forth' mapping diagrams (Blackburn et al. 1993) as depicted in Figure 2.3.

Diagrams of this form set up a special kind of connection between two formally distinct 'domains' and are similar in intention to the kind of mappings given for inter-semiotic 'contextualising' processes by O'Halloran (2007: 91). The connections defined in 'back-and-forth' diagrams are *structure preserving* in the very precise sense that it is possible to define a mapping between domains (the arrows marked z in the diagram) such that if a particular relation holds between entities in the 'source' domain (e and e′ on the left-hand side), then a relation also holds between the *corresponding* entities, i.e. the entities reached by the mapping—$z(e)$ and $z(e′)$—in the target domain. In the example of Figure 2.3(a), we see this spelled out for the discourse semantics of the text-flow semiotic mode. The left-hand domain refers to the significant features imposed on the physical substrate, the one-dimensional ordering of material; the right-hand domain refers to the discourse semantic interpretation of this spatial ordering, i.e. for text-flow, a basic text-structuring organisation. The essential idea informing this view is that if it is possible to establish a formal mapping across different domains, then one can use one domain to provide an interpretation, or 'semantics', of another. In this case, the domain on the right-hand side (text structuring) is used to interpret the one-dimensional sequencing relationship found on the physical page.

The semantics of the text-flow mode then contrasts with the superficially similar situation found in the static image-flow semiotic mode as well as with the very different organisation found in page-flow. These distinctions are captured in the additional back-and-forth mapping diagrams shown in Figure 2.3(b) and 2.3(c). In Figure 2.3(b), we see that although the physical substrate is still only coding one-dimensional precedence as before, the discourse semantics involved is now drawn from a completely different area— i.e. the network of potential of conjunctive relations. For Figure 2.3(c), the page-flow mode, we find composition relations (i.e. spatial layout) brought together with the possibilities of rhetorical structure theory: in short, the

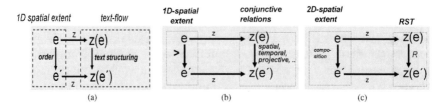

Figure 2.3 Formal back-and-forth mappings between the page and semantics in distinct semiotic modes: (a) the text-flow semiotic mode, (b) the image-flow semiotic mode and (c) the page-flow semiotic mode.

hierarchical composition structure is placed in correspondence with hierarchical rhetorical organisation (cf. Bateman 2008, Chapter 4).

Defining formal relations between different domains in this way allows meanings made in one domain to be put in correspondence with meanings made in another. If we can establish a structural/semantic relationship across domains that conform to the formal characteristics of a 'back-and-forth' mapping, then meaning can 'flow'. This organisational scheme provides a foundation for inter-semiotic translation, i.e. translation between sign systems, in general. Most current proposals for relating distinct semiotic modes can be couched in its terms. It subsumes equally cases where, for example, spatial extent (left-to-right, foreground-background, etc) is mapped to temporal development, or where, by further composition, spatial extent is mapped to narrative concerns (cf. Stöckl 2002; Kraft et al. 1991; Wolf 2003).

We can now use this framework to identify distinct kinds of relationships across semiotic modes. Perhaps the two most obvious kinds are composite modes and hybridised modes. This distinction is analogous to O'Halloran's (2005) consideration of multi-channel (e.g. Web sites) and multi-semiotic texts. In her account, multimodality is applied to the former, while the latter incorporates single-channel texts (e.g. printed documents) that encompass several semiotic systems (e.g. image, language). The precise allocation of a form to one or the other category is, however, an empirical issue and develops and changes over time. Moreover, we need also to distinguish within the 'multi-channel' area between modes where the multiple channels and their associated semiotic modes remain separate (i.e. composite) and where the multiple modes and their semiotic modes actually combine to form new meaning possibilities beyond a synchronisation of individual contributions (i.e. hybridise).

In short, composite modes are considered here to be modes which are made up of contributing semiotic modes whose discourse semantics are co-present without interacting. In contrast to this, hybridised modes represent a far closer combination of semiotic modes. Here a new discourse semantics is constructed from the contributing modes and represents, in a sense similar to constructs explored within cognitive linguistics and some branches of formal semiotics (cf. Goguen 1999; Fauconnier and Turner 2003), a genuine *blend* with new meaning potential. This is suggested graphically in Figure 2.4, where I use the formal notion of blend developed by Goguen. Hybridisation of this kind works as follows. Two domains may be 'blended' by considering each as a formal theory ($T1$ and $T2$ in the figure) and finding a set of statements that they *both* make about the 'world' (the 'common ground'). Given this common ground, it is possible by a mathematical operation to 'project' a further combined theory. This corresponds in a very literal sense to Lemke's (1998) idea of multiplying meanings but does not rely on any restriction such as Lemke's proposal that, in order to be meaning-expanding, distinct kinds of semiotic modes (e.g. topological vs. typological-categorial) need to be combined.

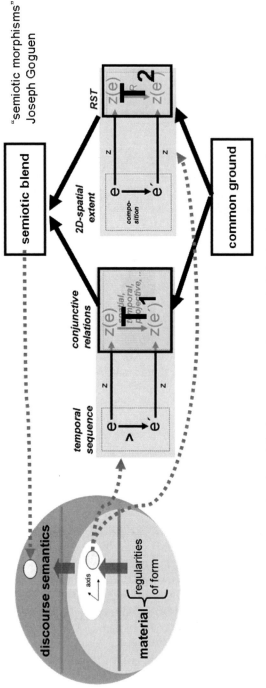

Figure 2.4   Combination of formal back-and-forth mappings within a single-hybridised semiotic mode.

The precise details of the discourse semantics being combined in such blends will lead to distinct particular cases, some of which are already being discussed in the literature (e.g. O'Halloran 1999, 2008). Moreover, one formal property of the process of forming such blends is that they will rarely be unique: precisely *which* blend is formed then opens up the door to a proper inclusion of cultural and genre constraints (cf., also, Forceville 2006: 392). There is also a clear relationship to be drawn with discussions and formalisations of 'metaphor' in at least two senses: first, in metaphor there is also typically a structured relationship established across domains and, second, this relationship is *meaning-generating* (cf. Black 1968; Schofer and Rice 1977; Lakoff and Johnson 1980; Gentner 1983; Fauconnier and Turner 2003). The approach set out here therefore shows considerable overlap with Forceville's (2006) argument that metaphor be applied across modalities; the formal mechanism employed here is considered entirely compatible with such work. There are also very close relationships to be drawn with O'Halloran's (2005) work on the complex multimodal semiotic system of mathematical discourse and the central role that *semiotic metaphor* plays in her account (cf. O'Halloran 1999, 2008). The mechanism developed here is therefore considered essential both for any description of complex semiotic modes and also for accounts of the mechanisms by which hybridised semiotic modes develop.

In this section, we have characterised hybrid semiotic modes as having their own integrated discourse semantics capable of bringing into relation contributions from distinct semiotic modes. Each of the three semiotic modes described above as active within the page, the modes of text-, image- and page-flow, are of this kind—although the complexity of the combinations taken up is different in each case. This characterisation now encourages a finer decomposition of semiotic modes than that typically pursued. However, it remains to be shown that this extra work brings returns. Although we cannot establish this beyond all doubt within the scope of the present paper, the next section provides one suggestive example of benefits that can accrue from this differentiated approach to semiotic modes.

EXAMPLE OF ANALYSIS

As one particularly clear example of multiple modes at work, I consider an analysis of some proposed difficulties for document interpretation related to multimodal literacy discussed by Unsworth (2007). Figure 2.5 shows the artefact at issue, taken from the Dorling Kindersley *Eye Wonder* series for younger readers. Unsworth suggests that this page leads to unintended 'misrepresentation' because of a divergence between text and image, which he then includes as one of an entire network of potential image-text relationships that he is attempting to construct. According to Unsworth, the divergence in this case arises because the *text* clearly indicates the depths at which the three zones begin and their very unequal extents (0–150 m, 150–1000 m and 1000–6000 m, respectively), whereas their *depicted sizes on the page* are the same. This is then coded by Unsworth as a case of a text-image relationship of 'complementarity' and 'divergence'. It is suggested that such a relationship unintendedly 'misrepresents' and so may present children with interpretation difficulties.

While it may well be the case that some children readers (and not only children readers!) may obtain a false message from this page, the precise kind of 'divergence' at issue here can be usefully unpacked in more detail. In fact, what is really at issue appears to be an ambiguity in the semiotic modes that apply to the page. It is then relatively straightforward for a multimodally inexperienced reader to select the wrong combination of semiotic modes—and, indeed, not even to be aware that there is a correct combination to apply. I will argue that it is this lack of 'literacy' in the semiotic modes available for guiding interpretation that leads to problems.

The page under discussion is a typical example of a Dorling Kindersley design. It is a highly sophisticated visual construct demanding the recognition of a range of modal combinations to be read successfully. It presents naturalistic drawings in vibrant colours of the creatures to be found within the various ocean zones, set against fairly natural backgrounds. These drawings are themselves additionally distinguished by clear framing within the layout into three areas. Each area shows a parallel structure with minor internal variation (cf. Figure 2.5 lower right). The invariant parts consist of a small

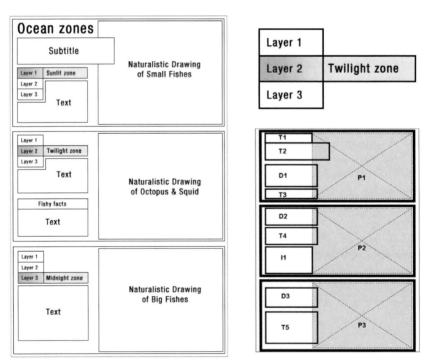

Figure 2.5   Page describing ocean zones taken from Gray, S. (2001, *DK Eye Wonder: Ocean*. London: Dorling Kindersley) discussed in Unsworth (2007: 1192) together with a close-up of one of the inset diagrams and a schematic layout representation of the page.

diagrammatic re-representation of the entire page and some explanatory/ descriptive text. The small diagrammatic re-representations themselves form a closed paradigmatic set, each member of which picks out one of the three ocean zones by a visually clear label (cf. Figure 2.5 upper right). This layout can therefore be described as a hierarchical structure constructed visually by framing and visual parallelism as set out in detail in Bateman (2008).

What this layout representation does *not* say is how it is to be interpreted, i.e. what meanings it is licensed to carry. For this, as described above, we need to add in the discourse semantic component of any semiotic mode considered applicable. In this respect the page sends several mixed messages. The naturalistic images suggest modalities of drawing and lifelike pictorial representations, but the framing and the schematised repeated diagrams, echoing the page organisation as a whole, suggest both modalities of diagrammatic representation and the modality of page-flow introduced above. The conflicts can then be summed up as follows: is this page a page-flow within which information is given about ocean zones and the animals that live in them, is it a diagram with additional lifelike elements for embellishment or is it a picture with minor diagrammatic elements positioned in it for elaboration? Naively, these alternatives may not seem to make much of a difference, but actually the interpretations possible for the distinct readings are completely divergent.

If the page is read as a page-flow, then the spatially represented layout structure communicates that there are three subtopics to be discussed within the overall page topic of ocean zones and that these subtopics are of approximately equal importance for the rhetorical goal at hand. The diagram mode allows rather more to be read out of the page: for current purposes, we can simplify somewhat and relate diagrams of this kind to Kress and van Leeuwen's (1996: 88) 'classificational' or 'analytic' visual process type used for realising conceptual representations. Such diagrams capture type-subtype or part-whole relationships. In the present case, one could consider whether we are seeing the ocean divided into parts or the definition of three subtypes of ocean zones. Regardless of this further specification, conceptual relationships of this kind make no commitments to spatial relationships in the domain represented: the spatial relations present in the page are used for realising relationships of hierarchy and composition. Again, under this semiotic mode, no conclusions about the relative sizes of the depicted regions are licensed. Finally, however, the picture reading is quite different. According to the norms of the pictorial semiotic mode, metric, topological and topographic relations on the page, including size and relative position, are used to assert correspondences in the represented domain. Under this semiotic mode, therefore, conclusions about the relative sizes of the depicted ocean zones certainly would be justified. Figure 2.6 summarises the properties of the primary modes discussed here as competing for attention using our abstract scheme for semiotic modes.

This then highlights quite precisely the interpretative challenges being made in this page design. We are not dealing with a clear exemplar of any of the individual semiotic modes on offer. We do not have an abstract

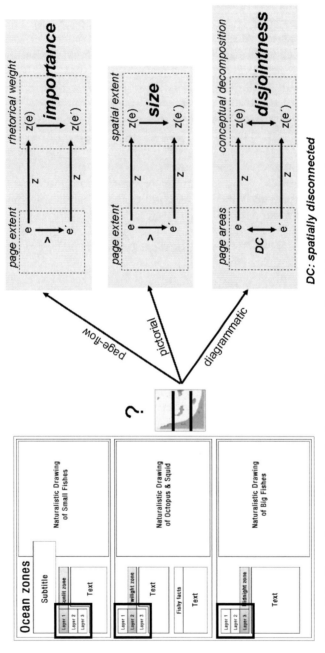

Figure 2.6   Competing semiotic modes for providing interpretations of the ocean zones' page.

diagram within which it would be unlikely to transfer properties of size and location, we have a hybrid pictorial-diagrammatic mode in which some properties are maintained (for example, the vertical spatial dimension on the page for representing iconically the relative spatial position of the ocean zones) and others are not (their relative size). It is this combination, I suggest, that really makes the page potentially 'difficult'. The divergence focused on by Unsworth is only there once particular semiotic modes have been applied. The multimodal competence required is then precisely that of learning which modes there are and how they impact on the inferences that can be made on the basis of the information presented.

There are also clear lessons for both design and analysis. Whereas the discussion above has focused on the interpretative consequences of selecting one semiotic mode rather than another as applying to a multimodal arte-fact, we can equally address the kinds of *evidence* that artefacts themselves bring to the interpretative process. That is, the selection of one semiotic mode rather than another needs to be motivated by the semiotic choices evident in the artefact itself. We touched briefly on these issues above when the selection of a pictorial semiotic mode was discussed with respect to the naturalistic drawings present, or when the diagrammatic mode was discussed relative to the schematised ocean zone representations presented. Establishing just what evidence is 'admissible' for constraining semiotic mode choice will itself require considerable detailed empirical investiga-tion. Moreover, for many document genres, it may justifiably be assumed that their designs should more or less clearly indicate just what semiotic modes are going to be appropriate for interpretation: to the extent that this does not occur, unintended misinterpretations will remain a problem. As Tufte expresses it:

> The danger of multifunctioning elements is that they tend to generate graphical puzzles, with encodings that only be broken by their inventor. Thus design techniques for enhancing graphical clarity in the face of complexity must be developed along with multifunctioning elements. (Tufte 1983: 139)

Here I have embedded 'graphical clarity' within multimodality more gener-ally as just one manifestation of the need, when combining semiotic modes, to give sufficient support to intended interpreters so as to allow them to follow the compositions being proposed.

CONCLUSION AND OUTLOOK

It has been argued that multimodal artefacts commonly employ a host of fine-grained semiotic modes whose meanings need to be combined to locate the meanings being made. To identify such modes, the article constructed a particular definition of semiotic mode that emphasises both the material substrate and a mode-specific notion of discourse semantics as essential components. A formal framework for describing the composition of distinct semiotic modes was introduced, and relations set out to existing and previous work. For the future, it is hoped that the kind of fine-grained decomposition of semiotic modes suggested here can contribute significantly to issues of multimodal and visual literacy, to the achievement of a tighter analytic focus and to the formalisation of the distinct but related semantics that each semiotic mode brings to the meaning-making process.

REFERENCES

Asher, N. and Lascarides, A. (2003) *Logics of Conversation*, Cambridge: Cambridge University Press.

Bateman, J. A. (2008) *Multimodality and Genre: A Foundation for the Systematic Analysis of Multimodal Documents*, London: Palgrave Macmillan.

—— (2007) 'Towards a grande paradigmatique of film: Christian Metz reloaded.' *Semiotica* 167(1/4): 13–64.

Bavelas, J. and Chovil, N. (2000) 'Visible acts of meaning: an integrated message model of language in face-to-face dialogue.' *Journal of Language and Social Psychology* 19(2): 163–194.

Biber, D. (1988) *Variation Across Speech and Writing*, Cambridge: Cambridge University Press.

Black, M. (1968) *The Labyrinth of Language*, Encyclopedia Britannica Inc.

Blackburn, P., Gardent, C. and de Rijke, M. (1993) 'Back and Forth through Time and Events.' In *Proceedings of the 9th Amsterdam Colloquium*, 14–17 Dec 1993. Amsterdam, The Netherlands, pp. 161–175.

Bordegoni, M., Faconti, G., Maybury, M. T., Rist, T., Ruggieri, S., Trahanias, P. and Wilson, M. (1997) 'A standard reference model for intelligent multimedia presentation systems.' *Computer Standards and Interfaces: International Journal on the Development and Application of Standards for Computers, Data Communication and Interfaces,* 18(6–7): 477–496.

Branigan, E. (1984) 'Point of view in the cinema: a theory of narration and subjectivity in classical film.' Number 66 *in Approaches to Semiotics*, Berlin: Mouton.

Fauconnier, G. and Turner, M. (2003) *The Way We Think: Conceptual Blending and the Mind's Hidden Complexities*, New York: Basic Books.

Forceville, C. J. (2007) 'Book Review: Multimodal Transcription and Text Analysis: A Multimedia Toolkit and Coursebook by Anthony Baldry and Paul J. Thibault.' *Journal of Pragmatics* 39: 1235–1238.

—— (2006) 'Non-verbal and multimodal metaphor as a cognitivist framework: agendas for research.' In Kristiansen, G., Achard, M., Dirven, R. and de Mendoza Ibanez, F. R., ed. *Cognitive Linguistics: Current Applications and Future Perspectives*, Berlin/New York: Mouton de Gruyter: pp. 379–402.

Gentner, D. (1983) 'Structure-mapping: a theoretical framework for analogy.' *Cognitive Science* 7: 155–170.

Goguen, J. (1999) 'An introduction to algebraic semiotics, with applications to user interface design.' In Nehaniv, C. ed. *Computation for Metaphors, Analogy and Agents*, number 1562 *in* 'LNAI', Berlin: Springer: pp. 242–291.

Gray, S. (2001) *DK EyeWonder: Ocean* London: Kindersley Dorling.

Halliday, M. A. K. (1993) 'The construction of knowledge and value in the grammar of scientific discourse: Charles Darwin's *The Origin of the Species.*' In Halliday,

M. A. K. and Martin, J., eds. *Writing Science: Literacy and Discursive Power*, London: The Falmer Press, pp. 86–105.

—— (1978) *Language as Social Semiotic*, London: Edward Arnold.

Holden, P. (1996) *Birds of Britain and Ireland*. Collins Wild Guide. London: Harper Collins.

Kieslowski, K. (1993) (Director) *Three Colours: Blue*. Film Produced by Marin Karmitz and distributed in USA by Miramax.

Kraft, R., Cantor, P. and Gottdiener, C. (1991) 'The coherence of visual narratives.' *Communication Research* 18: 601–616.

Kress, G., Jewitt, C., Ogborn, J. and Tsatsarelis, C. (2000) *Multimodal Teaching and Learning*, London: Continuum.

Kress, G. and Van Leeuwen, T. (2001) *Multimodal Discourse: The Modes and Media of Contemporary Communication*, London: Arnold.

—— (1996) *Reading Images: The Grammar of Visual Design*, 1st ed, London and New York: Routledge.

Lakoff, G. and Johnson, M. (1980) 'The metaphorical structure of the human conceptual system.' *Cognitive Science* 4(2): 195–208.

Lemke, J. L. (1998) 'Multiplying meaning: visual and verbal semiotics in scientific text.' In Martin, J. and Veel, R., eds. *Reading Science: Critical and Functional Perspectives on Discourses of Science*, London: Routledge: pp. 87–113.

Mann, W. C. and Thompson, S. A. (1988) 'Rhetorical Structure Theory: Toward a Functional Theory of Text Organization.' *Text* 8(3): 243–81.

Martin, J. R. (1992) *English Text: Systems and Structure*, Amsterdam: Benjamins.

Martin, J. R. and Rose, D. (2003) *Working with Discourse: Meaning Beyond the Clause*, London and New York: Continuum.

McCloud, S. (1994) *Understanding Comics: The Invisible Art*, New York: Harper Perennial.

Möller, K. D. (1978) 'Schichten des Filmbildes und Ebenen des Films. ' In 'Die Einstellung als Größe einer Filmsemiotik', number 7 in 'papmaks', Münster: MAKS (Münsteraner Arbeitskreis for Semiotik) Publikationen: pp. 37–81.

Moriarty, S. E. (1996) 'Abduction: a theory of visual interpretation.' *Communication Theory* 6(2): 167–187.

O'Halloran, K. L. (2008) 'Systemic Functional-Multimodal Discourse Analysis (SFMDA): Constructing Ideational Meaning using Language and Visual Imagery.' *Visual Communication* 7(4): 443–475.

—— (2007) 'Systemic functional multimodal discourse analysis (SF-MDA) approach to mathematics, grammar and literacy.' In McCabe, A., O'Donnell M. and Whittaker, R. eds. *Advances in Language and Education*, London and New York: Continuum: pp. 75–100.

—— (2005) *Mathematical Discourse: Language, Symbolism and Visual Images*, London and New York: Continuum.

—— (1999) 'Interdependence, interaction and metaphor in multisemiotic texts.' *Social Semiotics* 9(3): 317–354.

Ong, W. J. (1982) *Orality and Literacy: The Technologizing of the Word*, London: Methuen.

Oviatt, S. L. (1999) 'Ten myths of multimodal interaction', *Communications of the ACM* 42(11): 74–81.

Schofer, P. and Rice, D. (1977) 'Metaphor, metonymy and synecdoche revis(it)ed.' *Semiotica* 21(1–2): 121–150.

Stöckl, H. (2004) 'In between modes: language and image in printed media.' In Ventola, E. Charles, C. and Kaltenbacher, M. eds. *Perspectives on Multimodality*, Amsterdam: John Benjamins: pp. 9–30.

—— (2002) 'From space to time into narration—cognitive and semiotic perspectives on the narrative potential of visually structured text.' In Todenhagen,

C. and Thiele, W. eds. *Investigations into Narrative Structures*, Frankfurt am Main: Peter Lang: pp. 73–98.

Tufte, E. R. (1983) *The Visual Display of Quantitative Information*, Cheshire, Connecticut: Graphics Press.

Twyman, M. (1979) 'A schema for the study of graphic language.' In Kolders, P. A., Wrolstad, M. E. and Bouma, H. eds. *Processing of Visible Language* Vol. 1, New York and London: Plenum: pp. 117–150.

Unsworth, L. (2007) 'Image/text relations and intersemiosis: Towards multimodal text description for multiliteracies education.' In Barbara, L. and Sardinha, T. B. eds. Proceedings of the 33rd International Systemic Functional Congress (33rd ISFC), Pontifícia Universidade Católica De Sao Paulo (PUCSP), Sao Paulo, Brazil, 10–15 July 2006, pp. 1165–1205. Available at: http://www.pucsp.br/isfc (last access: 10 Dec 2010).

Wahlster, W., ed. (2006) *SmartKom: Foundations of Multimodal Dialogue Systems*, Springer, Heidelberg, Berlin: Cognitive Technologies.

Wolf, W. (2003) 'Narrative and narrativity: a narratological reconceptualization and its applicability to the Visual Arts.' *Word and Image* 19(3): 180–197.

3 Speech and Writing
Intonation within Multimodal Studies

Bradley A. Smith

INTONATION: SPEECH AND WRITING

Consider the following text (Text 1), an excerpt from a conversation between two sisters[1], transcribed using conventional orthographic resources but without punctuation:

> *speaker one:* hows your new oven
> *speaker two:* its fine its fine
> *speaker one:* youre not in love with it

There is something unusual about this text. The first speaker asks a question of speaker two about her new oven to which the second speaker appears to respond with a positive appraisal, 'its fine its fine'. Yet, the first speaker's response to this answer suggests that speaker two's answer was not in fact positive but construed a negative or perhaps qualified appraisal of the oven's value. There was clearly something in speaker two's reply not represented in the transcribed text above that speaker one has picked up on. It could have been a look, gesture or something in the 'tone of voice': one cannot say from the information available to us in the transcription[2].

In fact, whatever else was occurring during the original face-to-face spoken exchange, each of the two clauses in the reply of the second speaker was accompanied by a pronounced falling-rising pitch movement in her voice. It was this that the first speaker took to signal that 'all is not well' in her sister's otherwise positive assessment of her new kitchen white-good. The tone of voice and the meaning that the distinctive falling-rising pitch contours made, belied the meaning being communicated through the words alone: there was more going on in the original exchange than what is represented above in the conventional orthographic transcription[3].

The pitch contours in speaker two's reply indicated a sense of uncertainty with respect to the polarity of her declarative statement, to the 'isness' of her proposition (Halliday 1963/2005; Halliday and Greaves 2008): whether or not her new oven really 'is fine'. Speaker one's response to this communication of propositional 'uncertainty' was accompanied by the intonation commonly known as the 'high rising terminal' or 'HRT' (e.g. Guy and Vonwiller 1984). Here the HRT indicated to speaker one that what was on the face of it (without the intonational information) a statement, as realised by the declarative mood (Subject-Finite structure: see Halliday and Matthiessen 2004) was in fact intended as a question. The rising pitch contour added to the declarative proposition—'you're not in love with it'—the interrogative meaning 'is this [my proposition] true?'.

Although a substantial proportion of daily language use in contemporary literate societies occurs through writing, when we read language purporting to represent the 'spoken word'—whether as transcript, literature or e-chat—we are not getting the full picture: the orthographic resources of writing do not and can not give (nor were originally intended to give) an accurate transcription of the full meaning potential of spoken, dialogically constructed English text (Halliday 1985). For further exemplification of this, it may be noted that in speaker one's initial question the major pitch movement fell not where we would (without any other information than is given in the above excerpt) expect, on the final lexical item 'oven,' but on the premodifier 'your': there has been previous talk of other new ovens; the speaker now wishes to turn the talk to this specific ('your') new oven. One would not be able to infer this choice from the written text without prior textual information (for a discussion of this aspect of the reading aloud of written text, see Davies 1986); and in the case of the different types of pitch contour discussed above even the co-text might not give clues sufficient to a successful interpretation. Furthermore, these choices, obligatory in the spoken interpretation of the written text, are clearly more than just nuances of reading performance: both the type of pitch contour and the location of that contour in the flow of information form part of the essential meaning of the dialogic text.

These issues, of the 'recording' of speech via writing, and translation of written text into speech, are thus of significant cultural import. Although on the whole the functions for which writing systems were originally developed—recording and distribution of wealth, laws and religious declaration—were such as to make intonational meaning redundant (Halliday 1985), there are a range of text types, or 'registers' of discourse (e.g. Halliday et al. 1964; Halliday and Hasan 1985) within English culture wherein the interpretation of pitch movements such as those identified above—their type and location—can be crucial to the understanding of texts of those types. Such registers are legal discourse, including written transcripts of police interviews, witness statements and cross-examination; plays, film and television scripts and any literary discourse purporting to render speech in the written mode; political discourse, including public speeches and parliamentary debates; advertising; Internet and other forms of electronically mediated chat; transcripts of medical and other professional discourses (for example, psychological counselling and other medical interviews); and, of course, all historical documents purporting to record spoken text. These and many other types of language use constitute impoverished versions of the speech they purport to represent—typographic resources such as punctuation notwithstanding—and thus their interpretation from the written back into the spoken form raises serious questions as the interpretive process required.

Thus the view expressed in the following Carlyle quotation (1966: 160), articulating the importance written language had to him in his time, is problematic when one considers what is lost in the process of recording via writing, particularly when purporting to represent authentic dialogic discourse, where intonational meanings can be crucial:

> [italics and uppercap initials in original]: Certainly the Art of Writing is the most miraculous of all things man has devised . . . In Books lies the *soul* of the whole Past Time; the articulate audible voice of the Past, when the body and material substance of it has altogether vanished like a dream . . . All that Mankind has done, thought, gained or been: it is lying as in magic preservation in the pages of Books.

In our own time, even with recording technologies whereby semiotic phenomena such as intonation can also be made to lie 'in magic preservation' in records, tapes and bytes, the written form remains of particular importance to contemporary literate societies. First, the cultural heritage of ages prior to the invention of sound and dynamic visual (film and video) recording technologies is still preserved in the written form only and thus maintains the cultural importance of the written language regardless of contemporary shifts in communicative fashions. Second, it is clear that audiovisual digital media, far from relegating writing to the history books, have been the catalyst for perhaps the historically most dramatic increase in its use, via electronic discourse (short message service (SMS), e-mail, Internet chat, blogging, Facebook etc). These more dialogic social uses of writing put further pressure on the resources of the written language, particularly in that writing lacks the intonational resources which are so important for dialogic interaction (cf. Halliday and Greaves 2008). The written language is undoubtedly evolving as a result (see Thurlow and Pof 2009 for a discussion) but not yet to the point where there is a consistent conventional representation of intonational resources in the orthography.

The above observations are not intended to deny that important cultural communication takes place across time and space via writing, including mathematical and musical written languages: the magic of writing praised by Carlyle is indeed certainly that, for without it we would have no record of Shakespeare's, Newton's or Beethoven's works, for example, but only their oral and performance transmission through the centuries, subject to the vagaries and adulterations (but also, it must be noted, the inventiveness!) of interpretations by subsequent generations. The richness of cultural transmission enabled via the technologies of writing and of the past century cannot be denied. Rather, I wish to draw attention to the (usually unconscious) assumptions regarding intonational systems made in reading aloud a written text and the socio-cultural consequences of such assumptions. These issues have relevance to the emerging domain of multimodal studies: in particular, to the challenges of transcription and analysis and the theoretical underpinnings of these and also to the increasing interest in the social-semiotic functions and affordances of different semiotic resources.

In the next section I explore the analytical results of the application of two different theoretical perspectives to the interpretation of the same written text; and then return to suggest, extending the work by Davies (1986), how one's knowledge of intonational phenomena can inform interpretation of valued written texts within English language culture. I will then conclude by a discussion of issues in the study of speech and writing within the emerging field of multimodal communication.

INTONATION AND THEORY: DIFFERENT PERSPECTIVES, DIFFERENT PHENOMENA

> (Ladefoged 1997: 589): . . . before we can begin discussing the [phonetic] parameters themselves, we must consider what belongs in the phonology of a language. We must decide which differences in utterances are part of the language, and which are extra-linguistic. This is sometimes not as simple as it might seem, as speech conveys many kinds of information simultaneously.

One might have expected that the precise phonetic and phonological description of intonation would have been made easier by the availability during the twentieth century of increasingly powerful technologies—particularly computational—for analysing the sound signal. Yet although technical resources have certainly enabled a more detailed and accurate view of material aspects of intonation phenomena, such as fundamental frequency and temporal duration, both instrumentally (e.g. as output of algorithms) and manually (e.g. as platform for minute observation and analysis), even at the phonetic level of description, there is not, to this day, full agreement about the description of the physical phenomena that realise phonological systems of intonation, nor yet of the phonological categories such physical phenomena realise. As Halliday and Greaves (2008: 19) write, in fact, 'modern computer-based techniques . . . make the human investigator's work more complex—but also more thorough and more revealing'.

Phonetic description of features of the sound signal is inextricably intertwined with the issue of their interpretation as the expression of phonological (distinctive) systems so that different theoretical approaches to phonological description result in differences in the identification and valuing/interpretation of acoustic/auditory phenomena. As an example of different phonological interpretations of the same phenomenon, pitch movement is of course implicated in most if not all intonation descriptions, but there has been a longstanding debate about whether to interpret and represent pitch movements as a sequence of independent but related pitch events (segmental perspective) or as unitary events, as pitch contours (prosodic perspective). Ladd (1996: 44) illustrates his argument for the segmental approach by comparing two utterances that in the contour approach would be analysed as having the same, in the segmental approach, different phonological descriptions. Each utterance is a response to the same observation, "I hear Sue's taking a course to be a driving instructor", each spoken with what Ladd describes as a rise-fall-rise pitch movement (Ladd 1996: 43) "that can be used in English for a strongly challenging or contradicting echo question". The first response is a single word and syllable "Sue!?"; the second three words and several syllables, "A driving instructor!?".

According to Ladd, from the perspective of a segmental theory of intonation (Ladd 1996: 44), in the second response [italics in original]:

> We are not dealing with a global rise-fall-rise *shape* that applies holistically to an entire utterance . . . The rise-fall-rise shape that spanned the entire one-syllable utterance in *Sue!?* is not simply stretched out over the six-syllable utterance here. Instead, the contour is seen to consist of a sequence of at least two discrete events, an accentual feature consisting of a rise through a prominent syllable (here *driv-*) followed by a fall, and an edge tone consisting of a rise during the last few tenths of a second of the utterance. The low level stretch on the syllables *-ing instruct-* is simply a transition between these two events . . . A description in these terms gives us a simple but accurate way of describing how the tune in question is applied to texts with varying numbers of syllables and different stress patterns.

Ladd goes on to write (1996: 44–45):

> By breaking down the contour into component parts in this way, we do not, of course, preclude the possibility of larger units . . . In the example just given, we have not questioned the existence of a 'rise-fall-rise' nuclear tone in English, but have simply been more explicit about its internal structure. The rise-fall-rise unit can be seen as a composite or superordinate unit . . .

For Ladd, these distinctions are 'phonological', in the sense of phonology as the organisation of sound. But although in the second utterance it is clear that there are, in acoustic (phonetic) terms, two 'discrete events'—in pitch: a rise-fall, and another rise—and that one can thereby decompose the tone into its 'internal structure', these phonetic 'facts' are not themselves however necessarily the only determining factor for the phonological description: meaning (semiotic function) can also play a role. Ladd does suggest that there are alternative perspectives on these utterances, but in calling only one perspective 'phonological' and the other 'functional' is to reveal a particular view of what phonology is. From the multiple perspectives of Michael Halliday's systemic functional linguistic ('SFL') approach to the description of intonation phonology (e.g. Halliday and Greaves 2008), there are several things going on at once in both of the utterances quoted from Ladd in the previous section and from the semantic perspective, also a functional unity between both responses.

In terms of their functional correspondence, the (rise-[4]) fall-rise in both responses serves to add an identical sense of challenge, demanding a response to the information given. This tone choice is in fact a variation of the rising tone (HRT) found in Text 1, one which adds additional force to the sense of query realised by the high-rising pitch contour[5]. This sense of challenge/ query is an instance of interpersonal meaning: the enactment of social relations through the demand for (propositional) information (cf. Halliday and Greaves 2008). From this perspective, the fact of the phonological choice (the rising contour) that collaborates with the declarative mood to realise this meaning being (phonetically) realised differently in the two utterances is in fact a result of the difference in the (lexicogrammatical content of the) utterances themselves, not of any phonological difference between the intonation choice in the two responses. The phonological description, in SFL, is a product of semantic, grammatical and phonetic considerations: it is the description of the functional organisation of sounds.

Furthermore, this type of meaning—interpersonal—is prosodic in nature (cf. Halliday 1979/2002, Halliday and Greaves 2008): interpersonal meaning is relevant to the whole unit of which it is a part, such that its realisation tends to 'spread' (as iconic of the prosodic meaning it encodes) over the entire unit within which it functions. In this case, the pitch contour extends over the tone group such that the final rise of the fall-rise contour comes right at the end of this unit (although the final rise in fact begins on/has as its locus the accented syllable 'struct-'). The rise itself does not add any further (interpersonal) meaning beyond its being part of the unitary pitch contour realising the interpersonal meaning just discussed and cannot be considered apart from the rest of the contour.

The presence of distinctive contour shapes realising interpersonal choices in the two utterances is distinct from there being one accent in the first utterance and two in the second. The latter fact—the presence and location of accents—is a realisation of textual meaning: the organisation of meanings as coherent text, including the assignment of levels of relevance to certain items of discourse through accentual highlighting (cf. van Leeuwen 1992; Smith 2008). In the first utterance there is one only one accent possible; in the second utterance the potential for accent is greater, and both the words 'driving' and 'instructor' are given textual highlighting through accentuation of their respective primary stressed syllables 'dri-' and '-struct-'. The location of accent can be further differentiated from the location of the pitch contour itself—or rather, the (syllabic) locus of expression of the contour—which falls upon the first accent, 'dri-'. This assignment of a pitch contour to a particular location is also a realisation of (a higher) textual status additional to that of accent[6], sometimes called 'sentence stress' or 'nuclear accent', and in SFL called the focus of 'New' information (cf. Halliday and Greaves 2008; Bowcher 2004).

For other examples of textually functional intonation choices, in the initiating statement in Ladd's example ('I hear Sue's . . . instructor'), there may (or may not, depending upon one's reading) be an accent made to fall upon the personal pronoun 'I', without that pronoun necessarily also being the locus of the (presumably falling) pitch contour for the entire phrase. In this case the accent would be to suggest a textual relation to some prior information given by another interactant about Sue and her doings (which Smith 2008 terms, following Brazil (1978: 55), the realisation of 'information prominence'); otherwise, one would assume an accent on 'Sue' only, without the accent on the personal pronoun. The assignment of New status would presumably fall on the final content item 'driving instructor'[7], but in Text 1 at the beginning of this article, in the first utterance the pitch contour—New—falls upon the personal pronoun 'your' rather than on the head of this nominal group 'oven'.

One may say then that the Ladd interpretation *anatomises* (phoneticises) the phonological description of the utterances; Halliday's *functionalises* (semanticises) it. The Ladd interpretation is located within a particular theoretical tradition with its own purposes and perspectives (explicitly not meant to be an invalidation of the 'contour' perspective, but to (Ladd 1996: 45) 'cast [it] in a new light'): the term 'phonology' is to be interpreted as an abstraction from significant patterning of events in the sound stream, a view, which provides the basis for a description of the component parts of intonation phenomena, and one thus clearly productive for computational representations and analyses of such phenomena (cf. Teich et al. 2000).

The different theoretical views not only uncover different interpretations of the same phenomena but in fact give descriptive status to different phenomena. The segmental approach lends descriptive acknowledgment to the important fact of there being two accents—a status largely ignored in Halliday's description of intonational resources—such that in this tradition much of significance in the phenomenon of accent, lost to Halliday's SFL approach, has been uncovered (cf. Pierrehumbert and Hirschberg 1990; cf., also, on the social semiotics of accent and juncture, van Leeuwen 1992). In Halliday's prosodic perspective, semantic and phonological similarities and differences between contour types not recognised in the segmental description are distinguished; as are functional differences such as that between the type (interpersonal meaning) and location (textual meaning) of the pitch contour. For an example of the former, while the (sharp) falling-rising contour in the Ladd example is clearly similar phonetically to the (more rounded) fall-rise shape found in Text 1 at the beginning of this article, not only the phonetic expression of each but the meanings they realise are distinct. In the sharp fall-rise, the sense of challenge is in fact related to the sense of query of the simple rise seen in the HRT, while both are distinct in meaning and expression from the sense of propositional uncertainty found in the (smooth but pronounced) fall-rise used by speaker two in the earlier text (cf. Halliday 1970 for audio and descriptive examples of these phonetic, phonological and functional distinctions).

Each approach has its own way of interpreting and indeed uncovering phenomena in the sound signal, determining not only the interpretation of data in the sound signal but also what gets counted as 'data' for observation and comment. Thus neither one can be said to be superior nor the final word in the description of what is significant and worthy of attention and why. The relevance to multimodal studies in general is clear: the invention of increasingly powerful technical resources for the study of multimodal discourse (cf. O'Halloran et al 2010 for a discussion of digital technologies for multimodal studies; O'Halloran 2003; O'Donnell and Bateman 2005), and our attention to an increasing range of semiotic phenomena, does not exempt us from consideration at all points of the eternal issues of transcription/annotation, theory and its application and development.

INTONATION: AN ACTOR'S GUIDE

The discussion in Intonation and Theory: Different Perspectives, Different Phenomena raises questions about the cultural effect on literate societies of variation in interpretations of written text into speech, both in the academic sphere, and in the wider society, as for example in theatrical performance of a script. I first became aware of this issue when attending a reading from the transcripts of the trial of Oscar Wilde (Holland 2003), with Wilde's grandson, Merlin Holland playing Wilde and a descendant of Lord Alfred Douglas, Australian Queen's Counsel (QC) Francis Douglas playing Carson, hosted by the University of New South Wales (NSW) at the Sydney Justice and Police Museum[8]. I was particularly interested in the way in which the (non-professional) actors interpreted this historically important transcript, featuring two speakers famed for their oratorical abilities, in this Wilde's most dramatic performance. I had earlier studied this same text in terms of the dual registers within which Wilde seemed to assume he was speaking: for the cross-examination, the type was clearly legal discourse only, but for Wilde, there seemed also to be an artistic, theatrical discourse to engage in, a misconception that the cross-examiner (an old school-friend) seemed to play to his advantage (drawing Wilde into a false sense of security and cultural power).

One suspects that a reading and appreciation of this text, its humour and poignant tragedy, depends to some degree upon one's interpretation of the intonational choices used by the speakers in the original spoken dialogue, as in the following exchange (Text 2):

Carson:	Listen, sir. Here is one of your 'Phrases and Philosophies for the Use of the Young': 'Wickedness is a myth invented by good people to account for the curious attractiveness of others'
(Laughter)	
Wilde:	Yes.
Carson:	Do you think that is true?
Wilde:	I rarely think that anything I write is true.
(Laughter).	
Carson:	Did you say 'rarely'?
Wilde:	I said 'rarely'. I might have said never.

Was Wilde's first reply a simple falling tone statement of assent, perhaps spoken after a pause (a 'deadpan' reply); or a rising tone challenge (meaning 'yes, what of it?')? If the former, was it a low-falling or high-falling tone (cf. Halliday and Greaves 2008), encoding 'mild' (and even more deadpan) or 'strong/contrastive' interpersonal force, respectively? Was Carson's next question spoken with a rising tone, as is the unmarked choice for polar interrogatives (Halliday 1967), a straightforward demand for information, or was it in fact intoned with a falling pitch contour? Halliday and Matthiessen (2004: 142) call the latter choice (the combination of polar interrogative mood and falling tone) the realisation of a 'peremptory question', in which the propositional certainty encoded in the falling tone belies the interrogative function of the Finite-Subject syntagm, creating a more complex interpersonal meaning.

Wilde's subsequent response, we can confidently say from the immediate prior co-text of Carson's question, would most likely have had the lexical item 'anything' as New, with the rest afterward treated as 'Given' information (Halliday 1967), and we may surmise the 'neutral' (Halliday 1967) tone choice for this statement, the falling pitch contour. But of these interpretations we cannot be sure, as speakers are at liberty to choose from the available phonological potential as they please, each choice with its own contribution to meaning. There may have been two pitch contours, a falling pitch on 'anything' and the pronounced falling-rising contour found in Text 1 above on 'true' or 'anything' may have been accented only, and there may have been an accent on the personal pronoun 'I', adding contrast between the speaker's view of his work and his interlocutor's. Carson's final question might also have used the sharp fall-rise discussed earlier, adding further interpersonal force to the query. And in Wilde's final response, 'said' may have been accented, drawing attention to the contrast between this and the following modalised choice ('might have said'), or not. All of these interpretive choices, and many more potential choices one could consider even in this short excerpt, can be motivated by the meaning they would create (reading each version aloud helps appreciate their respective interpretations), and how that meaning would fit in with one's interpretation of the text, its context and its type.

Upon what basis may we propose what the actual choices were? I propose that it is via an understanding of a text as a member of a functional text-type—a 'register' of language, a semantic constraint corresponding to a particular, culturally distinct type of context—that one can come closest to making confident decisions. The term 'context' here is taken to mean an abstraction from the events, participants and circumstances of the environment in which the text takes place and to which the text relates (cf. Halliday and Hasan 1985; Butt 2003) and includes such phenomena as the social relations of the speakers (for example, from Butt 2003, hierarchic/non-hierarchic relations and social distance between the interactants) and the role language plays in that situational environment (for example, whether it is face-to-face dialogue in real-time—prototypical spoken discourse—or monologic and delayed/edited—prototypical written discourse).

These and other aspects of the context are taken to be related to the language that is used within such contexts: indeed, as a semiotic abstraction, context is created by the language, or rather, by the language (and other semiotic resources) in its relation to the relevant phenomenal environment of the text. Within particular types of context—for example, the social relations of the courtroom, or of a dinner party—one finds that language use falls into patterns of meaning and linguistic expression which correspond to the characteristics of that context—in fact, create or 'realize' them. Knowledge of patterns of use of intonation within particular registers such as courtroom cross-examination or comic repartee can therefore inform decisions as to how to interpret into speech a (literary or other) written text purporting to represent spoken language.

Such an approach does not, of course, amount to the determination of a 'correct' intonational interpretation for any written transcript of literary dialogue, nor is such the aim. Rather, in this way one is explicit about the means by which one arrives at interpretations. Particular intonational choices gain value from their consequences for the semantic and contextual meanings they realise, and from one's empirical knowledge of patterns of choice within spoken texts of the types (registers) within which a particular text has been categorised. It is, in this sense, the 'system' Stanislavski (2008) aimed to produce for actors but derived from the discipline of linguistics and the field of multimodal studies.

Of course there is nothing new in these observations of text-context relations and registerial description and prediction. What is relevant to the present discussion is that it is through the empirical profiling of patterns of choice in intonational and other semiotic systems within particular registers that one builds a basis from which we can begin to make principled decisions about how to interpret written transcriptions of spoken texts from the same or similar contexts. More importantly, this not only then forms a key to unlock, in a theoretically motivated way, a new perspective on the literary cultural heritage of the English language but provides the means to question the nature and role of one semiotic resource—writing—within our overall social-semiotic cultural potential and practice. Writing is itself explicable in registerial terms, as a type of language, in fact as a particular semiotic resource, with its own characteristics and typical social functions, against which functions we may calibrate its affordances and constraints and vice versa.

INTONATION, SPEECH AND WRITING WITHIN MULTIMODAL STUDIES

As a student of the semiology of intonation, I can sometimes feel myself to be in an awkward position with respect to the field of multimodal study, as also with respect to other more established disciplines such as linguistics and the phonetic and phonological sciences. With respect to the study of multimodal communication, intonation phenomena can be treated either as part of language or as systemic resources for communication distinct from, although related to, those traditionally considered part of language (those realised through articulatory systems: consonants and vowels, realising phonemes, morphemes etc). The latter approach allows intonation phenomena to be explored and analysed in relation to other auditory phenomena such as melody and rhythm in music (and in terms of rhythm, in the visual mode as well: cf. for example the studies of rhythm in O'Toole 1994/2010, this volume; and Martinec 2000) and instrumental and vocal qualities (often referred to under the heading of 'timbre') in music and speech (e.g. Crystal 1969; van Leeuwen 1999). To treat intonation phenomena as a distinct semiotic resource from language also reflects and allows participation in a wide range of intellectual and discursive traditions that, in the case of van Leeuwen's influences (cf. van Leeuwen 1999, 2005), includes such diverse scholars and studies as Roland Barthes (on, amongst other things, the semiotics of music, the voice: cf. Barthes 1977), Michael Halliday (linguistics and semiotics) and the composer and music theorist R. Murray Schafer (cf. Schafer 1986).

Michael Halliday includes intonation systems within his overall framework for language description, as a set of phonological systems that realise a variety of grammatical systems in the English language—the latter which he collectively labels 'intonational systems' (1963/2005: 239). In this approach, the student of intonation is primarily a grammarian, alongside those studying the various other systems and syntagms of the lexicogrammar of language. Most other linguists are more cautious in ascribing grammatical status to intonation phenomena. The issue of the relation of intonation and grammar and (conceptions of what constitutes) language has been a bone of contention for many decades (cf., for example, Bolinger 1958, 1964/1972; Crystal 1969). To my knowledge Halliday is alone in assigning full grammatical status within his description of the English language to all intonational phenomena. For some, the statement that intonation is a part of language is problematic (cf. title of Bolinger's 1964/1972 paper 'Around the edge of language'), although many linguists have engaged in the study of this set of phenomena.

Intonation has also of course been studied within the disciplines of the phonological and phonetic sciences, and here one often finds work by scholars working within entirely different disciplines to that in which the study of language (at least, language as meaning) is conducted (cf. Halliday and Greaves 2008 for a discussion of various approaches to and purposes for studying intonation phenomena). The student of intonation within these traditions is often a 'laboratory', 'experimental' phonologist, studying intonation as an abstraction from phonetic patterning, or a phoneticist, studying intonation in terms of the physical characteristics of its realisation in sound (acoustic phonetics), the perception of such (auditory phonetics) or the articulatory aspects of production (articulatory phonetics).

As demonstrated earlier in this paper, the theoretical tradition within which one works will to a large extent determine and limit the type of description one will produce and indeed the scope of one's enquiry. My own experience has been that many grammarians/linguists are reluctant to enter the forbidding realm of phonological science considered essential to study the use of intonation, and so intonation is often overlooked where it is clearly significant to a linguistic analysis; and phonologists, or those linguists working on the phonology of intonation, on the whole prefer to approach the study of intonation in terms of the reassuringly 'concrete' aspects of the sound signal, working towards phonology via consideration of phonetic patterning, such that, even though, according to the linguist Crystal (1969: 18), 'Most linguists would agree that statements of meaning are, in fact, their ultimate business', nevertheless 'procedurally, considerations of meaning . . . do not enter in until a stable basis of formerly defined features has been determined'.

Although this view, from a prominent linguist, may be contrasted to that espoused by that most famous of phoneticists, Ladefoged, quoted at the head of section two of this article (cf also Ladd 1996: 98), for Ladefoged, as for many others, many of the intonation contrasts identified by a scholar of intonation such as Pierrehumbert (1980), for example, (Ladefoged 1997: 590) 'are not what we would consider to be linguistically contrastive'. The point here is, as suggested earlier, that one's own theoretical and disciplinary approach is an intimate influence upon one's conception and indeed perception of the minutae of the sound signal and their significance (in the same way that learners of a foreign language tend not to perceive phonetic contrasts not significant in their language of origin). The 'grounding' of phonetic science in the study of concrete physical signal (instrumentally, computationally accessible and verifiable) does not ensure that all doubts about the empirically based scientific foundation for one's research are thus erased[9].

These are all issues that have relevance to the emerging field of multi-modal studies. In the present paper I have tried to show firstly that in the present endeavour to understand multimodal discourse—the characteristics and social functions of different semiotic modes and resources alone and in concert—it is worthwhile to explore and take into account the affordances and constraints of different theoretical and even disciplinary approaches to its study, including those developed for and traditionally associated with the study of (spoken and written) language. I have then shown how the application of register theory, in particular, forms a useful empirical basis for 'translating' a written text into the spoken mode, by relating a text to its context and thus offers a basis for thinking about the roles, affordances and constraints of different semiotic resources within literate cultures in general. And I have problematised the place of intonation within multimodal studies as a field, as a means to suggest that there are many (theoretical, institutional) issues of fundamental importance to the emerging domain of multimodal studies which, in many ways, echo those faced (or not faced) by scholars of language in the twentieth century.

Considering that all multimodal studies ultimately involve the production of (academic) discourse, in the metatheoretical as for the theoretical domain; therefore, the concept of register provides a useful starting point for exploring the characteristics and roles of different (disciplinary and theoretical) approaches in the study of contemporary multimodal text. As Matthiessen (1993: 282) suggests 'we find that insights into register variation in language can also be projected one order up in abstraction and be explored as principles concerning register variation in metalanguage'. When testing and calibrating different theoretical approaches to the study of multimodality therefore, a useful question is, 'what is the purpose or function of the study, and how does this purpose influence the types of approach taken?'. Our metadiscourse may usefully be subjected to the same analysis and theoretical treatment as the discourses we study.

NOTES

1. This text is taken from the Macquarie-UTS corpus of spoken Australian English.
2. Although the repetition may also be suggestive of a 'double meaning', it is unlikely that this alone would have resulted in speaker one's follow-up response.
3. It is not clear how one might have used the conventional punctuation resources of the written English language to transcribe either the pitch movement or its

meaning. A question mark, for example, which can be used with declaratives to indicate the semantic choice of 'question' (queclaratives: cf. discussion of Speaker 1's follow-up response), does not capture the sense here.

4. The initial rise may in fact be treated as non-significant in the phonological description, being merely a product of articulatory constraints (reaching the high initial pitch).

5. Note Ladd's attempt to capture both the sense of query and of additional interpersonal force through his punctuation: "!?".

6. Cf. van Leeuwen (1992) for an alternative interpretation; Smith 2008 for a discussion.

7. Without any 'good reason' for another interpretation (Halliday 1967) one assumes the primary stressed syllable of the last content lexical item as the locus of the pitch contour/assignment of New status: in this case 'dri-', as the primary stressed syllable of 'driving instructor'. Note also: there may be two (or more) pitch contours assigned to this utterance—another type of textual meaning potential realised through intonation (cf. Halliday and Greaves 2008).

8. http://www.unsw.edu.au/news/pad/articles/2004/sep/Oscar_Wilde.html

9. Cf. Ladd's (1996: 13) comment: 'Because of the general lack of agreement and the notable absence of instrumental evidence for impressionistic descriptions, adherents of the instrumental approach have often felt that their work is somehow more rigorous and more scientific . . . '.

REFERENCES

Barthes, R. (1977) *Image, Music, Text*, London: Fontana.
Bolinger, D. L. (1958) 'Intonation and grammar'. *Language Learning* 8: 31–37.
——— (1964/1972). 'Around the edge of language: Intonation'. *Harvard Educational Review* 34 (2): 282–293. Reprinted in Bolinger, D. L. M. ed. *Intonation: Selected Readings*. Harmondsworth: Penguin: pp. 19–29.
Bowcher, W. L. (2004) 'Theme and New in play-by-play radio sports commentating'. In Banks, D. ed. *Text and Texture: Systemic Functional Viewpoints on the Nature and Structure of Text*. Paris: L'Harmattan: pp. 455–493.
Brazil, D. (1978) *Discourse Intonation II*, Birmingham: English Language Research, University of Birmingham.
Butt, D. G. (2003) *Parameters of Context: On Establishing the Similarities and Differences Between Social Processes*, Mimeo, Sydney: Macquarie University.
Carlyle, T. (1966) 'Lecture V. The hero as a man of letters: Johnson, Rousseau, Burns'. In Neimeyer, C. ed. *On Heroes, Hero-Worship and the Heroic in History*. Lincoln; London: University of Nebraska Press: 154–195.
Crystal, D. (1969) *Prosodic Systems and Intonation in English*. London: Cambridge University Press.
Davies, M. (1986) 'Literacy and Intonation.' In Couture, B. ed. *Functional Approaches to Writing: Research Perspectives*, Norwood, New Jersey: Ablex: pp. 199–220.
Guy, G., and Vonwiller, J. (1984) 'The meaning of an intonation in Australian English.' *Australian Journal of Linguistics* 4: 1–17.
Halliday, M. A. K. (1985) *Spoken and Written Language*, Waurn Ponds, Victoria: Deakin University Press.
——— (1979/2002) 'Modes of meaning and modes of expression: Types of grammatical structure and their determination by different semantic functions.' In Allerton, D. J., Carney, E. and Holdcroft, D. eds. *Function and Context in Linguistic Analysis: A Festschrift for William Haas*, Cambridge: Cambridge

University Press: pp. 196–218; reprinted in Halliday, M. A. K., and Webster, J. eds. *On Grammar*, London: Continuum: pp. 57–79.

—— (1970) *A Course in Spoken English: Intonation*, Oxford: Oxford University Press.

—— (1967) *Intonation and Grammar in British English*, The Hague; Paris: Mouton.

—— (1963/2005) 'The tones of English', *Archivum Linguisticum*, 15 (1): 1–28; reprinted in Halliday, M. A. K., and Webster, J. eds. *Studies in English Language (Collected Works, Volume 7)*. London: Continuum: 237–263.

Halliday, M. A. K., and Greaves, W. S. (2008) *Intonation in the Grammar of English*, London: Equinox.

Halliday, M. A. K., and Hasan, R. (1985) *Language, Context and Text: Aspects of Language in a Social-Semiotic Perspective*, Waurn Ponds, Victoria: Deakin University.

Halliday, M. A. K., and Matthiessen C. M. I. M. (2004) *An Introduction to Functional Grammar*, 3rd ed, London: Arnold.

Halliday, M. A. K., McIntosh, A. and Strevens, P. (1964) *The Linguistic Sciences and Language Teaching*, London: Longmans.

Holland, M. (2003) *Irish Peacock and Scarlet Marquess: The Real Trial of Oscar Wilde*, London New York: Fourth Estate.

Kress, G., and Van Leeuwen, T. (2001) *Multimodal Discourse: The Modes and Media of Contemporary Communication*, London: Arnold.

Ladd, D. R. (1996) *Intonational Phonology*, Cambridge, New York, Melbourne: Cambridge University Press.

Ladefoged, P. (1997) 'Linguistic phonetic descriptions.' In Hardcastle, W. J., and Laver, J. eds. *The Handbook of Phonetic Sciences*, Oxford; Cambridge, Massachusetts: Blackwell: pp. 589–618.

Martinec, R. (2000) 'Rhythm in multimodal texts.' *Leonardo* 33 (4): 289–297.

Matthiessen, C. (1993) 'Register in the Round: Diversity in a Unified Theory of Register Analysis'. In Ghadessy, M. ed. *Register Analysis: Theory and Practice*, London: Pinter: pp. 221–292.

Moore, A. (in press) 'Surgical teams in action: a contextually sensitive approach to modelling body alignment and interpersonal engagement.' In Baldry, A., and Montagna, E. eds. *Interdisciplinary Perspectives on Multimodality: Theory and Practice*, Campobasso, Italy: Palladino.

O'Donnell, M., and Bateman, J. (2005) 'SFL in computational contexts: a contemporary history.' In Webster, J., Hasan, R. and Matthiessen, C. eds. *Continuing Discourse on Language: A Functional Perspective*, Equinox: London: pp. 343–382.

O'Halloran, K. L. (2003) 'Systemics 1.0: Software for Research and Teaching Systemic Functional Linguistics.' *RELC Journal* 34.2: 157–178.

O'Halloran, K. L., Tan S., Smith, B. A. and Podlasov A. (2010) 'Challenges in Designing Digital Interfaces for the Study of Multimodal Phenomena.' *Information Design Journal* 18 (1): 2–21.

O'Toole, M. (1994) *The Language of Displayed Art*, 1st ed, London: Leicester University Press.

—— (2010) *The Language of Displayed Art*, 2nd ed, London and New York: Routledge.

Pierrehumbert, J. B. (1980) *The phonetics and phonology of English intonation* PhD Thesis. Cambridge, Massachusetts: Massachusetts Institute of Technology, available online at http://hdl.handle.net/1721.1/16065 (accessed 15 December 2010).

Pierrehumbert, J. B., and Hirschberg, J. (1990) 'The meaning of intonational contours in the interpretation of discourse.' In Cohen, P. R., Morgan, J. and Pollack, M. E. eds. *Intentions in Communication*, Cambridge: MIT Press: pp. 271–311.

Schafer, R. M. (1986) *The Thinking Ear: Complete Writings on Music Education*. Toronto: Arcana Editions.

Smith, B. A. (2008) 'The language of the heart and breath: Bridging strata, bridging discourses of INFORMATION systems.' *Online Conference Proceedings for the 2007 ASFLA Congress: Bridging Discourses, held at Wollongong University*, 29 June–1 July 2007. Australian Systemic Functional Association, available online at http://www.asfla.org.au/2008/07/31/the-language-of-the-heart-and-breath-bridging-strata-bridging-discourses-of-information-systems/ (accessed 15 December 2010).

Stanislavski, K. (2008) *An Actor's Work*. Trans. J. Benedetti. Abingdon and New York: Routledge.

Teich, E., Watson, C. I. and Pereira, C. (2000) 'Matching a tone-based and tune-based approach to English intonation for concept-to-speech generation.' In *COLING 2000: Proceedings of the 18th International Conference on Computational Linguistics, July 31–August 4, Universitat des Saarlandes, Saarbrucken, Germany*. San Francisco, California: Morgan Kaufmann Publishers: pp. 829–835.

Thurlow, C. and Pof, M. (2009) 'The language of text-messaging'. In Herring, S. C., Stein, D. and Virtanen, T. eds., *Handbook of the Pragmatics of CMC*. Berlin and New York: Mouton de Gruyter.

University of New South Wales. (2008) "Oscar Wilde's Grandson at UNSW". Webpage, last updated 12 December 2008. http://www.unsw.edu.au/news/pad/articles/2004/sep/Oscar_wilde.html (accessed 15 December 2010).

Van Leeuwen, T. (1992) 'Rhythm and social context: accent and juncture in the speech of professional radio announcers.' In Tench, P. ed. *Studies in Systemic Phonology*, London; New York: Pinter Publishers: pp. 231–262.

——— (1999) *Speech, Music, Sound*, Houndmills: MacMillan Press.

——— (2005) *Introducing Social Semiotics*, London; New York: Routledge.

4 Visual Space and Ideology
A Critical Cognitive Analysis of Spatial Orientations in Advertising

Feng Dezheng

INTRODUCTION

After exploring the compositional meaning of visual space for the analysis of newspaper layout, Kress and van Leeuwen (1998: 218) admit that 'the major challenge to our approach is the epistemological status of our claim. For instance, how can we know that in western semiosis, left and right, top and bottom have the values we attribute to them, or more fundamentally, have any value at all?' They regard this as a legitimate challenge but don't provide an answer because, as they concede, 'we regard our efforts here as a beginning' (ibid).

To solve the problem, some scholars within the field of visual communication claim that we interpret spatial orientation in the way that we do because of our prior visual literacy (Berkeley 2003; Dyer 1989; Mitchell 2008). As Dyer (1989: 131) explains, 'we derive meanings from kinds of shots and other filmic techniques because we have learned the codes and conventions of photography and film practice'. However, this proposal requires further investigation because, as Messaris points out (1994: 9), 'the first time or inexperienced viewers should be able to make sense of the low-angle device and other spatial orientations'.

In this chapter the epistemological status of Kress and van Leeuwen's (1996) claim is explored from a cognitive perspective. Specifically, the question 'how do we know' is addressed by consideration of the Conceptual Metaphor Theory proposed by Lakoff and Johnson (1980), who claim that most abstract concepts are partially understood in terms of other (concrete) concepts. The concrete nature of spatial orientations makes it a perfect source domain for understanding abstract concepts like importance, power and emotions. This source domain is so important as to merit a metaphor category of its own: orientational metaphor[1], which means the understanding of abstract concepts in terms of spatial orientations, as in POWER IS UP and SAD IS DOWN (Lakoff and Johnson, 1980). Like all conceptual metaphors, the mapping of orientational metaphor is based on our embodied experience: the meaning of the visual space can be interpreted as the target domain of an orientational metaphor with 'experiential basis' as its grounding.

The introduction of orientational metaphor supports the association of spatial orientation and information value as proposed by Kress and van Leeuwen (1996). However, a further aim in this chapter is to use orientational metaphor to explore other meanings constructed through spatial relations and what ideology is thus conveyed implicitly. Through the examination of 100 car advertisements, it is found that, aside from organising information into a coherent whole, space orientations also construct 'power' (engine power, social power and image-viewer power relation) through vertical orientation and image-viewer interaction through horizontal orientation.

Car advertisements are chosen for their prevalent and innovative use of visual image. A total of 100 advertisements were collected mainly from Singapore's English daily newspaper, *The Straits Times*; a small number was selected also from local magazines and the Internet. Spanning a period of six months from August 2008 to January 2009, the selection of advertisements was randomly undertaken, excluding repeated copies of advertisements. The cars of the data set represented a combination of Japanese, American and European brands, all of which make extensive use of spatial relation as means of encoding ideology to enhance persuasive power.

A COGNITIVE APPROACH TO MULTI-SEMIOTIC CAR ADVERTISEMENTS

Framework of Visual Space

According to Kress and van Leeuwen (1996), spatial relation simultaneously involves three signifying systems: information value, salience and framing. Information value is signified by left/right, up/down and centre/margin spatial locations. The two-dimensional space proposed by Kress and van Leeuwen (1996) can be extended to a three-dimensional gestalt, including 'depth'. The depth of visual image is also discussed in Cross (2005: 184), who argues that the two-dimensional heuristic does not include all the directions/positions for physical space. In the car advertisements studied, the third dimension includes the foreground/background composition and the positioning of the car on the page. Due to their special features, cars may be positioned upward (front higher), downward (front lower), forward (front faces viewer) and backward.

Aside from the spatial relations among the visual elements and their positioning, there is another important dimension of visual space: the spatial relation between the object represented and the camera, which includes their distance and relative angle. Following Messaris (1994), we call this dimension 'camera positioning'. It encodes spatial relation through the high/low, front/oblique angles and close/long shots.

Hence, spatial relation can be sub-categorised as layout of elements, positioning of the car and camera positioning. For convenience of discussion, the orientation is divided into vertical and horizontal, but it should be noted that the two axes and the three spatial elements work together to encode meaning. The reworked spatial relation framework used for the analysis in this chapter is displayed in Table 4.1.

A Critical Cognitive Approach

From a critical point of view, the information encoded through spatial relations carries implicit visual persuasion. The two main ideological devices employed in advertisements are information value and image-viewer relations. The former attracts viewer's attention, making them focus on certain elements preferred by the advertisers. The latter adjusts the image-viewer interaction/distance, thus putting the viewers at a reading position intended by the advertisers in terms of both power relation and symbolic distance (see Table 4.2).

The semantic relations in Table 4.2 are realised *metaphorically* through spatial relations in Table 4.1, with the former as target domain and the latter as source. So Kress and van Leeuwen's (1996) descriptive model 'Left is Given' becomes, in the cognitive approach, GIVEN IS LEFT. This is a significant propositional change because, in systemic functional linguistic

Table 4.1 Framework of Visual Space in Car Advertisements

Visual space / Axis	Layout	Positioning	Camera positioning
Vertical	Up/down	Upward/downward	High/low angles
Horizontal	Central/marginal Right/left Foreground/background	Forward/backward Rightward/leftward	Front/oblique angles Close shot/long shots

Table 4.2 Semantic Relations Constructed through Visual Space

Visual / Axis	Layout	Positioning	Camera positioning
Vertical	Information value: *Ideal/Real*	Empowerment: *The car, the consumer* Accessibility	Image-viewer: *power relation*
Horizontal	Information value: *Importance* *Given/New*	Image-viewer: *Interaction*	Image-viewer: *Interaction* *Distance*

terms (Halliday 1994), what was 'given' (Token) in the first proposition becomes 'new' (Value) in the second. That is, in the first proposition we are assigning meaning to the visual space, and in the second we understand an abstract concept as it is realised through a concrete phenomenon. In this way, the meaning of the visual space is seen as a *macro metaphor,* which entails the submappings of dimensions of information value onto dimensions of visual space, as is shown in Tables 4.3 and 4.4.

According to Conceptual Metaphor Theory, the association between spatial orientations and their meanings is not arbitrary, rather, it is based on our physical and cultural experience, and a metaphor can only serve as a vehicle for understanding a concept by virtue of its experiential basis (Lakoff and Johnson 1980: 14). The experiential basis of metaphor is of special relevance here because it explains the 'how can we know' question. Seen as a metaphor, the validity of the association between visual space and semiotic value is determined by the existence and functioning of the experiential basis. It follows that the dispute about Kress and van Leeuwen's (1996) model should not be simply *whether* it is right or wrong but *when.* That is, when the experiential basis *exists* and *functions*, the model holds.

Let's take the left/right orientation as an example. In English-speaking cultures, we write and read from left to right, so we take the left as Given information and the right as New. This is a metaphorical process in that information value is understood in terms of spatial relations, according to our (culturally determined) experience of reading. The process can be captured by the metaphor: INFORMATION VALUE IS READING PATH, which entails GIVEN IS LEFT and NEW IS RIGHT. But the precondition is the experience of writing from left to right, so in cultures where people write from right to left (as in Ancient China or some Arabic countries) the model is questionable. Moreover, the experiential basis must be functioning with respect to other factors: that is, GIVEN IS LEFT is valid when the reading path is not interrupted or overwhelmed by other factors such as visual salience through size, font, colour etc.

It should also be noted that not every metaphor is grounded in immediate experience, rather, many are grounded indirectly through 'inheritance hierarchies' (Lakoff 1993: 241). Metaphorical mapping lower in a hierarchy can inherit its experiential basis indirectly from a mapping higher in the hierarchy. For example, GAINING POWER IS MOVING UP inherits the grounding of POWER IS UP.

Based on our physical and cultural experience, the meaning of the visual space is captured by orientational metaphors. In the following section, mappings between spatial relations and their metaphorical meanings are explored to investigate the semantics of visual space and the ideologies which result. The metaphor system represented in Tables 4.3 and 4.4 constitutes the major framework for this investigation, with a focus on the vertical axis in Vertical Orientational Metaphor and Ideology and the horizontal axis in Horizontal Orientational Metaphor and Ideology, respectively.

VERTICAL ORIENTATIONAL METAPHOR AND IDEOLOGY

The metaphor system, which serves as the framework for exploring the semantics of vertical visual space is represented in Table 4.3. As was shown in Table 4.2 earlier, 'layout' encodes information value through the metaphors IDEAL IS UP and REAL IS DOWN, while 'positioning' and 'camera angle' mainly encode power through sub-metaphors of the generic conceptual metaphor POWER IS UP.

Layout of Verbal and Visual

In the vertical layout of car advertisements, the uppermost part is usually the Headline, followed by the Main Image of a car, which is then followed by the Body Copy, and optionally, Sign-off and Logo (Landa 2004; see Image 1 of Figure 4.3). For analysis, the visual space is divided into two parts: the upper part, which includes the headline and the image, and the lower part, which includes the body copy and others. In accordance with Kress and van Leeuwen (1996), IDEAL IS UP and REAL IS DOWN are metaphors, capturing the meaning of the orientations 'up' and 'down', with the former entailing DESIRABLE IS UP, ABSTRACT IS UP and UNREALISTIC IS UP, and the latter entailing CONCRETE IS DOWN and REALISTIC IS DOWN. In the following discussion I will explain the experiential basis of each metaphor and unveil the ideological function of such visual arrangement.

What is ideal can be desirable, abstract and unrealistic, all of which can be understood through the orientation 'up', but they are based on quite different experiences. In accordance with Lakoff and Johnson's (1980) analysis of the metaphor GOOD IS UP, we can say that DESIRABLE IS UP is based on the fact that concepts of positive qualities are all up: HAPPY IS UP, HEALTHY IS UP, RATIONAL IS UP, POWER IS UP and so forth, which are further based on our physical experience: for example, HAPPY IS UP is based

Table 4.3 Vertical Orientational Metaphor System

Layout	Positioning	Camera angle

(i) IDEAL IS UP
    DESIRABLE IS UP
    UNREALISTIC IS UP
    ABSTRACT IS UP
 	
(ii) REAL IS DOWN
    CONCRETE IS DOWN
    REALISTIC IS DOWN
	(i) POWER IS UPWARD
	    ENGINE POWER IS UPWARD
	    MOTION
	    GAINING POWER IS MOVING
	      UPWARD
	
	(ii) ACCESSIBLE IS DOWNWARD
		(i) VIEWER POWER IS HIGH
		    ANGLE
		
		(ii) EQUALITY IS EYE-LEVEL
		    ANGLE
		
		(iii) IMAGE POWER IS LOW
		    ANGLE

on the habitual experience that an erect positioning (for example, bodily and facial posture) signals a positive emotional state.

The metaphors UNREALISTIC IS UP and ABSTRACT IS UP make use of another sense of 'up', that is, 'high'. We have to draw upon the metaphor ACCESSING (to something abstract, e.g. power, taste) IS GRASPING (something concrete), which entails the two metaphors UNDERSTANDING IS GRASPING and POSSESSING IS GRASPING. From experience, we know that what is high (e.g. stars) is difficult or impossible to grasp, and the metaphor UNDERSTANDING/PROCESSING IS GRASPING then entails DIFFICULTY OF UNDERSTANDING/PROCESSING IS DIFFICULTY OF GRASPING. In the last step, our cultural experience classifies what is difficult to possess as unrealistic and what is difficult to understand as abstract. The metaphor REAL IS DOWN, which entails REALISTIC IS DOWN and CONCRETE IS DOWN, is in antonymic relationship with IDEAL IS UP in the sense of ideal as 'unrealistic' and 'abstract' (note also the metaphor of 'grasping'). It has the same experiential basis as UNREALISTIC / ABSTRACT IS UP. Figure 4.1 shows the mapping of up/down orientation onto ideal/real value through experiential basis.

Having established the experiential grounding and metaphorical mapping of both IDEAL IS UP and REAL IS DOWN, the next step is to look into the ideological functions of the up/down orientation. Our main concern here is to find out the reason why in print advertisements headline and image are put in the upper part and the body copy at the lower part and the effect of this layout.

We adopt the generic structure potential of print advertisements proposed by Cheong (2004) to analyse the functioning of spatial layout. The terms are different from Landa (2004), but the meanings are similar, as is indicated in the brackets in Figure 4.2. Although Cheong (2004) may not intend to take spatial layout into consideration, her model roughly captures the up/down division of information arrangement (except that Announcement may appear uppermost). The visual and linguistic components interact

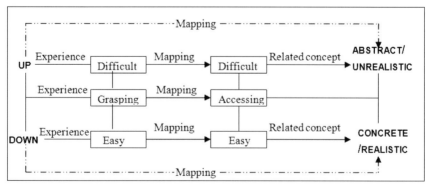

Figure 4.1   Grounding and realisation of ABSTRACT/UNREALISTIC IS UP and REAL IS DOWN.

(indicated by the bi-directional arrows) to create interpersonal, ideational and compositional meanings, but in terms of salience, the image in the upper part, which is interpersonal in function, is more salient (attracting attention) than the lower part, which is more ideational (providing information).

The ideology of this layout is threefold. First of all, the viewer is absorbed in the 'ideal world' in which you have power, freedom, success and so on. When the image is between the headline and the body copy, it serves as the bridge between the 'ideal' and 'real', suggesting that the 'ideal world' is made accessible by the car. As Vestergaard and Schroder (1985: 197) point out, advertisements do function on a fantasy level, but in order for people to find it relevant, the utopia visualised in advertisements must be linked to our surrounding reality by a causal connection. For example, in Image 1 of Figure 4.3, the headline 'wear your ego, drive the technology' is 'ideal', emancipating and empowering the viewer; the car, while still working on the ideal level in the sense that it illustrates the illusion built by the headline, points to the body copy through its heading. The illusion of accessibility is reinforced by the fact that the man is actually 'wearing' the car, which gives us the impression that the car is just an accessory (a watch).

The second ideological device is the vague meaning of 'ideal'. As is pointed out above, IDEAL IS UP entails DESIRABLE IS UP and UNREALISTIC IS UP. The ideology here is that 'desirable' is fully flagged, made salient through the headline and the image, but 'unrealistic' is suppressed, implicit in the layout. This goes perfectly with the objective of advertisements: they function on a fantasy level, constructing an imaginary world in which the reader is able to make come true those desires which remain unsatisfied in his/her everyday life (Vestergaard and Schroder 1985: 117). The suppression of 'unrealistic' makes the 'ideal world' reliable, and the reliability is reinforced by the high modality (full colour, real-life situation and sometimes human figures) of the image, which further suppresses the

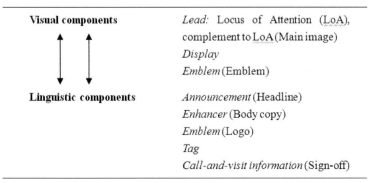

Figure 4.2   Generic structure of print advertisements (Cheong 2004: 165).

sense of 'unrealistic'. That the purchase of the car does not redeem this promise of the advertisement the consumers may well be aware of, but they are encouraged to enjoy a 'future endlessly deferred fantasy' (Berger 1972: 146).

Third, while the metaphors DESIRABLE/UNREALISTIC IS UP, REALISTIC IS DOWN function *interpersonally* to attract viewers' attention and involve their emotion through creating an 'ideal world', the metaphors ABSTRACT IS UP, CONCRETE IS DOWN function *ideationally* to describe the different information value assigned to the upper and lower sections. In the typical layout, the headline and the image are abstract, fancy and flowery, the body copy provides concrete information about the quality of the car, the call-and-visit information relates more immediately to reality by providing the information of the dealer and price, the logo/emblem closes the multimodal interaction by pointing to the manufacturer through the metonymy LOGO STANDS FOR MANUFACTURER. This structure is illustrated in Image 1 of Figure 4.3.

Metaphor and Ideology of the Positioning of the Car

This section is concerned with the positioning of the car. Our focus will be on the case when the car is (positioned as) a snapshot of the car in motion. The snapshot suggests motion through the metonymy SNAPSHOT OF THE CAR IN MOTION STANDS FOR THE MOTION. We will focus on the meaning of upward/downward motion. Two metaphors can be identified for the upward motion: (i) ENGINE POWER IS UPWARD MOTION and (ii) GAINING POWER IS MOVING UPWARD and one for downward motion: ACCESSIBLE IS DOWNWARD.

The Metaphor and Ideology of Upward Motion

(i) ENGINE POWER IS UPWARD MOTION. Cars have engine power, which defies natural forces (especially gravity) and thus engine power is an important feature, which the manufacturers (the advertisers) promote. From our world knowledge, we know that going up a slope requires more energy than going forward on flat ground or going downward, and this fact makes upward motion the proof of engine power. In other words, moving upward with ease is an index of engine power. This indexical relation between upward motion and engine power serves as the basis of the metaphor ENGINE POWER IS UPWARD MOTION, which enables us to understand the abstract concept engine power in terms of the concrete phenomenon of moving upward. (ii) GAINING POWER IS MOVING UPWARD. In the metaphor ENGINE POWER IS UPWARD MOTION, the 'motion' is understood literally. However, it can also be interpreted as moving upward along the 'social ladder', hence, the metaphor GAINING POWER IS MOVING UPWARD. The metaphor is an entailment of a more

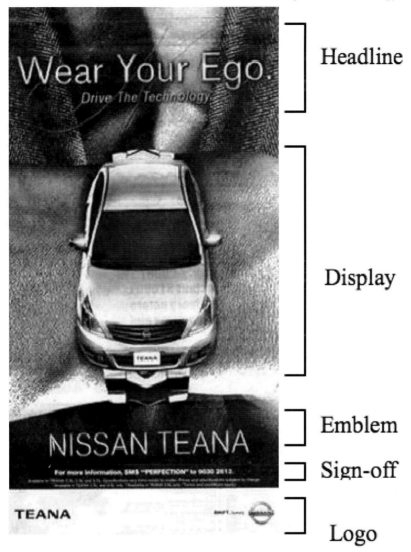

Figure 4.3   Car (Image 1)

generic metaphor POWER IS UP, and the experiential basis of POWER IS UP
serves as an indirect basis of GAINING POWER IS MOVING UPWARD.

When a car is displayed upward, both engine power and gaining social
power are suggested (see Image 2 of Figure 4.3). First of all, it implies
the engine power of the car without making an explicit assertion. As
far as cars are concerned, engine power is so crucial a criterion of car
quality that every manufacturer wants to claim their engine is the best.
However, as Vestergaard and Schroder (1985) warn, it is very dangerous

to make bold claims of the excellence of the product because consumers nowadays may react badly to direct propaganda. One solution is to construct the advertisers' claim implicitly through visual image. In Image 2 of Figure 4.3, the blurred wheel suggests it is a snapshot of the car in motion, impressing upon the viewer the view of the car as moving upward with ease (safety). The bumpy road with snow that makes the driving more difficult reinforces the excellence of the car. This interpretation is supported by the verbal element on the right, which reads 'Besides the *effortless strength of the new generation V6 engine*, the S-Class also comes with PRO-SAFE, the Mercedes-Benz holistic safety philosophy'.

The engine power carries you upward on the road, but when you drive the car you are not just moving up literally, but also metaphorically, along the 'social slope'. This is the second aspect of the ideology of moving upward: in a hierarchical society where consumers are assumed to be eager to move to a 'higher position', it creates an illusion that if you drive the car you will gain power with the same ease as the car moves upward, or the upward motion of the car may function for consumers as a sign of such upward social mobility. However, the upward motion alone cannot suggest the notion of power and has to be "relayed" by the language. In Image 2 of Figure 4.3, the fantasy of 'power', 'status' and 'superiority' is clearly represented in the verbal element: '[f]or over 30 years, it has

Figure 4.3   Car (Image 2)

Figure 4.3   Car (Image 3)

been *the choice of world leaders and celebrities.*' This constitutes the multimodal nature of the metaphor GAINING POWER IS MOVING UPWARD with its source depicted visually and its target expressed linguistically (Forceville 1996).

It should be noted that the upward motion may be formed by visual circumstantial elements, as in Image 3 of Figure 4.3 where the staircase configuration of light behind the car forms a strong vector pointing upward. This vector can be interpreted metaphorically as gaining power, given the knowledge that one normally moves to an upstairs office when he/she gets promoted. It is put in the background as a circumstantial element but also as a visual Theme, and the car is in the foreground as focus. The information is something like this: you have achieved power/status (as circumstantial Theme), now what you should do is to buy a Camry. This proposal is reinforced in the headline 'expect luxury when you *move up*'.

The Metaphor and Ideology of Downward Motion

Downward motion is not as common as upward motion probably because of the negative connotations of 'down'. However, it *is* used when a high-class car is newly introduced to market. The effect of downward motion is achieved through the metaphor ACCESSIBLE IS DOWNWARD. The metaphor

entails three submappings: THE STARTING POINT OF THE MOTION IS PRO-
DUCER, THE PATH OF THE MOTION IS PROCESS OF BECOMING ACCESSIBLE
and DESTINATION OF THE MOTION IS MARKET.

The metaphor is grounded in our experience of grasping: when something gets down, it becomes easier to grasp. The ideology is that the starting point is higher, indicating the superiority of the producer and excellence
of the product; the consumer, at the position of destination, looks up to
the coming of the car. The constructed reaction on the viewer's part is like
catching an illusive falling object, or from Chinese culture, like seeing a god/
goddess gracefully descending to earthly human, riding a piece of cloud. In
either case, the emotion elicited is one of happiness, gratitude and worship.
A relevant case in point is an advertisement for the Mitsubishi Pajero when
it enters the Chinese market. The car is depicted as going downward. The
starting point (Japan) is considered as higher than the destination (China)
as far as car quality is concerned. Thus Chinese consumers may welcome
the car like a descending god.

Metaphor and Ideology of Camera Angle

Vertical camera angles construct power relations between viewer and represented figure (e.g. Dyer 1989; Kress and van Leeuwen 1996; Messaris
1994; Zettl 1990). The meaning of camera angles on the vertical axis can
be discussed using following metaphors: (i) VIEWER POWER IS HIGHER
CAMERA ANGLE; (ii) IMAGE POWER IS LOW ANGLE. The grounding of these
metaphors is simple: on the one hand, it is related to POWER IS UP and
shares its experiential basis; on the other hand, it reproduces the structural
features of real-life situations in which we look up to powerful people and
look down upon weak people (Messaris 1994: 9).

The use of high angle and low angle are both prevalent in car advertisements, with their corresponding ideologies. When high angle is used,
the advertiser intends to build consumer power and to let the viewer feel
empowered; when low angle is used, the advertiser intends to build image
power and, to emphasise the superiority of the car.

In the corpus of car advertisements, 67% use high camera angle, which
suggests that advertisers attach much importance to the building of consumer power. The high angle may also create the illusion that the viewer
is the owner of the car on the ground that only the owner of an object has
power over the object and has a good reason to look down on the object.
Thus although the reader does not own the car, they are empowered
through the visual semiotics of the advertisements. If the reader identifies with and enjoys the feeling of being the (virtual) owner, they may be
more inclined to buy the car and become the owner in actuality.

Most advertisements make use of this strategy, except Mercedes-Benz
and other high-end cars. There are six advertisements of Mercedes cars,
five of which use low camera angle (see Image 2 of Figure 4.3). This

constitutes the second strategy: the building of product superiority. High-class cars are often associated with elitism, making themselves a symbol of status and wealth. Advertisers adopt low camera angle to trigger viewers' reverence toward status and wealth and project the reverence to the car. This appeals to the potential consumer of Mercedes-Benz: those who could afford a Mercedes are already well-established and care more about the manifestation of their power in symbolic form. The superiority of the car, visualised through camera angle, is just like the superiority of the consumers themselves, which thus makes it appealing.

HORIZONTAL ORIENTATIONAL METAPHOR AND IDEOLOGY

The metaphor system that serves as the framework for horizontal orientation is displayed in Table 4.4. On the horizontal axis, 'Layout' encodes information value in terms of importance, given/new, and past/present; 'positioning' and 'camera angle' encode image viewer interaction. 'Positioning' on the horizontal level is not considered in terms of motion. The forward, backward, rightward and leftward positionings are treated as static representation at different angles, which encodes image-viewer interaction. Since these interactions are achieved through camera angle, they are considered under the heading of camera positioning.

Layout of Verbal and Visual

In the layout, three pairs of relations are discussed: centre/margin, left/right and foreground/background. According to the orientational metaphor framework, these relations construct concepts of given/new, importance/unimportance and present/past.

Table 4.4 Horizontal Orientational Metaphor System

Layout	Positioning	Camera positioning
(i) left/right NEW IS RIGHT/GIVEN IS LEFT	IMAGE-VIEWER INTERACTION IS THE ANGLE OF REPRESENTATION *INVOLVEMENT IS FRONTALITY*	(i) SOCIAL DISTANCE IS SHOT DISTANCE
(ii) center/margin IMPORTANCE IS CENTRALITY	*DETACHMENT IS PROFILE*	(ii) IMAGE-VIEWER INTER-ACTION IS THE ANGLE OF REPRESENTATION
(iii) foreground/background IMPORTANT IS FOREGROUND		*INVOLVEMENT IS FRONT ANGLE* *DETACHMENT IS OBLIQUE ANGLE*

Right/Left Orientation

The meaning of left/right as given/new is conventional and is based on reading path (see A Critical Cognitive Approach). The values of both left and right are exploited in car advertisements. For the value of Given, Kress and van Leeuwen (1996: 183) argue in the analysis of an advertisement for Mercedes-Benz that the car photographed on the left is treated as an already known, 'given' symbol of status. For the value of 'new', Stenglin and Iedema (2001: 196) claim that advertisers pay higher rates to have their advertisements printed on the right-hand-side pages. However, the regular patterns in which the left contains an image and the right is verbal text should also be considered from the perspective of salience. As Kress and van Leeuwen (1996: 183) point out, the Given may be more salient visually than the New. We argue that when the left contains an image it is designed to be more salient for its size (normally the entire left side), colour (highly saturated) and high modality (true to life). Martin (2000: 334) also observes that the left is not simply Given, but has a positive forward-looking function, instigating and naturalising a reading position for the evaluation of verbiage/image texture that ensues. Therefore, aside from construing established status, the left image also attracts viewers' attention, as in Image 2, Figure 4.3.

The given and the new, organised by reading path, work as a coherent discourse with different affordances. They manipulate the viewers at three levels: first of all, the image of the car is given information, constructing its unarguable status (while it may well be arguable); second, the image does not simply work like linguistic *Theme*, it engages viewers' attention like the proposition 'this car you should buy' and also arouses viewers' desire for the car by its attractiveness; third, after the viewer's interest is aroused, the body copy/enhancer on the right comes into consideration to provide new information.

Centre/Margin Orientation

The association between central and important is so conventional that an account of its experiential basis seems to be unnecessary, and we only need to point out that it may arise from our biological feature of containing the most vital organs (heart and marrow) in the centre. In car advertisements, strict centre/margin layout is rare and most layouts polarise Given and New and/or Ideal and Real (Kress and van Leeuwen 1998: 196). However, if we were to see the middle of up/down and left/right polarity as centre and the rest as marginal, the centre/margin orientation is quite common. But it should be noted that in such a layout the difference between Given and New and/or Ideal and Real still exists. The power of centre/margin orientation is that it enables different orientations to work together to organise information according to their importance and function. Let's illustrate this point by an example.

Figure 4.3 Car (Image 4)

In Image 4 of Figure 4.3, the overall pattern can be seen as centre/margin, with the image of the car centralised and the rest marginalised. The central image apparently is the most important, not only because of its centrality but also because of other factors, such as large size, close shot and the angle of representation, which invests the car with the appearance of dynamism. As for the margin, there is perceived difference in their information value too, which can be interpreted in terms of Given/New and Ideal/Real. Among the marginal elements, headline right above the image is most important (highly valued, medium salience, according to Stenglin and Iedema 2001: 196), both owing to its 'ideal' position and its size and colour. Then follows the body copy in the right, which should be both highly valued and highly salient, but its salience is overridden by other elements. The last information, the price, is represented as given and realistic, which has the lowest salience. Such an arrangement is apparently ideologically motivated in that it is not in the accordance with the actual importance of buying a car (price may be first priority for many consumers).

Foreground/Background Orientation

Kress and van Leeuwen (1996: 201) treat foreground/background as one means of realising salience, and write that 'salience can create a hierarchy of

importance among elements, selecting some as more important, more worthy of attention'. Implicit in this proposition is that foreground information
is more important than background information, equal to the metaphor
IMPORTANT IS FOREGROUND. The notion of 'depth' explains this mapping.
Depth is 'the distance between the viewers' eyes and any point in the visual
field' (Messaris 1994: 51). So the foreground is read as near to the viewer
and the background remote to the viewer, which is in accordance with the
front-back z-axis proposed by Zettl (1990: 178). Our biological feature
of vision results in the different visual impacts of far and near objects:
we notice what is in the foreground first and take it as more important.
Normally, the car and the verbal text would be in the foreground and the
setting of the car in the background. The ideology of foreground is that it is
designed to be the focus of attention; the choice of background is ideological in that advertisers only choose backgrounds that go with the themes of
the advertisements, such as the choice of mountain to echo the themes of
status and adventure.

Sometimes however the setting communicates more information than
contextualising the car: it provides information about the 'past' while the
foreground is the 'present'. The foreground/background orientation in
this sense works in a similar way as the right/left one: it constructs the
established status of Given information and focus on the New; just the
background is not the departure of the discourse. For example, in Image
3 of Figure 4.3, the car (and other elements) is in the foreground as the
focus of attention, the staircase-like light arrangement forms the discursive topic of 'moving up', but it is constructed as 'past', as a presupposed
condition for the relevance of 'present'. Although not processed first, the
ideology of 'past' is the same as Given information: it represents 'success'
as well-established fact to entice the viewer while 'success' may in fact be
an aspiration.

Camera Positioning

Angle of Representation

The angles of representation can be categorised into the frontal angle,
which is the shot of the object at 90°, left/right angle, which is the shot
at 0° or 180°, and the oblique angle, which occurs in between. Following
Jewitt and Oyama (2001: 136), we will term the front-angle representation of the car as "frontality" and right/left orientation as 'profile'. Different angles of representation encode different social relations. Frontality
constructs maximum 'involvement' between the viewer and the image. As
Kress and van Leeuwen (1996: 136) point out, the frontal angle says, as it
were, 'what you see here is part of our world, something we are involved
with'. The representation of profile, on the other hand, constructs maximum detachment between the viewer and the image. The oblique angle,

working between these two polarities, constructs various intermediate degrees of interaction.

The association between social interaction and angle of representation is based on three important factors: the iconic nature of image, our knowledge of interpersonal communication and the personification of cars. According to Peircean semiotics, image is the primary means of iconic representation (Sebeok 2001). As a result, we tend to perceive images of concrete things as if they are real. That is why most people can decode visual representations without being taught (Messaris 1994), although their interpretation of the meanings of the image may not be critically informed.

Next, in real-life communication, we face the person we like to interact with, and most crucially, we gaze at him/her; we turn our face (gaze) away if we don't want to interact. So far, we have established that an image of a person directly gazing at the viewer is interpreted as interacting with the viewer (cf. Kress and van Leeuwen 1996). The third step is the personification of cars. The mapping between cars and human beings is a conceptual phenomenon and is prevalent in everyday language: we not only describe components of the car as organs of human beings (e.g. the headlights of the car) but also see a car as a person with emotion, charm and temper (Wernick 1991). Kress and van Leeuwen (1996: 118) also point out that although cars are not human beings, by being represented as looking at the viewer, they are represented as human. Thus, the front view of the car can be seen as direct gaze with maximum involvement, and the profile can be seen as no gaze with minimum interaction. The meaning can be represented as INVOLVEMENT IS FRONTALITY and DETACHMENT IS PROFILE, with the above as experiential basis.

As the angle of maximum involvement, front angle serves to align the viewer, to represent the car as interacting with the viewer. Through the personification of the car, frontality takes on the ideology of direct gaze: the car demands that the viewer enters into some kind of imaginary relation with it (Kress and van Leeuwen 1996). A surprisingly small number of advertisements use this angle. This may due to the fact that frontality makes the car 'aggressive without been attractive' (Vestergaard and Schroder 1985). The conscious avoidance of front angle may reflect the advertisers' awareness of consumers' resentment of direct command, which is somewhat like the avoidance of an imperative sentence.

Quite contrary to front angle, the shot of profile constructs minimum interaction between the image and the viewer. Thus represented, the car is purely a phenomenon to be observed, which appeals to the viewer aesthetically. The strategy is to attract views' attention and to arouse their positive judgment by providing aesthetic pleasure. The image usually has beautiful streamline body, fully saturated eye-catching colour and is medium shot perfect for viewing, which may strike us as an exhibited art work in a gallery. However, this kind of design is rare in car advertisements too (two out of 100 cases), understandably because the image of an advertisement is used for persuasion, not for appreciation like an exhibited artwork. The advertisers do not want too much interaction, but they do not want too little interaction either.

What fulfills advertisers' need is appropriate degree of interaction, or we can say, a blending of aggressiveness and attractiveness, which is achieved through oblique angle. Most of the car advertisements in the corpus use oblique angle (94%, see Image 2 and Image 3 in Figure 4.3), with varying degrees of obliqueness. Typically the car is represented at approximately 45°, showing one light, which can be read as 'half gaze'. The prevalence of oblique angle surely suggests its effectiveness in manipulating viewers' attitude. It appropriately constructs the interaction between the viewer and the image, engaging the viewer, yet not demanding interaction. Apart from the advantage of constructing appropriate interaction, oblique angle is also able to exhibit the beauty of the car, thus engaging viewers aesthetically at the same time. For example, in Image 3 of Figure 4.3, the car is represented at 45 degrees, which interacts with the viewer with 'half gaze', on the one hand, while exhibiting the impressive streamlined design of the car, on the other.

Shot Distance

Kress and van Leeuwen (1996) categorise shot distance as close shot, medium shot and long shot, which are interpreted as representing the social distance between the viewer and the image. The understanding of shot distance as social distance, hence, the metaphor, SOCIAL DISTANCE IS SHOT DISTANCE, has similar basis to the understanding of camera angle, only the experience of facing (gazing) in interpersonal communication is changed to physical closeness (see Angle of Representation). The validity of this metaphor can be supported by its entailed mappings, SOCIAL ESTRANGEMENT IS LONG SHOT, INTIMACY IS CLOSE SHOT, and others, which further entail thousands of images, which instantiate these metaphors. The three shot distances typically used in car advertisements are close shot, long shot and medium-long shot. Based on Kress and van Leeuwen (1996: 124), close shot shows part of the car (head, light and seat), long shot shows the car as occupying half of the visual space and less and medium-long shot shows the car as occupying the half of the visual space and more.

Close shot, which only shows part of the car, constructs intimate viewer-image relationship, and it is rarely used as the main image. The unpopularity of close shot is understandable, considering the incomplete image of the car shown. However, the advertisers do not neglect this latter ideological resource so easily, using it frequently as illustration in the body copy (see Images 3 and 4 in Figure 4.3). These close shot objects provide specific information on the car. The intimate image-viewer relationship built by close-shot is reinforced by the fact that the images are mostly inner parts of the car (the seat, the engine and the stereo), which the driver of the car interacts with.

Long shot, which encodes social estrangement, is also rarely used in car advertisements (3%, see Image 3 of Figure 4.3). When it is used, the focus of the advertisement is on the setting of the car, and the strategy is to let the context 'talk'. As mentioned in Foreground/Background Orientation, the setting of the car in Image 3, Figure 4.3 is as important as the car and provides information about past accomplishments. A very good case in point is a magazine advertisement for BMW, which unfortunately cannot be reproduced for copyright issues. The image is a Chinese painting of a mountain, with a BMW on top and with the verbal text on the left saying 'Reaching the peak of perfection'. Obviously, the theme of the advertisement is to accentuate the status of the car, so the mountain peak, which fits the theme perfectly, is given prominence. Represented as such, the advertisement succeeds to impress the viewer about the excellence and insuperability of BMW, and it blends cultural tradition with contemporary technology.

The most common representation of the main image is medium-long shot, in which the full figure of the car is shown. According to the mapping between social distance and shot distance, medium-long shot constructs socially close relationship, which is somewhat between personal closeness and public distance, like friendship between business partners, teacher and students. The prevalence of medium-long shot indicates its appropriateness in the construction of image-viewer relationship. Meanwhile, the visual effect of the car, showing full figure with enough detail. This positioning complements the close shot of car components in the body copy. Thus designed, viewers learn more about the product as they engage with the advertisement and accordingly the relation between them changes from 'acquaintance' to 'intimate'. This strategy of engaging the viewers step-by-step is manipulative both emotionally (to get them involved deeper and deeper) and rationally (to let them know more and more).

CONCLUSION

This article explored the meaning and ideological implication of the spatial orientations of car advertisements as multimodal discourse. It argued that the epistemological status of Kress and van Leeuwen's (1996) association between spatial orientation and information value can be established by the cognitive theory of metaphor, especially the experiential basis of the mapping. After exploring the experiential basis of the mapping between spatial orientations of language-image layout, arrangement of the car, camera positioning and their respective meanings, the ideologies implicit in the spatial orientations were investigated. Through detailed examination of 100 car advertisements, it was discovered that the spatial layout of verbal and visual elements constructs information value, the positioning of the car and the camera positioning on the vertical axis construct product power or image-viewer power, and horizontal camera positioning constructs image-viewer interaction/distance. But it should be noted that although the orientations are separated for the purpose of analysis, the semiotic choices work together as a coherent whole to make meaning, and the meanings thus produced also work together to realise ideologies that aim to make the car an object of desire.

NOTES

1. Note that 'orientational' here refers to spatial orientation, which should be differentiated from Jay Lemke's use of 'orientational meaning' to refer to 'interpersonal' orientation.

REFERENCES

Berger, J. (1972) *Ways of Seeing*, Harmondsworth: Penguin Books and BBC.
Berkeley, G. (2003[1709]) *Towards a new theory of vision*. Available online at C. Green ed. York University, <http://psychclassics.yorku.ca/Berkeley/vision.htm> (access date: 2009.05.11).
Cheong, Y. Y. (2004). 'The construal of ideational meaning in print advertisements.' In O'Halloran, K. L. ed. *Multimodal Discourse Analysis*, London: Continuum: pp. 163–195.
Cross, J. (2005) 'Icon as Ideology: A Media Construction.' In Lassen, I., Strunck J. and Vestergaard, T. eds. *Mediating Ideology in Text and Image*, Amsterdam: John Benjamins: pp. 173–192.
Dyer, G. (1989) *Advertising as Communication*, London: Routledge.
Fairclough, N. (1989) *Language and Power*, London: Longman.
Forceville, C. (1996) *Pictorial Metaphor in Advertising*, London: Routledge.
Halliday, M. A. K. (1994) *An Introduction to Functional Grammar*, 2nd ed, London: Edward Arnold.
Jewitt, C., and Oyama, R. (2001) 'Visual Meaning: A Social Semiotic Approach.' In Van Leeuwen, T., and Jewitt, C. eds. *Handbook of Visual Analysis*, London: Sage Publications: pp. 135–156.
Kövecses, Z. (2002) *Metaphor: A Practical Introduction*, Oxford: Oxford University Press.
Kress, G., and Van Leeuwen, T. (1998) 'Front Pages: (The Critical) Analysis of Newspaper Layout.' In Bell, A., and Garrett, P. ed. *Approaches to Media Discourse*, Oxford: Blackwell: pp. 186–219.
——— (1996) *Reading Images: The Grammar of Visual Design*, 1st ed, London: Routledge.
Lakoff, G., and Johnson, M. (1980) *Metaphors We Live By*, Chicago: University of Chicago Press.
Lakoff, G. (1993) 'The contemporary theory of metaphor.' In Ortony, A. ed. *Metaphor and Thought*, Cambridge: Cambridge University Press: pp. 202–251.
Landa, R. (2004) *Advertising by Design*, New Jersey: John Wiley and Sons, Inc.
Martin, J. R. (2000) 'Fair Trade: negotiating meaning in multimodal texts.' In Coppock, P. ed. *The Semiotics of Writing: Transdisciplinary Perspectives on the Technology of Writing*, Belgium: Brepols: pp. 311–337.

Messaris, P. (1994) *Visual Literacy: Image, Mind and Reality*, Boulder: Westview Press.

Mitchell, T. W. J. (2008) 'Visual literacy or literary visualcy?' In Elkins, J. ed. *Visual Literacy*, London: Routledge: pp. 11–14.

Sebeok, T. A. (2001) *Signs: An Introduction to Semiotics*, 2nd ed, Toronto: University of Toronto Press.

Stenglin, M., and Iedema, R. (2001) 'How to Analyze Visual Images: A Guide for TESOL Teachers.' In Burns, A., and Coffin, C. eds. *Analyzing English in a Global Context*, London: Routledge: pp. 194–207.

Vestergaard, T., and Schroder, K. (1985) *The Language of Advertising*, New York: Blackwell.

Wernick, A. (1991) *Promotional Culture: Advertising, Ideology, and Symbolic Expression.* London: Sage.

Zettl, H. (1990) *Sight, Sound, Motion: Applied Media Aesthetics*, 2nd ed. Belmont, CA: Wadsworth.

5 The Music Table Revisited

Problems of Changing Levels of Detail and Abstraction in a Tangible Representation

Rodney Berry and Lonce Wyse

INTRODUCTION

Tangible interfaces have frequently captured the interest of those in search of more natural interactions between humans and computers. Building on the long-standing tradition of manipulable objects to aid young children's learning of mathematical and spatial concepts, a whole new generation of *computational objects* has come into being to extend this kindergarten style of interaction into the adult world. The abstract nature of musical structure, coupled with the visceral experience of music itself, make it no surprise that the design of tangible interfaces for computer-mediated music making has also become popular. Tangible musical interfaces offer intuitive ways to create and manipulate musical patterns and create new timbres, especially in an improvisation or performance setting where physical objects can act as live controls for various musical parameters. In addition, each object can represent some aspect of the music itself, be it an individual note or perhaps a component in a sound synthesis system. When music is represented in tangible form, it is possible to see and feel relationships between the objects that might not otherwise be apparent.

This dual role of control and representation is a distinguishing feature of tangible user interfaces (Ullmer, Ishii and Jacob 2005) and is perhaps part of their appeal to interface designers. Unfortunately, the very physicality that makes tangible interfaces so attractive also necessarily binds them to the laws of the physical world. Unlike images on a computer screen, real objects can not be made to simply appear and disappear or to be copied, pasted, shrunk or enlarged as needed. To accomplish these operations in the context of a larger music composition, we are forced to return to purely graphical onscreen representations.

Tangible objects are never purely tangible (Dourish 2001) but are usually visible and sometimes also audible. The tangible elements of computer interfaces are also typically accompanied by some form of visual augmentation. This can take the form of projected images directly on the objects, images on an adjacent screen or on the interaction surface, a head-mounted display or some kind of embedded display built into the object itself. The relationship between a tangible musical representation and its corresponding intangible graphical representation can affect the representative power of both combined. In fact, the two might better be thought of as a single multimodal representation with both tangible and intangible elements.

A traditional musical instrument also offers a physical means by which the sound of the instrument can be controlled. However an instrument also plays a less obvious role as a tangible representation of the space of all music possible on that particular instrument. This is especially true when used by the composer in the act of composition. In what follows, we will review different tangible approaches to music manipulation, analyse some of the limitations and suggest other strategies from the world of augmented reality that might expand the expressiveness of this kind of musical interaction, particularly for larger compositions.

COMPOSITION: INSPIRATION AND EXECUTION

Imagine you are Beethoven sitting at the piano. You have just returned from the doctor with the news that your recent hearing loss will continue to get worse. Your fingers echo the proclamation on the keyboard, "da-Da-da Dah . . .", you mutter to yourself as you recall asking the doctor, *"How much worse?"* Your fingers wander down the keyboard to the spaces between the notes you just played. "da-Da-da Dah . . .". " . . . *much worse, you'll probably lose your hearing completely."* Those first four notes have become a theme, a motif that will later become your Fifth Symphony, but for now, you are just testing the motif to see where it can go. The motif has become a movable shape in your hands, and the orchestra in your head plays it in unison and fortissimo, with a dramatic pause.

> You group multiple appearances of the theme into larger movable chunks and the beginnings of a larger structure start to appear. Your mind has now left piano-space and moved out into the larger space of an orchestral piece and you need to start writing this down . . . (see Figure 5.1a)

Of course, this fictional Ludwig is only Beethoven the archetype. The real Beethoven spent four years writing his Fifth Symphony in between work on other pieces for various patrons. Claims about the origins of the themes and his working methods can never be verified, and stories of the theme representing 'fate knocking at the door' are probably apocryphal. However, our archetypal Beethoven is acting out a romanticised version of the composition process common in the Western European art tradition for the past 400 years using the chief tools of the trade: a piano, a pen and a piece of manuscript paper—two different kinds of representation: one physical and tangible, the other, visual and symbolic.

In the broadest sense, a musical *composition* can be any set of circumstances and constraints that leads to music being produced. Parallels are often drawn between musical form and the narrative curve of a story that presents and develops themes toward a final resolution (Childs 1977). Although works exist that do not follow this model, many compositions do follow a comparable trajectory to that of a narrative. Composer Roger Sessions (Sloboda 1985) identifies two distinct phases in the composition process. The first he calls *inspiration,* where the composer first becomes conscious of an idea or theme. The second is *execution,* where the composer subjects the basic theme to a more deliberate process of extension and transformation to create a finished composition. Each phase requires a different way of thinking and therefore different kinds of tools.

Inspiration requires a style of thinking that could be characterised as 'breadth first', the musical equivalent of brainstorming, where numerous material is found and tested before settling on the fragments most suitable for development. This requires tools that allow the composer to spontaneously explore and select possible melodic and rhythmic phrases, themes, timbre combinations for later development. The composer also needs to immediately hear the results of this exploration in order to reflect upon, accept or reject new material. Traditionally, the tool for this creative phase has been a musical instrument, often a keyboard instrument such as the piano.

In contrast, *Execution* involves a more 'depth first' approach where the selected material is subjected to extensive formal manipulations. This calls for tools that can represent this material in a way that permits manipulation and development into larger structures. Although *execution* is more formalised, at times it also requires an explorative approach reminiscent of the *inspiration* phase but at higher levels of abstraction. This indicates a need for tools that facilitate connection with the methods and representations characteristic of the *inspiration* phase. Finally, there also needs to be a way for the piece to be reproduced at a later time for performance or for further modification.

In western music, *execution* is traditionally supported by the use of a written score (Sloboda, 1985b), punctuated by frequent returns to the instrument.

MUSIC AND REPRESENTATION

Musical notation takes different forms depending on context. For example, in *common music notation* (here the term refers to the notation system used in European art music from the Baroque to the present), the music is represented on paper as a two-dimensional space with pitch on the vertical axis and time on the horizontal axis. Sets of five horizontal parallel lines provide a reference for determining pitch and vertical lines mark out divisions of time. The round points show at what time and pitch individual notes should occur. Various modifications of these symbols yield information about phrasing and articulation of notes. Other symbols signal repeated sections and other aspects of performance.

Common music notation focuses on the music itself so that the music can be reproduced on any instrument. It is left to the individual performer to translate this into the physical actions needed to play it on a particular instrument. Tabulature, on the other hand, is written for a specific instrument and shows in detail how a composition is to be performed (see Figure 5.1b).

The tablature shown in Figure 5.1b is for a lute-like instrument called a *Chitarrone* and shows a player exactly where to put his fingers for each note in order to precisely reproduce a piece of music on that instrument. If applied to another instrument, the notation would become meaningless.

Figure 5.1(a)   Beethoven manuscript (1808).

Figure 5.1(b)   Example of tablature notation (Kapsberger 1604).

Although less 'portable' than common notation, tablature enables musicians to develop compositions around the mechanical logic of the instrument and the body of the player.

THE COMPUTER AS A COMPOSING TOOL

In computer music, the process of sound generation is decoupled from the physical act of making and controlling the sound. This allows other ways of working reflectively with musical material. The Musical Instrument Digital Interface (MIDI) is a standardised protocol that represents note events, as well as other expressive changes in the sound, as data to be passed between computing devices and peripherals. The MIDI represents note events in terms of when and how hard a key is pressed on the keyboard. Several data channels carry note events and other control changes associated with a particular instrument sound. It is also possible to select from a number of instrument timbres to be used in the music.

In most commercial composition programs, the user can either 'play' the notes in from a MIDI source, usually a keyboard, so that notes are 'recorded' as if on tape or the notes are entered by modifying an on-screen visual representation of the music. This is usually combined with an editable piano-roll style representation of the notes on the screen or a traditional *common music* notation with word-processor-style cut, copy and paste editing. More recently, these programs manipulate actual sound files as well as midi note events; however, the representations used remain conceptually similar to those used in software from the early 1990s. In fact, the working process for composers is still quite similar to that of their nineteenth-century counterparts. The composer first explores using a MIDI piano-style keyboard or perhaps some other controller resembling a guitar or wind instrument, to find basic raw material for development. These fragments are captured by the computer ready for editing, then developed upon using the graphical interface (with mouse and computer keyboard), occasionally returning to the keyboard to test new ideas.

INSTRUMENT AS REPRESENTATION

For analysis and composition, western music has traditionally favoured the general form of notation, in which the music exists independent of the physical realities of any particular instrument. It is rare however for a composer to work purely using a score without at least periodically referring to a real musical instrument such as a piano. The layout of the piano keyboard is naturally suited to a representational role and has remained unchanged for centuries. Its whole range of notes is laid out from left to right in ascending order of pitch, and the harder a key is struck, the louder the resulting sound.

An instrument both affords and constrains various kinds of moves about its physical form. These moves translate into musical events, gestures and patterns as they become sound. Because of this, musicians speak of being able to 'feel' various chordal and melodic patterns under their hands, as well as a sense of how such patterns are physically manifest as hand movements. In this way, musical gestures often begin as gestures on the instrument before their musical consequences are revealed when sound is produced.

This reflects a highly physical style of thinking that we more commonly associate with early school-age children. However, the practice of music perhaps demonstrates its continuing importance in adult life.

THINKING THROUGH THE HANDS

Piaget, based on his observations of children in the 1950s, claims that we progress through three principal developmental stages, each character-ised by distinctly different kinds of thinking (Inhelder and Piaget 1958). Between what he calls the *pre-operational* thinking of the infant and the *formal operations* thinking of the young adult, Piaget sees a transitional stage, from around seven to twelve years, that he calls *concrete operations*. The *concrete operational* child begins to develop and practice adult formal thinking but always with the aid of a physical representation of some kind. This is the age of obsessive block play and finger counting. The traditional progression of the composer at the piano, trying out fragments of melody to writing them down and developing them on manuscript paper recapitulates the childhood transition from playful, physical, open-ended experimenta-tion to the adult world of formal, abstract and directed activity.

Turkle and Papert (Turkle and Papert 1990) argue that far from being simply stages in our maturational process, concrete and formal operations are styles of knowledge that can be used by an individual in different kinds of situations and in varying ways between individuals. For them, the transition from concrete operations to formal operations is not simply maturational but also social. They see *formal operations* as the dominant accepted mode of thinking in our society, while *concrete operational* thinking is consid-ered childish, with no proper place in the adult world. As a result, *concrete operational* thought is not something that we grow out of, rather, we actively suppress it in order to fit in to society. Resnick (1998) uses the term *lifelong kindergarten* to underline the importance of physically grounded abstraction in adult thinking and activities. Through *computational objects* (physical, tangible things that ideally contain sophisticated computing systems that can sense and respond to manipulation by the user) Resnick revives Montessori and Froebel's legacy of "manipulatives" (Zuckerman and Arida 2005) to help us span both concrete and formal styles of thinking.

TANGIBLE INTERFACES: REPRESENTATION AND CONTROL

The term *Tangible User Interface* (TUI) came into common usage after a paper by Ishii and Ullmer (1997) entitled: *Tangible Bits: Towards Seamless Interfaces between People, Bits and Atoms*. The authors paint a picture of a free-flowing exchange between cyberspace and the physical world, in contrast to what they see as a severely constricted passage afforded by the traditional graphical user interface (portrayed as *painted bits*). They call for a *coupling of bits and atoms* in the form of graspable objects (cards, books, models etc.) paired with digital information pertaining to or represented by them. Elsewhere (Ullmer and Ishii 2000), they highlight the roles of *representation* and *control* in tangible user interfaces. In a graphical user interface, the mouse and keyboard are in fact tangible input devices that provide control, but the representation of that which is controlled by using them is only visible on the screen. In contrast, a tangible interface element can physically embody both a path for control (moving an object might change several parameters in the computer) as well as the main information-bearing, representational aspect of the interface (images projected on the object, light or sound emanating from the object itself and, most importantly, the physical position and orientation of the object). They see the abacus as an ideal tangible device because it makes no separation between representation and control. The abacus is not an input device and has no explicit input and output. Instead, its entire physical structure and operation serves as a representation of abstract numerical values and operations. At the same time, it provides a way to control and manipulate those same associated values and operations. However, the abacus is highly constrained to its appointed task and can by no means be considered 'expressive'.

Traditional musical instruments and the abacus have several things in common: they serve as a tangible representation of the space of possibilities they serve to navigate; they accomplish this without any intermediate representation (such as data in the computer), and their means of representation and their means of control are intertwined.

Because the rules involved in mathematical operations are fixed, the abacus' representation can scale to an immense degree. In contrast, musical rules and possibilities are less well defined and can vary greatly between musical styles. This presents a challenge for those who wish to make computer-assisted composition a tangible experience.

TANGIBLE MUSIC

One well-known tangible music system is the *reacTable** (Kaltenbrunner, Geiger and Jordà 2004). The *reacTable** consists of a round, translucent tabletop on which the player places and manipulates a number of objects in order to control a software-based sound synthesiser (see Figure 5.2a). In addition, the system is able to make projected images follow each object around the tabletop. Each object represents a sound-processing component. Some generate sound while others process the sound from other signal generation objects. With its ability to encapsulate collections of devices as a single object, the *reacTable** allows some movement between levels of abstraction. The *reacTable** also includes modules that can store and play short sequences of notes, or control values for filters and other modifiers, in emulation of the sequencers used in pre-digital electronic music. However, the *reacTable** is aimed at improvised performance rather than the composition of larger-scale structures over time. Longer structures are possible but only as defined by processes that generate sonic events rather than the definition of the events themselves.

The *scoreTable** (Jordà and Alonso 2006) uses the same table and marker system as the reacTable* to create an environment specifically for composing note-based compositions (see Figure 5.2b).

The representation used imitates the western score notation, complete with clef and time signature. The round marker objects imitate the round note-heads of the conventional score and the projected images show the note-stems to indicate the duration of the note. In keeping with the circular table, the lines of the staff notation are bent around in a circle to facilitate cyclical repetitions of note patterns. The marker objects are placed on this staff to represent and control the positions of notes. Repeat markers (:ll) provide a limited means of extending the piece by causing marked sections to repeat instead of simply continuing on to the end. A metronome object allows control over the tempo of the piece.

Costanza's Augmented Musical Stave allows the player to build a simple melodic pattern by rearranging blocks on a paper stave on a tabletop (Costanza, Shelley and Robinson 2003). Its purely tangible interface illustrates both the advantages and limitations of a purely tangible representation of music. Control and representation are entirely contiguous without a mouse, keyboard or screen in sight, but it can only create a short fragment of melody at one time.

The following example, the Music Table (see Figure 5.3a), is described in more detail because one aim of this paper is to explore the problem of changing levels of detail and of abstraction evident in this kind of interface. The Music Table (Berry et al. 2003) is a tabletop music system developed by Rodney Berry along with graphic designers, Mao Makino and Naoto Hikawa and programmer, Takashi Furuya at Advanced Telecommunicaton Research (ATR) Media Information Science Research Laboratories in Kyoto from 2001–2004. The system consists of a tabletop with several blocks on it, each with a computer-readable marker attached. An overhead camera allows the computer to read the positions and orientations of the marked blocks.

The player arranges the blocks in order to form musical patterns that are immediately played back by the computer. The position of a block towards or away from the player determines the pitch of the note while its left-to-right

Figure 5.2(a)   reacTable*

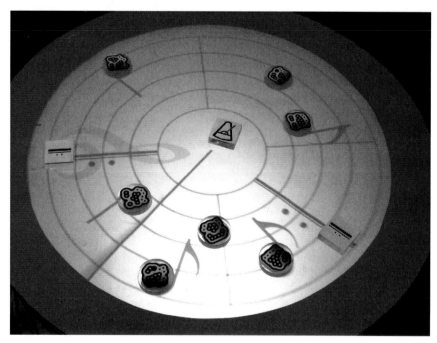

Figure 5.2(b)   scoreTable*.

position determines its order of occurrence in relation to the other notes/ blocks. The tabletop is divided from left to right into eight sections so that notes will always fall precisely on one of eight possible beats. These eight beats repeat over and over according to the arrangement of the note objects. The pitch axis is also divided into the notes of a major scale.

When the player places a block on the table, the computer checks the block's position on the plane of the table and schedules a note event at the appropriate time and pitch. Tilting the block to the right or left makes the duration of the note become longer or shorter (see Figure 5.3b). Rotating the block makes the note louder or softer in imitation of a volume knob.

Computer-generated images are superimposed directly on top of the image of the markers so that, when viewed on a large screen behind the table, they appear to be present in the real world along with the blocks, tabletop and the player's hands. Cartoon centipede-like walking creatures represent each note event and grow longer or shorter in proportion to their note length and become spikier as notes become louder. This aspect of the representation is partly a result of the original Music Table being designed for children but is also a result of following Japanese convention of using cute animated characters in adult-targeted interfaces. Bright flashing circles of light show which notes are currently playing. A larger cube with markers on all six sides can be rotated to select different instrument sounds.

Figure 5.3(a)   The Music Table.

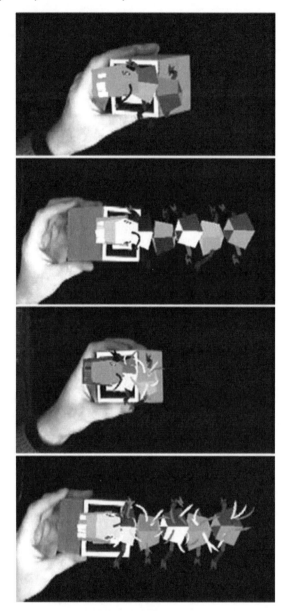

Figure 5.3(b)   Music Table features.

The player can place a phrase object on the table in order to save the current pattern before using the existing note blocks to make a new pattern (see Figure 5.4b). Like the individual note blocks, the overall loudness of each phrase can be adjusted by rotating the object clockwise or counter-clockwise.

Four saved phrases can play simultaneously, each using a different instrument sound (see Figure 5.4a) and volume level. In an earlier version of the Music

Table, there was also an 'edit' object that, when placed next to a phrase object, would cause all the contained notes to appear on the screen as if they were attached to note blocks. The edit object was then used to drag the note objects to new locations or to delete them (by raising them up toward the camera).

The ability to save the current state of the representation and retrieve earlier ones is not well supported in the Music Table or any of the other tangible music systems reviewed here. As we saw earlier with the abacus, one of the special qualities of a physical representation is that it can preserve some aspects of its physical state even while the computer is switched off. Of course, putting it into that state to begin with requires physical intervention from the user, and returning to an earlier state likewise requires physical intervention and the loss of the current state.

PHYSICALITY: STATES AND CONSTRAINTS

For a computer-based tangible interface to retrieve earlier states and manifest them physically, the computer would ideally be able to move objects around in space, make them appear and disappear at will, as well as to change their shape, colour and texture. Although not capable of all these things, Patten's Physical Intervention in Computational Optimization (PICO) project (Patten and Ishii 2007) extends his earlier tangible interfaces by using arrays of electro-magnets to move objects around on the surface of a table. Once the physical interface elements are in motion, possibilities for using physical forces as natural constraints become apparent. For example, two objects might be surrounded by a rubber band that keeps them a maximum distance from each other, or a draughtsman's flexible curve might limit travel beyond its boundary. Detergent spread on one area of the table causes rapid crossings of that area where a patch of sticky honey might offer greater friction. This friction might change if the user were to heat up the honey with a hairdryer. Rosenfeld approaches the same issues as Patten, but this time using several tiny robots (Rosenfeld et al. 2004) that can be manipulated by the user but can also rearrange themselves on the table as directed by the computer. Both approaches allow the tangible elements of a physical representation to return to their locations from a previous time. The robots can also reproduce their orientation in relation to the table.

There is no reason (apart from perhaps the cost of materials and maintenance) that this approach could not also be applied to music composition and performance. The ability to preserve and edit not only fixed states but also the transitions between them makes this very attractive. In the case of Patten's PICO, a rubber band or a ruler could force groups of notes into certain ranges but allow freedom of movement within the constraints, or different slippery or sticky materials could affect the kinds of transitions possible between note patterns when executed by the user's hands or by the computer.

The importance of constraints is highlighted by Ullmer (Ullmer, Ishii and Jacob 2005) who couples the idea of constraints with the idea of tokens that can be placed and manipulated within or outside the confines of constraints. For example, an arrangement of tokens might represent a pattern of musical notes. If one were to place them in or attach them to a larger container object, they could be manipulated as one object by manipulating the constraint instead of its component tokens. The surface of a table provides a constraint for objects placed upon it in that objects can only fall as far as the table surface permits and the quality of the surface may vary in its level of friction. The objects themselves can also provide their own constraints. For example, flat-bottomed objects will tend to retain their position in comparison to round, easily rolled

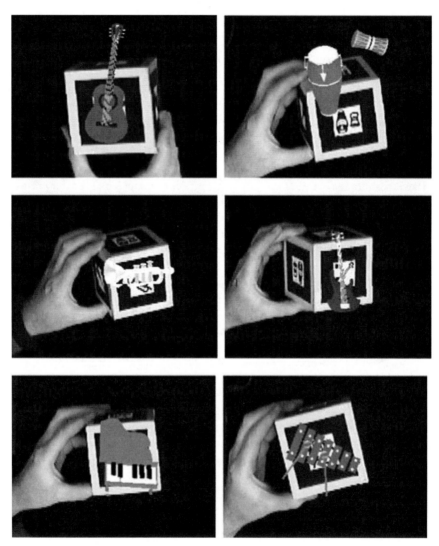

Figure 5.4(a)   More Music Table features.

Figure 5.4(b) More Music Table features.

objects. It is not hard to imagine musical notes represented by objects that fit together Lego-style or with magnets to make phrases or motifs that could be moved as a whole.

Since most pieces of music reuse and transform one or more basic motifs, the ability to represent re-usable groupings of notes as one transformable object is a key requirement for any system used to develop a longer piece.

DESCRIPTION, PRESCRIPTION, ABSTRACTION

None of the tangible music systems described above can explicitly represent more than a few bars or phrases of music, although some allow vertical complexity in the form of multiple layers of sound. The reacTable* can produce patterns that change over a longer period of time but such patterns result from generative processes and not from any explicit representation of the musical events themselves. However a generative approach could certainly be applied to musical events of over a period of time.

For example, if one were to make a computer program especially to produce the first movement of Beethoven's Fifth Symphony, one approach might be to make a list of every note in the order that they occur against some kind of timeline or schedule. This might be analogous to so-called 'mark-up' languages such as HyperText Markup Language (HTML). Groups of notes could be encapsulated into phrases and groups of phrases into sections, much as repeated lines of a poem or song might be copied and pasted using a word-processing program. Essentially, commercial music composition programs work in this way. However, if the crucial first four notes were to be changed, it would then be necessary for almost every group of four notes in the whole piece of music to be similarly altered, since most are derived from this first motif.

Alternatively, knowing what we know about the relationships between phrases in the piece, it would be more programmer-like to simply define the basic theme then define the various transformations used to produce its variations throughout the rest of the piece. These transformations would include diatonic sequencing, mirroring, transposition, augmentation, diminution etc. This would lead to a more compact description, in effect a prescription to unpack the entire piece from the basic motif. Any changes made to the initial motif would then see the change automatically propagate throughout all the variations generated by the transformation objects.

Both kinds of representation could even operate in parallel, the literal representation of the whole piece being continually re-generated by the algorithmic representation. It could be possible to make changes to the explicit representation directly in ways that might be counter to the dictates of the algorithm. These changes could be made immune from the effects of the generating algorithm so as to remain undisturbed by changes higher up in the procedural hierarchy.

A tangible interface using such an approach would be possible, but, inevitably, some compromises would be necessary because of the natural physical limits of the physical space and the objects in it. In the case of the Music Table, it will require a review of the affordances and constraints implicit in the technological and physical environment and how they might be accommodated into a new design.

THE MUSIC TABLE REVISITED

The Music Table uses overhead camera-based tracking of fiducial markers to find the position and orientation of marked objects on the tabletop. This means that, in order for a marker to be tracked, it must be visible to the camera. If another object, including the player's hand, passes between the object and the camera, the occluded object will no longer exist as far as the computer is concerned. This is why many tangible interfaces (The reacTable* and scoreTable*, for example) use a special glass-topped table with a projector and camera underneath to prevent occlusions. This method also creates a spatially contiguous relationship between the tangible and intangible elements of the interface, whereas the Music Table creates a once-removed contiguity by combining the 'real' and computer-generated images on a separate screen. The Music Table's split representation allows the player to focus only on the physical elements when dealing with the parts of the music that are adequately represented by the blocks' positions on the table, namely pitch and timing. In addition, the player can effectively control the loudness and length (articulation) of notes by rotating and tilting the blocks without needing to look up at the screen. If sound and touch are insufficient feedback, then a glance at the screen provides graphical confirmation of these two states.

The use of an overhead camera also allows full three-dimensional tracking of objects and thus opens up the space above the table for interaction, not just the surface of the table. It is also potentially cheaper and usable in situations where a special table would be inconvenient. Occlusion continues to be an issue in the Music Table, but since children using the original one quickly learned to mute notes by deliberately covering the associated markers, there are clearly positive ways to work with occlusion in an interface design.

Another factor is that, as one gets closer to the camera, the field of view decreases and the number of objects that can be tracked becomes proportionately less. Once a marker gets so close to the camera that it fills the whole picture, nothing else is visible. For this reason, if the space above the table is to be fully exploited, this must be accommodated in the design. For example, it would make sense to reserve the space close to the camera for rarer operations that have wide-ranging effect. In the original Music Table, this space was used purely for erasing whole phrases where a deliberate, unmistakable action was required and a separate 'trash-can' object would have added unnecessary clutter. Major changes in modes of operation or representation might be appropriate to use in this region. Less 'high-level' operations, but where several objects might need to be visibly manipulated, could take place closer to the tabletop.

One of the main attractions of a three-dimensional working space is that some kinds of melodic manipulations can be more simply described in spatial terms than as a set of commands or operations. For example, such transforms as transposition (moving up or down) inversion (turning upside-down), retrograde (reversal), augmentation (stretching) and diminution (squashing), all describe changes to a musical phrase on a plane with pitch on one axis and time on the other. However, it should be possible to pick up a musical phrase, stretch it, turn it upside down and move it 'upwards' in the pitch space, effectively achieving in one action a combination of operations as expressed in the above terms. In addition, many 'in-between' operations and sets of states would be unwieldy to describe in a more conventional manner—much in the same way that the shadow of a three-dimensional object on the wall changes considerably while the object itself is simply rotated. This action could conceivably be recorded and made into a new object or tool that can be used to perform the same set of operations on any other phrases in future.

As the complexity of a physical representation increases, so too does the potential for physical clutter until manipulation becomes impossible. Fortunately, a tangible element is only needed when the player needs to actually make changes to whatever the element represents and controls, otherwise it could easily be represented by a purely graphical object. There will be times when the player will want every physical note object present for hands-on editing of a detailed phrase. There will also be times when none will be needed, or perhaps just one physical object could be used, as we might currently use a mouse, to make an adjustment and move on. Therefore it is necessary to be able to detach a physical element from its graphical counterpart in order to make the most of the scrolling, zooming, deletion and duplication possible with a purely graphical interface. This can be seen to some extent in James Patten's Audiopad (Patten, Recht and Ishii 2002), a tabletop environment where small pucks are placed on top of graphical control elements to act as control knobs for the parameters represented but can be easily removed and applied to another point of control. This is essentially how the original Music Table's edit object worked but it was never implemented effectively. Although the representational aspect of Audiopad is concerned with showing points of control for various audio mixing parameters and not the specification of a piece of music, it demonstrates that control and representation can be smoothly coupled and decoupled in a tangible interface. For the Music Table, the current representation mutes a note when the tangible block is removed or covered with the hand. If this is to be retained, it will require a distinctive action to detach the block from the note instead of treating it as a simple occlusion. This will require careful use of the space above the table and clear graphical feedback to show that the decoupling has or has not occurred.

Essentially, the proposed extensions to the Music Table centre around the idea of the music itself being represented mostly in two dimensions, sited on the surface of the table itself. The actions and operations required in order to edit and structure the music on a higher level would be represented in three dimensions and take place in a hierarchical layering of the space between the tabletop and the camera.

CONCLUSION

Tangible representations of musical events and patterns echo a hidden representational role traditionally played throughout history by musical instruments in the hands of composers. The power to simultaneously represent and control the music with a mixed representation, made of both tangible and graphical elements, potentially subsumes the compositional roles of both instrument and score.

However, so far there appear to be no tangible composing tools that allow an explicit representation for development of a longer piece of music. Since a representation rooted solely in the physical world can only be extended by physical means, a larger piece of music will quickly exhaust all spatial and material resources. Even when graphical augmentations are added, the physical elements cannot simply disappear when they cease to be convenient.

To overcome this, a degree of compromise is unavoidable, but, with careful management of the coupling and decoupling between physical and graphical elements, an orderly use of the table surface and its relationship with the space above it and three-dimensional interactions with the representation on the tabletop, a reasonable balance should be achievable.

In this way, it may be possible to support both inspiration and execution, with their attendant concrete and formal thinking styles, in the same working space, thus allowing a more natural interplay between the two. Ideally it should be possible to retain the physical immediacy and playfulness of a tangible representation while adding some of the plasticity of a screen-based representation.

The Music Table began its life as a demonstration of the potential of new technologies and tangible interfaces for creative expression but also brought to light a new set of problems. It is fitting then that, almost seven years later, the Music Table begins a new life as a space in which to explore, map and hopefully overcome this same set of problems.

REFERENCES

Beethoven, L. van. (1808) *Symphony No. 5 Op. 67 in C Minor*: Staatsbibliothek zu Berlin.

Berry, R., Makino, M., Hikawa, N. and Suzuki, M. (2003) *The Augmented Composer Project: The Music Table*. Paper read at *The 2nd IEEE and ACM International Symposium on Mixed and Augmented Reality*, 8–10 October, 2003, Tokyo, Japan.

Childs, B. (1977) 'Time and Music: A Composer's View.' *Perspectives of New Music 15* (2): 194–219.

Costanza, E., Shelley, S. B. and Robinson J. (2003) 'Introducing audio d-touch: A tangible user interface for music composition and performance.' In *DAFX-03: Proceedings of the 6th International Conference on Digital Audio Effects*, 8–11 September 2003, London, UK.

Dourish, P. (2001) *Where the Action Is: The Foundations of Embodied Interaction*, Cambridge, Mass: MIT Press.

Inhelder, B., and Piaget, J. (1958) *The Growth of Logical Thinking from Childhood to Adolescence: An Essay on the Construction of Formal Operational Structures*, New York: Basic Books.

Ishii, H. and Ullmer, B. (1997) 'Tangible bits: Towards seamless interfaces between people, bits and atoms'. *Proceedings of ACM CHI 97 Conference on Human Factors in Computing Systems*, Los Angeles, USA, April 18–23, 1997, volume 1 of papers: Beyond the Desktop: 234–241.

Jordà, S., and Alonso, M. (2006) 'Mary had a little scoreTable* or the reacTable* goes melodic', In *Proceedings of the 2006 Conference on New Interfaces for Musical Expression*, Paris, France: IRCAM Centre Pompidou: pp. 208–211.

Kaltenbrunner, M., Geiger, G. and Jordà, S. (2004) 'Dynamic Patches for Live Musical Performance'. Paper read at *4th Conference on New Interfaces for Musical Expression (NIME 04)*, 3–5 June 2004, in Hamamatsu, Japan.

Kapsberger, J. H. (1604) *First toccata from Libro primo d'intavolatura di chitarone*, Venice: Wikimedia Commons.

Patten, J., and Ishii, H. (2007) 'Mechanical constraints as computational constraints in tabletop tangible interfaces.' In *Proceedings of ACM CHI 2007 Conference on Human Factors in Computing Systems*, San Jose, California, USA: ACM Press, pp. 809–818.

Patten, J., Recht, B. and Ishii, H. (2002) 'Audiopad: a tag-based interface for musical performance.' In Jacko, A. and Sears, A. eds. *NIME '02: Proceedings of the 2002 Conference on New Interfaces for Musical Expression*, Singapore: National University of Singapore, pp. 1–6.

Rosenfeld, D., Zawadzki, M., Sudol, J. and Perlin, K. (2004) 'Physical Objects as Bidirectional User Interface Elements.' *IEEE Computer Graphics and Applications* 24 (1): 44–49.

Sloboda, J. A. (1985) 'Composition and Improvisation.' In *The Musical Mind: The Cognitive Psychology of Music,* Oxford [Oxfordshire], New York: Clarendon Press; Oxford University Press, pp. 102–138.

Turkle, S., and Papert S. (1990) 'Epistemological pluralism: Styles and voices within the computer culture.' *Signs: Journal of Women in Culture and Society* 16 (1): 128–157.

Ullmer, B., and Ishii, H. (2000) 'Emerging frameworks for tangible user interfaces.' *IBM Systems Journal* 39 (3–4): 915–931.

Ullmer, B., Ishii, H. and Jacob, R. J. K. (2005) 'Token+ constraint systems for tangible interaction with digital information.' *ACM Transactions on Computer-Human Interaction (TOCHI)* 12 (1): 81–118.

Zuckerman, O., Arida, S. and Resnick, M. (2005) 'Extending tangible interfaces for education: digital montessori-inspired manipulatives.' *SIGCHI Conference on Human Facors in Computing Systems*, 2–7 April 2005, Portland, Oregon: ACM Press, pp. 859–868.

6 Enregistering Identity in Indonesian Television Serials
A Multimodal Analysis[1]

Zane Goebel

INTRODUCTION

This paper theorises the role of representations of personhood found in Indonesian television serials in enabling audiences to socially identify others as belonging to a particular group of persons. In doing so, I add to a growing body of work on language ideologies and semiosis (e.g. Agha 2007; Errington 2001; Inoue 2004; Kroskrity 2000; Schieffelin, Woolard and Kroskrity, 1998) by exploring how representations of personhood in Indonesian television serials figure in the construction and circulation of knowledge relating to ethnicity and social relations.

In line with linguistic anthropological work on semiotics, interaction and socio-cultural reproduction and change (e.g. Agha 2007; Wortham 2006) such knowledge can be conceptualised as semiotic registers, which are made up of constellations of linguistic and non-linguistic signs. In particular, and drawing on insights offered by scholars of multimodality and social interaction (e.g. Goodwin 2006; Gumperz 1982; Hymes 1974; Norris 2004; Scollon and Scollon 2003; Van Leeuwen 2005), I show how a multimodal analysis of televised representations of personhood and social relations allows us to tease out how television serials can *potentially* add dimensions to personhood that are not easily circulated via other mass-mediated text-based messages.

Here I emphasise "potentially" because of the need to understand whether and to what extent such signs are interpreted as such by viewers, as pointed out by scholars of social interaction and the media (e.g. Fairclough 1995; Friedman 2006; Ginsburg, Abu-Lughod and Larkin 2002; Gumperz 1982). Even so, I will not pursue matters of reception and interpretation in this paper for reasons of space. After looking a little more closely at recent work on semiotics and interaction, I will then briefly describe the methodological approach. The bulk of my paper, of course, will be devoted to a multimodal analysis of the representations of personhood found in an episode taken from a television serial.

REPRESENTATIONS OF IDENTITY AND ENREGISTERMENT

In a series of publications linguistic anthropologist, Asif Agha (2003, 2005, 2007) has described how various types of social interaction figure in the creation and reproduction of relationships between signs and persons. His main concern relates to how particular signs become emblems of identity or personhood across time and space. The starting point for such (re)production processes—which he terms 'enregisterment'—is a 'semiotic encounter'. In such encounters communication is not a product of a face-to-face meeting, but rather whether and to what extent participants orient to signs (Agha 2007: 69). In this sense signs only become signs if those used by a sender are recognised by the receiver. Often such sign ratification is seen in the types of repetition discussed by Tannen (1989). Where signs are ratified and/or appropriated and recontextualised (e.g. Bauman and Briggs 1990) we have the formation of what Agha (2007) terms a 'semiotic register' (SR), defined as a category of signs that include both linguistic and non-linguistic signs, such as facial expressions, gesture, prosody, pause, space and so on.

The links between these signs and the SR of which they are a part are such that the use of one sign implicates the SR to which it belongs (Agha 2007: 81; see also Ochs 1996 on this). As with signs, SRs should also be seen as emergent because the very nature of SR production means that the constellation of signs making up a SR will change in a speech chain (i.e. from speech event to speech event) because place, participants and so on will differ from one speech event to the next. In this sense, SR formation always draws upon pre-existing signs from other SRs that exist within a system of SRs (e.g. Agha 2007; Bakhtin 1981; Silverstein and Urban 1996).

Continued semiotic encounters over time and across speech events also enables the reification of some linguistic signs from an emerging SR. Typically, such signs are associated with particular types of persons, settings, social practices and so on. In other words, despite the emergent nature of SRs, some SRs and the signs associated with them become more stable and perdure over time through such processes of enregisterment. In addition to being a product of face-to-face semiotic encounters across speech events, the enregisterment of SRs can be a result of meta-pragmatic discourses about language usage and users found in dictionaries and prescriptive grammars, more widely accessible books on etiquette, novels, newspapers, magazines, radio and television (e.g. Agha 2007: 190–232; Inoue 2004). In the case of mass-mediated representations of language use, the signs linking such usage to performable social personas and relationships are harder to falsify or question (Agha 2007: 74–77). This is so for two reasons. The first is that this type of speech chain does not allow the type of questioning and/or ratification of such stereotypes that are possible in face-to-face talk, and second, the audience of such representations is also much larger (Agha 2007).

Competence to perform or comprehend SRs varies from person to person because of their interaction in different communities of practice (Wenger 1998) and their access to different forms of media (e.g.

Fairclough 1995; Friedman 2006; Ginsburg et al. 2002; Spitulnik 1996). That is, people have different trajectories of socialisation. While this points to the fragmented nature of people's understanding of signs, these divergent trajectories also represent different processes of enregisterment which produce competing SRs (Agha 2007). Thus, although there will always be dominant SRs within a system of such registers—especially those that are institutionally authorised, as in the case of use of signs associated with a *Standard Language* in state-owned/run schools and broadcasters (e.g. Spitulnik 1998)—there will also, necessarily, be competing SRs (e.g. Agha 2007). Thus, in any semiotic encounter participants' familiarity with a SR and its constellation of signs allows them to socially identify the user as belonging to a particular category of persons according to the participant's knowledge of sets of semiotic registers (e.g. Irvine 2001).

In summarising the above theory of semiotic register formation, it is important to point out that to date most of the work done in this framework has focused upon meta-pragmatic commentaries about a person's sign usage in printed media or television news (e.g. Agha 2003; Inoue 2004; Miller 2004). With the exceptions of Meek (2006) and Goebel (2008a), work on semiotic register formation in films and serials is still quite rare, despite the potentially large audience that such representations may reach. This is also surprising given the way in which audio-visual media of this type enables the linking of personhood with concrete hearable and observable signs in ways not possible through the type of written representations one finds in novels, etiquette magazines, letters to the editor in newspapers and so on. In this sense, audio-visual representations are perhaps 'worth a thousand words'. This is so because they provide audiences of such representations the opportunity to breathe life into the type of 'imagined' (Anderson 2006 [1991, 1983]; Appadurai 1996) personas found in written sources, providing much more depth to what can be interpreted as a type of "demeanour" (Goffman 1967) associated with particular persons.

METHOD

When I recorded the television serial that I present below, I did not record it with the intention of using it in the type of analysis undertaken in this paper. It was recorded as part of larger linguistic anthropological fieldwork project on inter-ethnic relations in urban Indonesia conducted from December 1995 until August 1998 (e.g. Goebel 2002a, 2005, 2010). For a long time afterwards this and other serials became examples of 'authentic' teaching material to help learners of Indonesian become acquainted with the type of variation that they would encounter in Indonesia (e.g. Goebel 2002b; Black and Goebel 2002). In this sense there was no special reason why I recorded this serial.

Because I am interested in how televised representations of sign usage in semiotic encounters figure in processes of enregisterment, there are two main methods that seem especially suited to the task. These include those offered in the broad field of ethnomethodology and studies of embodied interaction (e.g. Antaki and Widdicombe 1998; Birdwhistle 1972; Goodwin 2006; Haviland 2004; Kendon 1985; Sacks 1995; Schegloff 2007) and the ethnography of communication (e.g. Hymes 1974). This combination is by no means new and has been fruitfully tried and tested by many scholars working in the fields of language socialisation, learning and language use in situations of inter-cultural contact (e.g. Gumperz 1982; Ochs 1988; Philips 1983; Wortham 2006).

Although Hymes (1974) framework has been critiqued due to a lack of attention to interpretation processes relating to 'norms' (e.g. Gumperz 1982); nevertheless, his notions of speech events, speech situations and his SPEAKING[2] framework provide a useful guide for the systematic documentation of signs and comparison between each set of signs. Drawing on ethnomethodological insights allows us to establish whether and to what extent sign usage by one character in a serial or film is oriented to by other characters in their semiotic encounter. Moreover, combining this analysis with Hymes' framework allows us to see how such sign usage relates to other signs within a particular televised serial.

Indeed, attending to semiotic encounters as part of a larger chain of semiotic encounters across speech events and speech situations enables further insights into participants' interpretations of ambiguous signs (e.g. Wortham, 2006) together with insights into how viewers might be able to interpret such sign usage. In the above sense, the methodology presented here falls within the type of multimodal analysis found in the work of Scollon and Scollon (2003) and Norris (2004), as well as that found in Systemic Functional Linguistics (e.g. O'Halloran 2008; O'Toole 1994/2010; Van Leeuwen 2005).

While my analysis will focus on the use of multiple linguistic and non-linguistic signs, I also need to be clear about some of my ideological biases relating to transcription and classification (e.g. Ochs 2006 [1979]). In particular, I need to provide a note about initial transcription procedures and how this figured in my classification of code choice in this serial. Initial transcription was carried out by two Indonesian research assistants, both of whom reported to be from Sundanese-speaking West Java. Indeed, I chose them because their language background would enable them to transcribe the talk in the serial I present here. In asking them to transcribe the dialogues I asked them to put in bold any forms that they considered were regional languages. Thus, part of my categorisation of linguistic forms relied upon 'native speaker' judgments. This process was not unproblematic insofar as each consultant often provided different classifications. Even so, one way in which these ambiguities could be bracketed was via reference to conversation analytical insights (e.g. Gafaranga and Torras 2002), which allows us to see whether and to what extent participants orient to certain linguistic sign usage (e.g. language choice). In doing so, this ethnomethod-ologically inspired analysis offers insights into how such sign usage is inter-preted by participants in the televised representations of interaction.

THE ENREGISTERMENT OF ETHNOLINGUISTIC DIFFERENCE IN INDONESIA

Elsewhere I have explored the historical development of semiotic registers that contained 'languages other than Indonesia' (LOTI) and region, within their constellation of signs amounting to essentially region-based ethno-linguistic categories of personhood, such as Javanese, Sundanese, Balinese and so on (Goebel 2008a). Accordingly, here I will not cover this ground in detail but merely sketch out some of the main points of my argument, which covered the role of political discourses, schooling, language policy, enumeration practices and representations of language use in the popular mass media.

To provide some brief examples of each I shall start with the politi-cal-scholarly discourses of the late 1920s. During this period public prac-tices of discernment and choice that explicitly mentioned Indonesian and LOTI helped enregister two semiotic registers. The first contained within its category of signs LOTI, ethnicity and region, while the second con-tained Indonesian and the potential new state. This treatment of ethnicity as something linked with region and language continued after Indonesia gained independence from its Dutch colonial masters in the late 1940s. For example, regional leaders saw shared language as a sign of ethnic group membership, which could be used to gather support for their efforts to gain more autonomy visà-vis the Jakartan political elite in the mid-1950s (Feith 1962: 522). By the early 1980s this idea was already part of the Indonesian constitution, which explicitly states the need to preserve *bahasa daerah* "regional languages" (e.g. Anwar 1980).

In putting into practice these constitutional ideas—which essentially amounted to a language policy document—successive governments have attempted to realise this language ideology through the centralised and decentralised curriculum dealing with the teaching of regional languages in primary and secondary schools (e.g. Lowenberg 1992; Nababan 1991). However, as has been recently documented, the success of such efforts appears to be patchy at best (e.g. Kurniasih 2007). Even so, in other ways schooling also helped contribute to the enregisterment of semiotic registers, which had within their category of signs region-based personas who spoke a specific LOTI.

For example, Parker (2002) has observed that by the third grade of primary school children can identify all the provinces in Indonesia along with their capital cities. This together with the labelling processes that goes with teaching, textbooks, and timetabled subjects may contribute to children's understanding of language as a named object tied to stereo-typical performable identities. These processes will not only help children name the languages that they speak but also enable them to imagine themselves as a member of a particular group of people who are defined as such by way of residence and language usage, as suggested by Nababan (1991).

In other words, children's exposure to such discourses about regions, languages and their users and uses will help enregister LOTI with ethnicity. As such, a child's emergent semiotic register—which might initially contain signs such as linguistic tokens and utterances, intimacy, family, local spaces—might also include 'ethnicity', 'us', and 'region'.[3] This relationship between language and ethnicity will be further enhanced through the learning of Indonesian at school, especially where Indonesian is portrayed as the language of unity and communication among geographically dispersed ethnic groups with their own LOTI. Indeed, the propagation of Indonesian at schools as the language of national unity also brings into focus further criteria for defining communication with members of other ethnic groups as 'a communicative practice requiring Indonesian'. That is to say, Indonesian is required for communication with the 'ethnic other'.

In summary, all of the above processes and practices have helped formulate SRs that index Indonesian and LOTI with various contexts, including region, stranger, ethnicity and so on. Figures 6.1 and 6.2 summarise the discussion by providing a multi-dimensional picture of these signs making up these SRs where the use of one sign can invoke the SR to which it belongs.

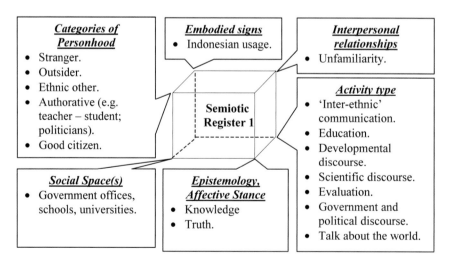

Figure 6.1   Semiotic Register 1: Indonesian and its constellation of signs.

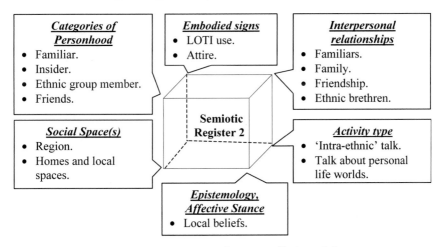

Figure 6.2   Semiotic Register 2: LOTI and its constellation of signs.

ANALYSIS

The data that I will use to exemplify my argument is drawn from an episode titled *Cipoa* "Con artist" of a series called *Noné* (Missy), broadcast nationally in 1995 by the state-owned educational television station Televisi Pendidikan Indonesia *(TPI)*. In this setting a young woman (Susi) has travelled by taxi to a house she wishes to rent. I will point to transcription conventions as I move through the analysis (see complete list of transcription conventions[4]). I have also taken one frame to exemplify embodied language usage and starting from Frame 3, the new frame is placed to the left of the dialogue where changes in gesture, posture and facial expression co-occur with a change in participant constellations and/or a new speaker turn (all frames are taken from the episode of *Cipoa* noted above).

In the talk that accompanies Frame 1 (Figure 6.3) the young woman (Susi) refers to the man (Ucup) as *Mang* (literally uncle), and the man refers to Susi as *Neng* (literally Ms). The occurrence of LOTI terms of address within a primarily Indonesian conversation may present signs of difference, especially for those unfamiliar with these terms. In isolation these fragments may leave open the question as to just which LOTI. However, recourse to co-occurring signs allows viewers to use knowledge—such as that about provinces and cities—to make guesses as to which LOTI. For example, the taxi's number plate is prefixed with a "D" meaning it is from Bandung, West Java, and the name of the taxi company "Bandung Taxi Company" is at the bottom of the driver's door (see the oval in Frame 1). In cases where there are multiple viewers, some of these viewers may be neighbours who originate from the particular province, as was sometimes the case in the two neighbourhoods where I conducted linguistic

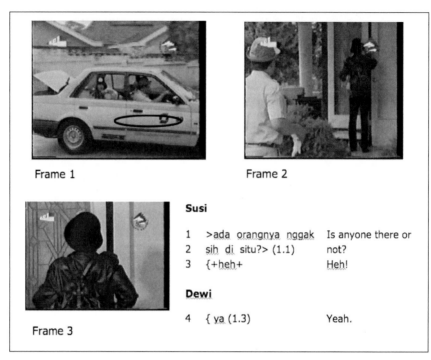

Frame 1   Frame 2

Susi

1   >ada orangnya nggak   Is anyone there or
2   sih di situ?> (1.1)   not?
3   {+heh+   Heh!

Dewi

4   { ya (1.3)   Yeah.

Frame 3

Figure 6.3   Frames 1–3.

anthropological fieldwork (reported in Goebel 2002a; 2005). Alternatively, they may be someone who has followed the serial and thus has had access to other signs that have disambiguated just which LOTI. It may also be the case that one of the characters actually identifies themselves as coming from a particular region.

As importantly, viewers' access to subsequent interactions may also provide further signs that help disambiguate just which LOTI, while also simultaneously reproducing LOTI-region links and indexing embodied behaviour with particular LOTIs and with Indonesian. Consider for example, the interaction that occurs around Frame 2 (Figure 6.3). In this interaction Susi moves away from her interaction with Mang Ucup to ring the doorbell of the house. In doing so, this provides potential signs as to what the relationship might be between her and the occupant of the house. For example, we can read an unfamiliar or stranger relationship between Susi and the house's occupant because Susi has no key and rings the doorbell. Such a reading, however, is ambiguous without recourse to the interaction that ensues.

There are also other signs that offer particular readings about other aspects of character identities. For example, in the talk surrounding Frame 1, Mang Ucup and Susi try to establish how Susi will pay for the fare. She offers a large denomination bill, to which Mang Ucup says not only that he can't provide change for it but that he does not earn that much in a day. After Susi offers foreign currency—which Ucup does not want—Ucup asks for her stuffed toy, which Susi notes is worth more than his taxi. All of this talk and the material artefacts involved offer readings of a 'well-to-do' Susi. To solidify, however, such an identity requires further interactional work.

After ringing the doorbell again, Susi uses Indonesian in summoning the occupant. [See Frame 3, Figure 6.3] The occupant, Dewi, appears to orient to this Indonesian usage with *ya* "yes" (Frame 3, line 4). This co-occurs with long inter-turn pauses signalled by the number in seconds and tenths of seconds within parenthesis (lines 2 and 4). This orientation toward linguistic sign usage together with widely circulating signs that associate unfamiliar social relationships with Indonesian usage provides further evidence for a reading of a stranger relationship between participants. However, without recourse to subsequent interactions such a relationship is still rather ambiguous. As we will see in the semiotic encounters in Frames 4 onwards—Frame 4 occurs directly after Frame 3—this stranger relationship continues to solidify (see Frames 4 and 5, Figure 6.4).

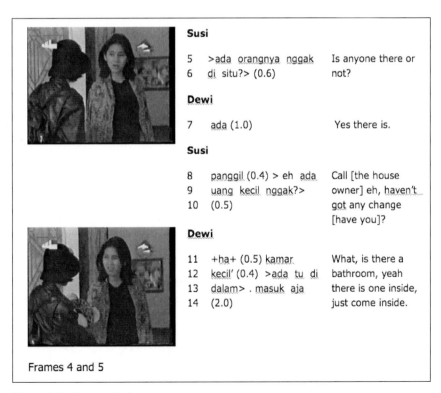

Susi

5	>ada orangnya nggak	Is anyone there or
6	di situ?> (0.6)	not?

Dewi

7	ada (1.0)	Yes there is.

Susi

8	panggil (0.4) > eh ada	Call [the house
9	uang kecil nggak?>	owner] eh, haven't
10	(0.5)	got any change
		[have you]?

Dewi

11	+ha+ (0.5) kamar	What, is there a
12	kecil' (0.4) >ada tu di	bathroom, yeah
13	dalam> . masuk aja	there is one inside,
14	(2.0)	just come inside.

Frames 4 and 5

Figure 6.4 Frames 4–5.

At Frame 4 the door is opened as Susi asks again if anybody is at home. The talk continues to be in Indonesian: notably without any terms of address or introduction. Inter-turn pause length also continues to be quite long ranging from half a second to two seconds. We can also see that in terms of facial expressions, Dewi does not appear to be very friendly (Frames 4 and 5). Again we cannot be sure about this interpretation unless we follow the interaction. We can also see that in terms of dress, Susi's leather coat and her expensive stuffed toy is noticeably different to that of Dewi, who is wearing a T-shirt and a sarong with a batik design. These differences may add to the potential differences in social status which seem to be implied through Susi's talk in lines 8–14 and the absence of introductions or terms of address.

Indeed, as we will see, Susi initially assumes that Dewi is a domestic maid. We can see some of this through what appears to be a false start (line 8) where Susi tells Dewi to call (*panggil*) someone (perhaps the house owner) before asking for change. What seems to be occurring across interactional time is both the solidification of stranger identities—which also help reproduce Indonesian usage-unfamiliarity associations—and the emergence of classed identities based upon possession of material goods and money.

After being invited in (Frame 5 line 13), Susi proceeds to comment on the aesthetics of the inside of the house primarily in Indonesian (Frame 6, Figure 6.5). In doing so, she uses a number of English tokens, while also referring to herself as an artist (at this stage this might mean either screen or music). This talk further disambiguates the 'stranger' relationship between Dewi and Susi insofar as Susi appears unfamiliar with the house. It is also interesting that much of the talk relates to the material world, which may produce links between it and Indonesian usage.

While Susi's use of English tokens "my god" (line 16), "trendi" (line 20) and "glamor" (line 26) may be a sign of 'the city' as against 'under-educated rural areas', here I suggest that it contributes to a solidification of Susi's monied-class identity insofar as English usage may suggest either an ability to engage in overseas travel, to study overseas, or to take special courses within Indonesia: all of which are expensive and out of reach of the type of low-income Indonesians with whom I am familiar (Goebel 2010). Susi's monied-class identity appears to further solidify together with Susi's interpretation of Dewi as a domestic maid. Susi's interpretation of 'domestic maid' is made more explicit when Susi asks Dewi to go and pay the taxi (Frame 7, lines 27–29). As we will see, from Frame 8 (Figure 6.6), the interaction between the pair of Dewi-Ucup contrasts markedly with that of Susi-Ucup and Susi-Dewi. This also helps to solidify the types of emerging identities discussed thus far.

In Frame 8 we see that Mang Ucup appears to recognise Dewi, through reference to her name, as she is standing at the door. We can also see that Ucup's facial expression, which ends in a smile, is reciprocated by Dewi in Frame 9, where she appears to also recognise Mang Ucup. In other words, the

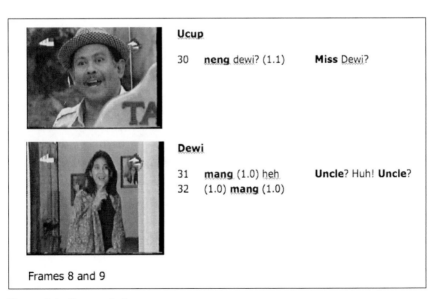

Susi

15	wadu::h' (0.3) +oh	Wow, oh **my god** this
16	**my god**+ (0.3) bagus	house is great yeah.
17	juga ini rumah ya? ya	But [we] need to
18	tapi mesti diganti lagi	change some of the
19	sama barang-barang	things [furnishings)]
20	yang lebih **trendi**'	with more **trendy**
21	(1.2) susi nggak suka	ones. Susi [i.e. "I"]
22	sama warna warna	doesn't like colours
23	kayak gini (0.3)	like this, they are not
24	kurang aktif (0.4) ya? .	active enough. Yeah if
25	kita kan artis mesti	its artists like us right
26	**glamor** gitu' . Eh (0.3)	[we] need [to be] **glamorous** right.
27	tolong dong dibayarin	Eh , please pay the
28	taksi dulu . +itu tu+	taxi first, that one, the
29	yang di luar ya? (9.0)	one outside, yeah.

Frames 6 and 7

Figure 6.5   Frames 6–7.

Ucup

30	**neng** dewi? (1.1)	**Miss** Dewi?

Dewi

31	**mang** (1.0) heh	**Uncle**? Huh! **Uncle**?
32	(1.0) **mang** (1.0)	

Frames 8 and 9

Figure 6.6   Frames 8–9.

smile appears to become a mutually recognised and ratified sign of familiar interpersonal relations. This embodied language co-occurs with increased body movement (e.g. the movement of Dewi's arm into a pointing gesture) and the use of LOTI linguistic tokens (in bold font), which when read in conjunction with the type of widely circulating stereotypes linking LOTI to intimacy discussed in the section The Enregisterment of Ethnolinguistic Difference in Indonesia might suggest a 'familiar' relationship between these two. The above sign usage also contrasts considerably with the earlier interaction between Susi and Dewi. In doing so, it also helps to solidify earlier identities and social relations between Dewi and Susi. For example, there is now the use of terms of address, names and smiles, which suggest a different type of social relationship. As with the previous interaction, however, the identities that such sign usage points to are still ambiguous.

In Frame 10 (Figure 6.7), we see that Ucup appears to be sure that the young woman is in fact the Dewi that he knows through the use of her name again. This also co-occurs with further smiling, him jumping up and down and waving his arm, continued use of a LOTI terms of address (in bold font), together with raised volume (indicated by the "+" surrounding an utterance or word) and laughter (line 34). Such sign usage is also oriented to by Dewi who continues to use LOTI terms of address while smiling, running towards Ucup (Frame 11) and raising the volume of her talk (line 35). In doing so, the identity of familiars continues to solidify. This is also achieved across time when contrasted with the interactions between the two prior participant pairs of Susi-Mang and Susi-Dewi, which can be

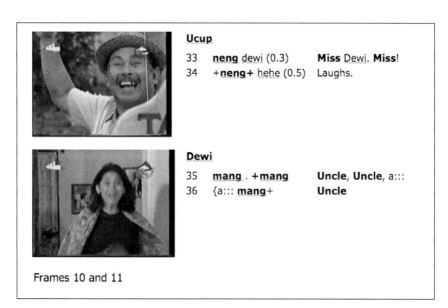

Ucup

| 33 | **neng** dewi (0.3) | **Miss** Dewi. **Miss!** |
| 34 | **+neng+** hehe (0.5) | Laughs. |

Dewi

| 35 | **mang** . **+mang** | **Uncle, Uncle,** a::: |
| 36 | {a::: **mang+** | **Uncle** |

Frames 10 and 11

Figure 6.7   Frames 10–11.

affectively characterised as business and indifference, respectively. More-over, the co-occurrence of these new embodied behaviours are potentially linked or indexed with the LOTI being used.

In Frames 12 to 14 (Figure 6.8), we can see that both Ucup and Susi begin to be heavy users of LOTI linguistic signs. This co-occurs with continued smiling, raised volume, laughter, pointing at each other and

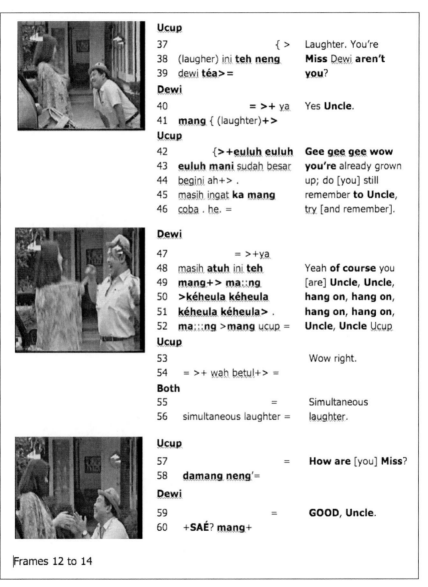

Ucup

37	{ >	Laughter. You're
38	(laugher) ini **teh neng**	**Miss** Dewi **aren't**
39	dewi **téa**>=	**you**?

Dewi

40	= >+ ya	Yes **Uncle**.
41	**mang** { (laughter)**+>**	

Ucup

42	{**>+euluh euluh**	**Gee gee gee wow**
43	**euluh mani** sudah besar	**you're** already grown
44	begini ah+> .	up; do [you] still
45	masih ingat **ka mang**	remember **to Uncle**,
46	coba . he. =	try [and remember].

Dewi

47	= >+ya	Yeah **of course** you
48	masih **atuh** ini **teh**	[are] **Uncle, Uncle,**
49	**mang+>** ma::ng	**hang on, hang on,**
50	>**kéheula kéheula**	**hang on, hang on,**
51	**kéheula kéheula**> .	**Uncle, Uncle** Ucup
52	**ma:::ng** >**mang** ucup =	

Ucup

53		Wow right.
54	= >+ wah betul+> =	

Both

55	=	Simultaneous
56	simultaneous laughter =	laughter.

Ucup

57	=	**How are** [you] **Miss**?
58	**damang neng'=**	

Dewi

59	=	**GOOD, Uncle**.
60	+**SAÉ**? **mang**+	

Frames 12 to 14

Figure 6.8   Frames 12–14.

much less space between their bodies than was the case with the other two pairs. Moreover, their bodies also directly face each other, which again contrasts with the previous pairs where this was not the case, as in Frames 15 and 16 (Figure 6.9). Frame 15 is taken from the interaction that occurred between Frames 1 and 2, while Frame 16 reproduces Frame 5.

In the interaction that occurred around Frame 12, Dewi repeats Ucup's propensity for jumping up and down (Frame 10). This potentially indicates a mutual recognition of this activity as a sign of familiar inter-personal relations. Just as importantly we also see mutual orientation to a new set of signs that occur across Frames 12 to 14. These include overlap (the start of which is indicated by a parenthesis "{"), latching (that is, no perceivable pause between turns indicated by an equals sign "="), rapid speech (indicated by a ">" surrounding words/utterances) and touch. We also see that in Frame 12, Dewi confirms that she is indeed the Dewi that Ucup thinks he knows (lines 38–41) and that in Frame 13, Dewi is able to remember Ucup's name (line 52).

In Frame 14 (lines 57–60) we also see that a LOTI is used to ask about personal life worlds as compared with earlier Indonesian usage which was about the material world (e.g. Frame 6, lines 15–26). All of this sign usage helps further solidify the identities of Dewi and Ucup. In this case it is now clear that they are LOTI-speaking familiars whose affective stance toward each other can be characterised as one of rapport (in Tannen's 1984, 1989 sense) or intimacy. There is also Ucup's lowering of his body in Frame 14 and Dewi's use of what can be classified as a 'politeness' form "saé" 'good/well', which are all signs of hierarchical social relationships. Again, for reasons of space I will not analyse this here.

In summary, we can say that this emergence of identities was 'built up to' in an ethnomethodological sense (Antaki and Widdicombe 1998),

Frame 15   Frame 16

Figure 6.9   Frames 15–16.

while also relying on the existence of widely circulating signs (e.g. Figures 6.1 and 6.2) together with contrasts of sign usage from one speech event to the next. In doing so, these semiotic encounters also potentially index a new set of signs with LOTI users and usage. I have summarised these signs as Semiotic Registers 3 and 4 (Figures 6.10 and 6.11), whereby the use of a sign can infer the semiotic register to which it belongs. The bold text indicates these new signs, while plain text represents pre-existing signs described in Figure 6.1 and Figure 6.2.

CONCLUSION

In this paper I have theorised how mass-mediated representations of person-hood and social relations not only reproduces signs from pre-existing semiotic registers, but how such representations potentially index non-linguistic signs, such as gesture, proxemics, prosody, intonation and so on with LOTI usage and users. In particular, I have argued that the association of LOTI with a region occurs regularly in such representations enabling those unfamiliar with a LOTI to guess just which LOTI it may be, while also reproducing categories of personhood, such as ethnicity and the non-LOTI speaking other or stranger. More importantly, however, is that the co-occurrence of other non-linguistic signs in such televised serials adds particular dimensions to personhood that

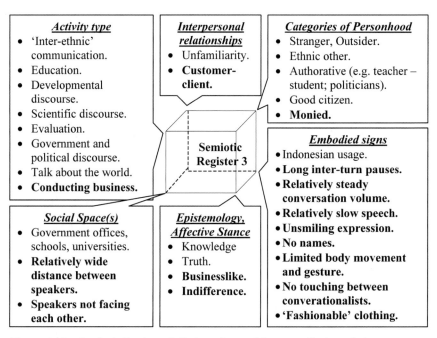

Figure 6.10   Semiotic Register 3: Indonesian and its constellation of signs.

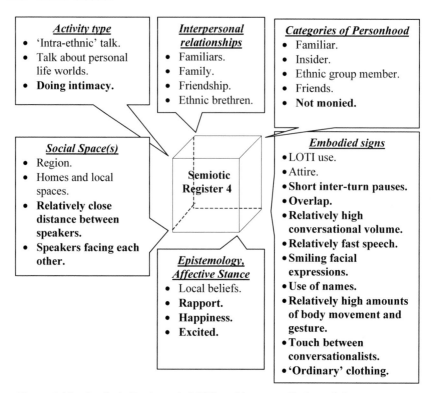

Figure 6.11   Semiotic Register 4: LOTI and its constellation of signs.

are much harder to produce if only in written form. In this sense, this allows viewers to imagine what a particular person of an ethnic group may be like: that is to say, they may have particular expectations about their demeanour. Indeed, it may be the case that in subsequent situated face-to-face interactions a viewer may make judgements about a person's background based upon the use of certain signs, as demonstrated in Agha's (2003) work on the linking of accent with culturally valued personas in Britain.

In closing I would like to make a number of points. First of all, in the beginning of my analysis I alluded to signs of class, which actually solidi-fied further in later interactions between Ucup, Dewi, Susi and one fur-ther participant, Ayu. However, for reasons of space I have not followed through with this theme. Second, I should re-highlight that what I have offered above is a theorisation of processes of enregisterment based in part on my own experiences in Indonesia. Without recourse to meta-pragmatic commentaries about these serials—either as found in the print media or actual viewers' comments as they watched this serial—we cannot be sure whether and to what extent the signs I describe in this paper are recognised by viewers. Again, for reasons of space I have not treated this issue here.

NOTES

1. This paper is a written version of a conference paper with the same title, which was presented at the Fourth International Conference on Multi-modality (4-ICOM) in Singapore on 1 August 2008. In this paper I build upon two other previous publications ('Enregistering, Authorizing and Denaturalizing Identity in Indonesia'. Journal of Linguistic Anthropology, 18 (1): 46–61 and 'Enregistering Ethnicity and Hybridity in Indonesia', Journal of the School of Letters [Nagoya University], 4, 37–50). I do so by exploring the multimodal aspects of interaction and their implication for studies of knowledge/cultural reproduction. I am indebted to my audience in Singapore, particularly Michael O'Toole, Volker Eisenlauer and Esther Joosa. I would also like to express my sincere gratitude to the Japan Society for the Promotion of Science for a grant (No. C20520380), which has enabled me to purse this research. Last but not least, I would also like to thank a team of Indonesian research assistants who have worked with me on this project, including Mbak Eni, Mbak Riris, Mas Inu and Mbak Puji. Of course, all errors and omissions remain my sole responsibility.
2. SPEAKING is an acronym covering the minimal types of data that Hymes' suggested are needed to understand what makes up participants' communicative competence. These include (S) Situation, (P) Participants, (E) Ends, (A) Act sequence, (K) Key, (I) Instrumentalities (or modes in the sense of those working in the area of multimodal interaction analysis) and (G) Genre.
3. Of course, this is a simplistic view of such relationships given that there may be many languages spoken in a household because of 'mixed' marriages, the presence of care-givers from different language backgrounds and so on.
4. The following is a list of transcription conventions used:

plain font	Indonesian (I)
Bold	LOTI
bold italics	forms that can be classified as a LOTI or I.
. between words	Indicates a perceivable silence.
outline	English tokens
BOLD CAPS	LOTI politeness tokens
brackets with a number (.4)	length of silence in tenths of a second.
=	no perceivable pause between speaker turns.
{	start of overlapping talk.
' after a word	final falling intonation.
? after a word	final rising intonation.
+ surrounding an utterance/ word	raising of volume
> at the start and end of an utterance	utterance was spoken faster than the previous one.
: within a word	sound stretch
Brackets with three?, i.e. (???)	word that could not be transcribed
[word] in English gloss	indicates implied talk.

REFERENCES

Agha, A. (2007) *Language and Social Relations*, Cambridge: Cambridge University Press.
———— (2005) 'Voice, footing, enregisterment.' *Journal of Linguistic Anthropology* 15(1): 38–59.
———— (2003) 'The social life of cultural value.' *Language and Communication* 23 (3–4): 231–273.
Anderson, B. R. O. G. (2006 [1991, 1983]) *Imagined Communities: Reflections on the Origin and Spread of Nationalism*, revised edition, London: Verso.
Antaki, C., and Widdicombe, S. (1998) 'Identity as an achievement and as a tool.' In Antaki, C., and Widdicombe S. eds. *Identities in Talk*, London: Sage Publications: pp. 1–14.
Anwar, K. (1980) *Indonesian: The Development and Use of a National Language*, Yogyakarta: Gadjah Mada University Press.
Appadurai, A. (1996) *Modernity at Large: Cultural Dimensions of Globalization*, Minneapolis: University of Minnesota Press.
Bakhtin, M. M. (1981) *The Dialogic Imagination: Four Essays*; trans. Emerson, C., and Holquist, M., Austin: University of Texas Press.
Bauman, R., and Briggs, C. (1990) 'Poetics and performance as critical perspectives on language and social life.' *Annual Review of Anthropology* 19: 59–88.
Birdwhistle, R. (1972) 'A kinesic-linguistic exercise: The cigarette scene.' In Gumperz, J., and Hymes D. eds. *Directions in Sociolinguistics: The Ethnography of Communication*, New York: Holt, Rinehart and Winston: pp. 435–453.
Black, P., and Goebel, Z. (2002) 'Multiliteracies and the teaching of Indonesian.' *Babel* 37(1): 22–26, 38.
Cipoa, (1995) *Noné* [television series]. Jakarta, Indonesia: Television Pendidikan Indonesia (TPI)
Errington, J. J. (2001) 'Colonial linguistics.' *Annual Review of Anthropology* 30: 19–39.
Fairclough, N. (1995) *Media Discourse*, London: Arnold.
Feith, H. (1962) *The Decline of Constitutional Democracy in Indonesia*, New York: Cornell University Press.
Friedman, S. L. (2006) 'Watching twin bracelets in China: The role of spectatorship and identification in an ethnographic analysis of film reception.' *Cultural Anthropology* 21(4): 603–632.
Gafaranga, J., and Torras, M.C. (2002) 'Interactional otherness: Towards a redefinition of codeswitching.' *The International Journal of Bilingualism* 6(1): 1–22.
Ginsburg, F. D., Abu-Lughod, L., and Larkin, B. (2002) 'Introduction.' In Ginsburg, F. D., Abu-Lughod, L. and Larkin, B. eds. *Media Worlds: Anthropology on New Terrain*, Berkeley: University of California Press: pp. 1–36.
Goebel, Z. (2010) *Language, Migration and Identity: Neighborhood Talk in Indonesia*, Cambridge: Cambridge University Press.
———— (2008a) 'Enregistering, authorizing and denaturalizing identity in Indonesia.' *Journal of Linguistic Anthropology* 18(1): 46–61.
———— (2008b) 'Enregistering ethnicity and hybridity in Indonesia.' *Journal of the School of Letters* 4: 37–50.
———— (2005) 'An ethnographic study of code choice in two neighbourhoods of Indonesia.' *Australian Journal of Linguistics* 25(1): 85–107.
———— (2002a) 'Code choice in inter-ethnic interactions in two urban neighbourhoods of Indonesia.' *International Journal of the Sociology of Language* 158: 69–87.
———— (2002b) 'When do Indonesians speak Indonesian? Some evidence from inter-ethnic and foreigner-Indonesian interactions and its pedagogic implications.' *Journal of Multilingual and Multicultural Development* 23(6): 479–489.

Goffman, E. (1967) *Interaction Ritual: Essays on Face-to-face Behavior,* New York: Anchor.

Goodwin, C. (2006) 'Human sociality as mutual orientation in a rich interactive environment: Multimodal utterances and pointing in aphasia.' In Enfield, N., and Levinson, S. eds. *Roots of Human Sociality,* London: Berg Press: pp. 96–125.

Gumperz, J. J. (1982) *Discourse Strategies,* Cambridge: Cambridge University Press.

Haviland, J. B. (2004) 'Gesture.' In Duranti, A. ed. *A Companion to Linguistic Anthropology,* Oxford: Blackwell: pp. 197–221.

Hymes, D. (1974) *Foundations in Sociolinguistics: An Ethnographic Approach,* Philadelphia: University of Pennsylvania Press.

Inoue, M. (2004) 'What does language remember?: Indexical inversion and the naturalized history of Japanese women.' *Journal of Linguistic Anthropology* 14(1): 39–56.

Irvine, J. (2001) 'Style as distinctiveness: The culture and ideology of linguistic differentiation.' In Eckert, P., and Rickford, J. eds. *Style and Sociolinguistic Variation,* Cambridge: Cambridge University Press: pp. 21–43.

Kendon, A. (1985) 'Some uses of gesture.' In Tannen, D., and Saville-Troike, M. eds. *Perspectives on silence,* New Jersey: Ablex: pp. 215–314.

Kroskrity, P. V., ed. (2000) *Regimes of Language: Ideologies, Polities, and Identities* (Advanced Seminar Series) Santa Fe, New Mexico: School of American Research.

Kurniasih, Y. K. (2007) 'Local content curriculum 1994: The teaching of Javanese in Yogyakarta schools'. Paper presented at The First International Symposium on the Languages of Java (ISLOJ), Graha Santika Hotel, Semarang, Indonesia, 15–16 August.

Lowenberg, P. H. (1992) 'Language policy and language identity in Indonesia.' *Journal of Asian Pacific Communication* 3(1): 59–77.

Meek, B. A. (2006) 'And the injun goes "How!": Representations of American Indian English in white public space.' *Language in Society* 35(1): 93–128.

Miller, L. (2004) 'Those naughty teenage girls: Japanese kogals, slang, and media assessments.' *Journal of Linguistic Anthropology* 14(2): 225–247.

Nababan, P. W. J. (1991) 'Language in education: The case of Indonesia.' International Review of Education 37(1): 113–131.

Norris, S. (2004) *Analyzing Multimodal Interaction: A Methodological Framework,* London: Routledge.

O'Halloran, K. L. (2008) 'Power, identity and life in the digital age.' In Amano, M., O'Toole, L., M., Goebel, Z., Shigemi S. and Song-Wei eds. *Identity in Text Interpretation and Everyday Life,* Nagoya: Nagoya University: 45–61.

O'Toole, M. (1994) *The Language of Displayed Art,* 1st ed, London: Leicester University Press.

O'Toole, M. (1994) *The Language of Displayed Art,* 2nd ed, London and New York: Routledge.

Ochs, E. (2006 [1979]) 'Transcription as theory.' In Jaworski A. and Coupland, N. eds. *The Discourse Reader,* London: Routledge.

—— (1996) 'Linguistic resources for socializing humanity.' In Gumperz, J. J., and Levinson, S. C. eds. *Rethinking Linguistic Relativity,* Cambridge: Cambridge University Press: pp. 407–437.

—— (1988) *Culture and Language Development: Language Acquisition and Language Socialization in a Samoan Village,* Cambridge: Cambridge University Press.

Parker, L. (2002) 'The subjectification of citizenship: Student interpretations of school teachings in Bali.' *Asian Studies Review* 26(1): 3–37.

Philips, S. U. (1983) *The Invisible Culture: Communication in Classroom and Community on the Warm Springs Indian Reservation,* New York: Longman.

Sacks, H. (1995) *Lectures on Conversation,* Vol 1 and 2, Oxford: Blackwell.

Schegloff, E. A. (2007) 'A tutorial on membership categorization.' *Journal of Pragmatics* 39: 462–482.

Schieffelin, B. B., Woolard, K. A., and Kroskrity, P. V., eds. (1998) *Language Ideologies: Practice and Theory*, New York: Oxford University Press.

Scollon, R., and Scollon, S. W. (2003) *Discourses in Place: Language in the Material World*, London: Routledge.

Silverstein, M., and Urban, G. (1996) 'The natural history of discourse.' In Silverstein M., and Urban G. eds. *Natural Histories of Discourse,* Chicago: University of Chicago Press: 1–17.

Spitulnik, D. (1998) 'Mediating unity and diversity: The production of language ideologies in Zambian broadcasting.' In Schieffelin B., Woolard K. and Kroskrity P. eds. *Language Ideologies: Practice and Theory*, New York: Oxford University Press: pp. 163–188.

—— (1996) 'The social circulation of media discourse and the mediation of communities.' *Journal of Linguistic Anthropology* 6(2): 161–187.

Tannen, D. (1989) *Talking Voices: Repetition, Dialogue, and Imagery in Conversational Discourse*, Cambridge: Cambridge University Press.

—— (1984) *Conversational Style: Analyzing Talk among Friends*, Norwood, New Jersey: Ablex.

Van Leeuwen, T. (2005) *Introducing Social Semiotics*, London: Routledge.

Wenger, E. (1998) *Communities of Practice*, Cambridge: Cambridge University Press.

Wortham, S. (2006) *Learning Identity: The Joint Emergence of Social Identification and Academic Learning*, Cambridge: Cambridge University Press.

7 The Semiotics of Decoration

Theo Van Leeuwen

INTRODUCTION

In the eighteenth and nineteenth centuries, fuelled by the industrial revolution and the questions it raised about the difference between handmade and machine-made objects, there were intense debates about the nature of decoration and its place relative to, on the one hand, non-decorated objects, and, on the other hand, the arts. In the late nineteenth century, this debate culminated in the arts and crafts movement to which I will refer later.

But in the twentieth century this changed. In a famous tract called *Ornament and Crime*, written over a hundred years ago, the Austrian architect Adolf Loos wrote:

> Herein lies the greatness of our age; that it is incapable of producing a new ornament. Ornament is no longer organically linked with our culture. The evolution of culture is synonymous with the removal of ornament from utilitarian objects. (cited in Brett 2005: 195)

One of the objects he discussed was clothing. 'So immensely strong is the individuality of modern man', he wrote, 'that it can no longer be expressed in articles of clothing':

> Modernity uses the ornaments of earlier or alien cultures as it sees fit, but no longer produces new forms of decoration. Objects are pure and functional, and expression moves away from the decoration of objects to fine art. (ibid.)

Somewhat later, Le Corbusier (1987: 188) stressed the need to remove ornamentation from interior decoration: 'Every citizen must replace his hangings, his damasks, his wallpapers, his stencils, with a plain coat of white ripolin.'

Such arguments revolved around functionality. In the late nineteenth century, new forms of architecture and design had emerged. Alongside the still heavily decorated settings and objects of the private sphere, plainer, functional forms of dress, of interior decoration, of architecture and so on had emerged in the industrial sphere. These purely utilitarian types of design were now preferred by the artist-designers of the Bauhaus in Germany, the Werkbund in Austria and so on, and paradoxically endowed with moral and aesthetic, rather than only utilitarian values, on the basis of discourses inherited from earlier puritan styles of dress and design. Indeed, functionality itself could become decorative in this context. Le Corbusier saw the steamship as a prime example of pure functionality—and then used elements of steamships to make buildings *look* like steamships, for instance by making the edge of a building pointed like the bow of a ship, or by using the grey steel of a battleship, or the red, yellow and blue colours of semaphore flags (Riley 1994: 212).

All this applies also to language, and to linguistics. In the early twentieth-century journalistic language stripped language of everything that was not functional in the transfer of information. In a 1915 brochure, Reuters already wrote of 'compressing news into minute globules" that would condense news stories to their absolute essence and use standard devices to guarantee facticity (Palmer 1998: 184). A study of an English language Vietnamese newspaper (Machin and van Leeuwen 2007) showed how the Western subeditors who introduced this style to local journalists discouraged the wordplay and poetic flourishes, which were prized by the Vietnamese journalists. And as for linguistics, in Prague school functionalism there had been a place for linguistic decoration, for the poetic, the ornamental side of language, which, as Jakobson showed (1963), exists not only in poetry but also in everyday uses of language. But in modern functional grammars such as systemic-functional grammar (e.g. Halliday 1985) linguistic decoration disappeared. The human ability to play with language, to create rhymes and assonances, no longer plays a role in understanding language here.

More recently, however, there has been somewhat of a revival of decoration. "Pattern is back", as the cover blurb of a recent book on the design of wallpapers, wrapping papers etc triumphantly announces (Cole 2007). Individuality, difference, contrary to what Loos predicted, is once again expressed through choices of clothing, interior decoration and so on, albeit now in the new environment of lifestyle marketing, of the creation, in selected areas of course, of the surface differences that mask the increasing homogeneity of precisely those things that are most decorated—buildings, clothes, certain key objects etc.

Again, this applies also to language. In PowerPoint presentations, for instance, a wide range of decorative designs can be chosen for one and the same underlying textual pattern (title plus list of bullet points) so that generic homogeneity, homogeneity of communicative practice, can be overlaid with the expressing of different identities.

There is another side to the re-emergence of decoration as well, a change of emphasis, in certain forms of public communication, from text to context, from forms of communication that require conscious, focused attention, to forms of communication that are embedded in everyday practices. The first signs of this emerged in the 1920s. Eric Satie, for instance, re-introduced the idea of ambient music in that period (re-introduced, because in the eighteenth-century composers like Telemann, for instance, were commissioned to write 'dinner music', music to be played in the background while the dinner guest ate and chatted). Satie had his 'ambient' composition played at the opening of an exhibition, but as soon as the musicians started, everyone fell silent and turned to the musicians, attending to the music as they would in a concert hall, and Satie, apparently, walked around urging them to keep talking and not to pay attention to the music (Murray Schafer 1994: 110). Visual artists, too, became interested in making posters, clothes, furniture and other objects, and, of course, buildings, rather than paintings and sculptures intended for display in galleries and museums. From the point of view of the public communication of key ideas, this can be an effective strategy. In a study of attitudes to Disney across the world, Silvia Lomina y Vedia interviewed seventeen- to twenty-one-year-old Mexican students about Disney. Many were critical, or denied any interest. Yet they would wear Disney socks, Disney T-shirts, Disney backpack patches and so on. When asked how it was possible to deny all contact with Disney and at the same time habitually use such objects, 'all responded with an initial moment of confusion. Some were surprised and said they hadn't noticed. Others that it was merely fashionable or "looked nice". A few others were at a loss what to say and walked away' (Wasko et al. 2001: 216).

Contemporary culture and cultural communication is as much, if not more, in the props and settings of our everyday practices as in the 'texts' that we consciously and concentratedly interact with. And for this reason, discourse analysts should pay as much, if not more, attention to 'context' as to 'text', to 'background' as to 'foreground'.

MEANING AND PLEASURE

Two themes dominated the nineteenth-century debate about decoration (or 'ornament'—both terms were used, and often interchangeably). The first is the opposition between meaning and pleasure. Immanuel Kant, in the *Critique of Judgment,* had argued for aesthetics as based on pleasure and subjectivity. To say "this is a beautiful jug" is, according to Kant, not a rational statement but a subjective expression of pleasure that says nothing about the jug but everything about the beholder's reaction to it. This view influenced one point of view in nineteenth-century writing about decoration. Owen Jones, for instance, in a mid- nineteenth-century book called *The Grammar of Ornament* (1856), said that

> Ornament . . . has no business beyond appealing to the eye, in order to entertain the imagination in free play with ideas, and engage actively in the aesthetic judgment independently of any end. (cited in Brett, 2005: 109)

William Morris, a key figure in the arts and crafts movement, on the other hand, insisted on meaning in *Some Hints on Pattern Design* (1895: 177):

> You may be sure that any decoration is futile when it does not remind you of something of which it is a visible symbol. As a Western man and a picture lover, I must still insist on plenty of meaning in your patterns . . .

And it was possible to express meanings with flowery wallpaper (plant forms were a key motif for the decoration of just about anything), both in terms of broader themes, such as the beauty of nature, and reconciling nature and technology, and in terms of more specific meanings, as dictionaries of the allegorical meanings of flowers were still in wide use at the time. Kate Greenaway's *Language of Flowers* (1884), for instance, had the spring crocus as signifying 'youthful gladness', the blue periwinkle as signifying 'early friendship', the zinnia as signifying 'thoughtfulness about friends', and so on (cf. Brett 2005: 108).

Like the Mexican students, and in the tradition of Kant, the first of these two views focuses on 'taste', on individual, subjective appeal, thereby allowing the cultural meanings embedded in decorations to be denied and ignored. The second acknowledges that wallpapers and fabrics have "plenty of meaning', even if that meaning is communicated differently, by just 'being there', being everywhere, by being the context of our life. As a semiotician, I am duty-bound to opt for the second view, but without denying that pleasure and meaning can live happily together, and that pleasure can play a key role in the successful communication of social and cultural meaning. As design historian David Brett (2005: 105) has put it, 'decoration, even of the most humble and everyday kind, acts as an integrator of individual pleasure with social life and its ideological commitments'.

A second key theme in nineteenth-century debates about decoration, is the opposition between the generic and conceptual on the one hand, and the specific and naturalistic on the other. Christopher Dresser, in *The Art of Decorative Design* (1857: 217), described decoration as a conventional art form and linked it to science:

> We are not to draw particular plants as they really exist—blown about and deformed—but as we know them to be . . . what Nature's production would be if they were unmodified by external influences. . . . the plant in a perfect state . . .

It is a view which can be found also in more recent literature on decoration. Design historian David Brett, for instance, says that 'the shapes of much-repeated decorative elements may play on the minimal cues we need for recognition, and so get basic concepts across even if they are not in full vision' (Brett 2005: 52).

John Ruskin, in *The Eagle's Nest* (1872) propagated a more empirical view (cited in Brett 2005: 114):

Art has nothing to do with structures, causes or absolute facts . . . In drawing, try only to represent the appearance of things, never what you know the things to be . . .

In Kress and van Leeuwen (2006), this contrast is understood in terms of the concept of modality. Conceptual, or 'abstract' modality, as they called it, represents objects in terms of their underlying, general truth, in terms of what we *know* they 'are' like, and measures truthfulness or realism by that standard, while 'naturalistic' modality represents objects in terms of what they look like (or sound like), in terms of what we would have been able to see (or hear) if we saw (or heard) them in reality, in specific circumstances, and it measures truthfulness and realism by that criterion. In contemporary communication, many still prefer naturalistic images in, for instance, film and television, and even in fantasy games that show things we could never see in reality. But decoration has long moved away from Ruskin's point of view towards conventionalised forms that repeat, over and over, the key motifs of contemporary culture. And even the use of formerly naturalistic media, such as photography, increasingly moves in the direction of more generic, decontextualised images that express concepts rather than depict specific people, places and things, for instance in the kinds of images now marketed to designers by image banks such as Getty Creative Images (Machin, 2004). Such images, too, are increasingly used, not as illustrations, but as decorations—decorative backgrounds or marginal elements of texts such as web pages, book covers etc.

It would appear that both these key themes from the nineteenth-century debate are still, or again, of high relevance today and deserve to be picked up again, as, not just of interest from the point of view of design history but also from the point of view of understanding the return of decoration in contemporary visual communication.

THE FUNCTIONALITY AND MULTIMODALITY OF DECORATION

Despite the classic opposition between functionality and decoration, writers on decoration do often describe it as functional as well as pleasurable. David Brett (2005: 47), for instance, insists on the role of decoration in 'providing comprehensibility of shapes'. What tends to be decorated he says, is edges, for instance rooflines, the hems of dresses, or, to add a modern example, the framelines which, in PowerPoint design templates, divide the titles of screens from their 'content' space. As we have seen already, he also follows Owen Jones 19th century 'grammar of ornament', in seeing the 'shapes of much-repeated decorative elements play on the minimal cues we need for recognition, and so get basic concepts across' (ibid.: 52). These functions of decoration could be seen as ideational, as in the service of representation, and Brett also argues for the cohesive effect of decoration (the mouldings in a building, for instance, can create a unity of style), and this could be interpreted as a textual function.

I am not sure whether such functional explanations are entirely convincing. Edges and hems may be the places where decorative elements are often found, but they can also be plain and unadorned, and they can be made more or less salient without having to be decorated. Nor is decoration only found at the edges or in the background. It can also enhance core elements, for instance, the lettering of a text, or the necktie that serves as focus for the outfit of a man-in-a-suit. Nevertheless, although there is a difference between the functionality of an object and the possible functionality of its decorative elements, decoration can add ideational meanings that bear no direct relation to the functionality of the decorated object, as well as enhance 'textuality' and cohesion and, of course, interpersonal communication, because of its ability to signify difference and bestow identity in different objects with the same functionality (for instance, different neckties).

Not only is decoration functional, it is also multimodal. Whatever kinds of objects we look at, wallpaper, fabrics, ornaments in architecture and so on, we find it involves not only abstract and figurative pictorial forms but also colour, texture and even movement. Cole (2007: 141), for instance, shows a fabric by Keira March, which has been made of canvas and painted with black and indigo hues and then has strips of lace and other elements sewn on it.

Second, even though I am dealing here primarily with visual examples, the concept of decoration can be applied to every semiotic mode. I have already alluded to linguistic decoration, but there is musical decoration as well (suspensions, runs, trills, grace notes, arpeggios and so on), and it may be that a study of musical ornamentation (as it is usually referred to in this context) in, for instance, Baroque music, or, for that matter, in jazz, can provide as many points of departure for the development of a new semiotics of decoration as our brief excursion into nineteenth-century design debates.

SOME NOTES TOWARDS THE ANALYSIS OF VISUAL DECORATION

Writers on decoration have classified decorative motifs in a number of different ways, first of all as non-pictorial (whether geometric or otherwise) and pictorial, which may include various subclasses such as, for instance natural forms, plant forms etc. Despite Alfred Loos' distinction between decoration and fine art, there does not appear to be a clear division between 'artistic' and 'decorative' motifs in the twentieth century, and art has in fact provided many key decorative motifs. Matisse's forms, for instance, which are neither quite pictorial, nor quite non-pictorial, have been a rich resource in many areas of design.

In non-pictorial decoration, meaning can be created either through connotation, when a cluster of design parameters has a clear cultural or historical reference, or on the basis of the principle of experiential metaphor (cf. Kress and van Leeuwen, 2001). Especially in the colonial era, not only exotic food and drink and fabrics, but also many decorative forms were introduced into Western culture from other parts of the world, especially from Islamic art—hence the word 'arabesque' for the kind of patterns which are common in that art. The connotations of such motifs will resonate with the 'orientalist' and 'exoticist' associations, which the world where the motifs came from have for the Western world into which they were adopted.

More abstract decorative motifs that do not have a recognisable provenance will have a meaning potential that rests on the meaning potential of their key formal qualities, representing qualities that are common to many objects. These qualities are likely to be much the same as those I have proposed in an earlier paper on typography (van Leeuwen 2006).

Curvature

An abstract motif can stress angularity, or it can stress curvature. The significance of curvature can be based on experiential and cultural associations with essentially round or essentially angular objects. Depending on the context, roundness can come to signify 'smooth', 'soft', 'natural', 'organic' 'maternal' and so on and angularity 'abrasive', 'harsh', 'technical', 'masculine' and so on. Both may be positively or negatively valued, depending on the broader cultural context. Clearly the field of possibilities is very wide. But it will be narrowed down by other, co-present features, and by the context generally, for instance by the kind of object it decorates. If there is little or no context to narrow down the meaning potential, it will signify the whole wide complex of related notions, although users may of course focus on a specific meaning that holds special appeal for them.

Salience

As with many of the other features discussed here 'salience' indicates a gradual contrast, a continuum of salience from thin decorative patterns that hardly stand out against the background to strong obtrusive patterns. High salience in decorative patterns can be made to mean 'daring', 'substantial', 'solid', 'assertive' and so on and its opposite 'timid' or 'insubstantial', but the values may also be reversed. High salience might also mean 'overbearing', 'domineering' and low salience 'subtle', 'delicate' and so on. Other, co-present signifying elements will narrow down the meaning potential and the values invoked, and make them more specific.

Density

Abstract decorative motifs may be condensed, narrow, squashed, tightly packed or expanded and wide. The metaphoric potential of this will relate to our experience of space. Expansion may be positive, providing a sense of room to breathe, room to move and condensing the opposite. Or expansion may be wasteful and condensed use of space economical and efficient.

Connectivity

Decorative motifs may be disconnected, separated by framelines or space, or they may be connected to each other, and this is, yet again, a matter of degree. The meaning potential again follows from what connectivity is and does. Disconnection can suggest 'atomisation' or 'fragmentation' and connection 'wholeness' or 'integration'. But the values may be reversed, and disconnection could suggest the individuality of each motif and connectivity the opposite. Motifs may be internally disconnected, in which case there is disconnection *within* the motif, with, for instance, the lines that trace the outline of, say, a dove, not connecting, not closing up, or externally, in which case there is disconnection and distance *between* the motifs.

Clearly a pattern can combine all these features, and even have angular as well as rounded aspects. The wrapping paper in Figure 7.1, for instance, has strict, precisely regimented lines, which stand up stiffly, hemming in more rounded forms. In addition there will be colours, textures and so on. It is therefore better not to follow the example of most writers on decoration, who produce overall classifications such as 'geometrical', 'abstract', 'natural' etc, but to see decorative patterns as clusters of features or parameters that may come together either in culturally patterned or novel ways and derive their meaning from the combination of these features, just as a good dish derives its taste from a combination of ingredients.

Repetition

In my work on music (1999), I described the difference between 'measured time' that has a regular pulse, and 'unmeasured time', a form of musical time that has no discernable regular pulse, but is a continuing, ongoing sound that at best fluctuates in more unpredictable waves of slightly increasing and decreasing dissonance and level. In the case of regular time, there is often a regular rhythmic motif that underlies and underscores the melodic message.

Most visual decorative patterns are regular and repetitive patterns. But the unpredictable, patterns of nature can also be used as decoration—the

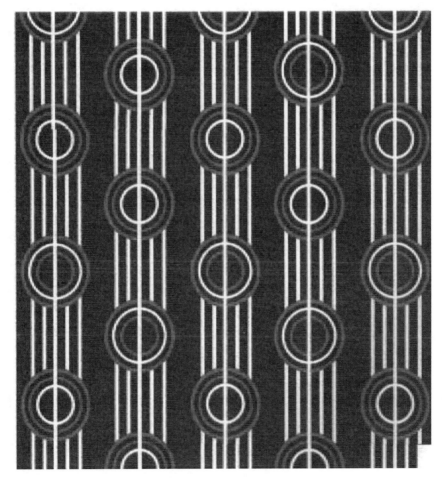

Figure 7.1   Wrapping paper (Marc Burton 2007).

swirls of marble, the grain of wood and so on, and sometimes such patterns are produced deliberately, as when glassblowers bring about deliberate accidents in firing, creating colourful swirly effects. Such unpredictable, irregular patterns became a key form of decoration in modernity. Even Adolf Loos, the author of *Ornament and Crime,* used it in a building he designed in Vienna, which is now known as the Adolf Loos Haus.

Regular repetitive patterns are not only a key feature of decoration, and of rhythmical patterns and 'riffs' in music, they are a fundamental feature of all human work, all human action. Rhythmic repetition in music is what makes music danceable, movable on, and visual patterns have a similar link to the movements of our hands as they doodles, spirals, zigzags and so translate repetitive action into the visual traces that are at the basis of decoration and on which more complex patterns begin to form regular variations.

Figure 7.2   "Day and Night" (woodcut, M. C. Escher 1938).

But there is another important aspect to repetition. When a pattern is repeated over and over, you do not have to see the whole. You can be secure in the knowledge that it will continue to be the same. You know you are in a stable world. Sigmund Freud understood this and expressed it memorably in his account of the *fort . . . da* game ('gone . . . there'), in which the child enacts the absence and reappearance of the mother by means of the repetitive manipulation of a wooden reel, with a great yield of pleasure and excitement. Repetition therefore induces pleasure in the constancy and stability of the environment in which we act and of the meanings that we find in there. And the pleasure of more complex repetitions is perhaps that we do not immediately notice them, and only after a while begin to see the pattern so that we can begin to stop worrying about where the pattern will lead us to and enjoy it for what it is here and now.

But repetition of course also opens up the possibility of non-repetition, not only in the sense we already described of random patterns, but also of the gradual transformation of at first sight repetitive patterns, of a mix of repetition and sequence and development, whether in reversible or non-reversible fashion, something of which M. C. Escher was perhaps the undisputed master (Figure 7.2).

AN EXAMPLE

The example in Figure 7.3 shows the 2007 Annual Report of the University of Technology, Sydney. Like many contemporary texts, it contains both

Figure 7.3   Cover of Annual Report (University of Technology, Sydney Library 2007).

words and what appear at first sight to be meaningless patterns, meaningless and hence purely decorative 'graphisms'. With the aid of the considerations, I have presented in this essay I will nevertheless try to 'read' these apparently meaningless graphic patterns. Let me begin with the colour, silvery grey, a colour that is a time-honoured symbol of value, whether applied to boxes of visiting cards or motor cars. Sleek, glossy, stylish, yet businesslike. Words such as 'access', 'absorb', 'resource', 'intellect', 'accumulate', 'research' are printed vertically, as ascending, aspirational words, indicating the key values the library seeks to embrace, and by being backgrounded and repeated, also on the back cover of the document, they become decorative elements, along with the geometric graphisms, part of the environment, rather than a text to read. Their role as decorative elements changes how they communicate—they are now enduring, stable concepts that are a permanent feature of the setting, as for instance in Islamic ornamentation, where words may also function as more or less isolated elements, and often sit at the edge between comprehensibility as words and being an apparently meaningless decorative motif.

Then there is very rigid, regular grid of thin white lines on which nevertheless some other elements are imposed. Big squares, more strongly framed, single out special zones, and arrows draw attention to them, and bring in a more dynamic, active element. Special moments of value, 'plus' signs, and circles, some coloured, appear as if in a brain scan where certain parts light up as they are activated. And different zones are of different degrees of lightness and radiation, almost as in a heat reading.

Thus, the library is, on the one hand, depicted as a rigid classificatory schema, executed in immaculate metallic sheen, and yet, within that, there are specifically distinctive features (the special zones), moments of activity (the arrows) and of affective engagement (colour and light). A strange machine, visually whizzing and burring, in which resources have been accumulated and classified and in which research can be accessed. Such backgrounds are a peculiar modern form of textuality to which we rarely pay much conscious attention, but in which some of the most crucial identities and values are nevertheless expressed, constantly, repetitively and almost subliminally. We would do well to extend our work in visual communication to include decorative elements of this kind.

REFERENCES

Brett, D. (2005) *Rethinking Decoration—Pleasure and Ideology in the Visual Arts*, Cambridge: Cambridge University Press.
Cole, D. (2007) *Patterns—New Surface Design* London: Laurence King.
Dresser, C (1857) 'Botany as Adapted to the Arts and Art Manufacturing.' *Arts Journal* Vol 20: 217–260.
Halliday, M. A. K. (1985) *An Introduction to Functional Grammar*, 1st ed, London: Arnold.

Jakobson, R. (1963) 'Closing Statement: Linguistics and Poetics.' In Sebeok, T. A. ed. *Style in Language,* Cambridge, Mass: MIT Press: pp. 350–377.

Kress, G., and van Leeuwen, T. (2006) *Reading Images—The Grammar of Visual Design,* 2nd ed, London: Routledge.

———— (2001) *Multimodal Discourse—The Modes and Media of Contemporary Communication,* London: Arnold.

Le Corbusier (1987 [1925]) *The Decorative Art of Today,* Cambridge, Mass: MIT Press.

Machin, D. (2004) 'Building the World's Visual Language: The Increasing Global Importance of Image Banks.' *Visual Communciation* 3(3): 316–336.

Machin, D., and van Leeuwen, T. (2007) *Global Media Discourse—A critical introduction,* London, Routledge.

Morris, W. (1895) *Some Hints on Pattern Designing,* London: Longmans.

Murray Schafer, R. (1994) *Our Sonic Environment and the Soundscape—The Tuning of the World,* Rochester, Vermont: Destiny Books.

Palmer, M. (1998*)* 'What makes news.' In Boyd-Barrett, O., and Rantanen, T. eds. *The Globalization of News,* London: Sage.

Riley, C. A. (1994) *Color Codes—Modern Theories of Color in Philosophy, Painting and Architecture, Literature, Music and Psychology,* Hanover: University Press of New England.

van Leeuwen, T. (2006) 'Towards a Semiotics of Typography.' *Information Design Journal* 14(2): 139–156.

———— (1999) *Speech, Music, Sound,* London, Macmillan.

Wasko, J., Phillips, M. and Meehan, E. R. (2001) *Dazzled by Disney?—The Global Disney Audiences Project,* London: Leicester University Press.

Part II
Domains of Multimodal Studies

8 Multimodality and Social Actions in 'Personal Publishing' Text

From the German 'Poetry Album' to Web 2.0 'Social Network Sites'

Volker J. Eisenlauer

INTRODUCTION

> Der Rundfunk wäre der denkbar großartigste Kommunikationsapparat des öffentlichen Lebens [. . .], wenn er es verstünde, nicht nur auszusenden, sondern auch zu empfangen, also den Zuhörer nicht nur hören, sondern auch sprechen zu machen [. . .].

> *Radio broadcasting would be one of the greatest means for public communication [. . .], if it could not only send but also receive, so that the listener could not just hear but also speak.*
>
> (Bert Brecht 1932, author translation)

In his speech about the functions of radio broadcasting, Brecht (1932) envisioned a new bi-directional form of mass media communication, which has come to fruition in the era of Web 2.0 technology. Most notably, in recent Web 2.0 applications, such as *Wikipedia, Blogger, YouTube, MySpace* or *Facebook*, ordinary people have become lexicographers, journalists, movie makers or digital writers. Only a few years ago, a basic knowledge of HTML was an absolute prerequisite to upload texts or other files to the Internet. Today it suffices to type content in Web 2.0 templates and upload it with just a few mouse clicks. As a particular feature such "user-generated" texts, also known as *personal publishing* texts, are by no means limited to verbal texts, but typically combine diverse representational formats (e.g. texts, photos, films and sounds) into rich multimodal artefacts. Some of these texts provide more factual information, such as Wikipedia entries or journalistic weblogs, and appear to have corresponding predecessors in ordinary mass media publications. Others however, stand out for their remarkable level of self-disclosure (cf. diary-like personal weblogs, photo- and video-sharing sites or social network sites [SNS]) lacking, at first glance, equivalent texts in traditional media. This paper directs its focus on one particular form of these conceptually private sites, namely SNS[1] and relates them to functionally related precursor texts, i.e. texts utilised for documenting and maintaining social networks before the advent of the Internet. Such a diachronic comparison is directed towards a reflective evaluation of the interrelations between multimodal representation patterns, contextual knowledge and media technology (cf. Eisenlauer and Hoffman 2008). Its aim is to contribute towards a critical understanding of contemporary, new media texts.

To cope with such a diachronic approach, this paper will first give a definition of *personal publishing,* introduce its underlying concepts and work out its most central characteristics (Introduction). Following this, it will discuss key features of SNS and point to two central functions, carried out in the documentation of a particular social network as well as in the textual self-presentation of individuals (Web 2.0, Social Software and Personal Publishing). It will then be demonstrated that on a functional level SNS bear some striking similarities to the *poetry album*[2] and its more recent equivalent, the *friendship book.* Drawing on the systemic functional understanding of *genre as social action* will then help to specify an intermedial comparison, accounting for the obligatory communicative stages bound to the respective texts (SNS as a Particular Form of Personal Publishing). Eventually the paper will sum up its central arguments and present an outlook on future research.

WEB 2.0, SOCIAL SOFTWARE AND PERSONAL PUBLISHING

In order to delineate the concepts and characteristics of *personal publishing*, it is necessary to situate it in relation to *Web 2.0* and *social software*.

As illustrated in Figure 8.1, at the most general level, we find *Web 2.0*. The term commonly refers to genuine interactivity "simply because people can upload as well as download"[3]. Furthermore Web 2.0 encompasses, as Richter and Koch (2007) emphasise, new technologies, new types of applications, new social formations and new business models. One specific aspect of these various phenomena is covered by *social software*: the term captures new Web 2.0 applications and points at the same time to its impacts on society. In this respect studies have emphasised new levels of text collaboration and the public display of social relations on the Internet.[4] The impacts of new applications on the individual user are covered by the term *personal publishing*. Former recipients of hypertexts have undergone a transformation to become empowered and self-publishing authors. While researchers in the humanities still discuss the power shifts inherent in "first generation hypertexts", where the reader chooses his/her individual way from node to node, thus becoming "co-author" of the text (e.g. Storrer 2000; Bucher 1998), *personal publishing* texts give evidence

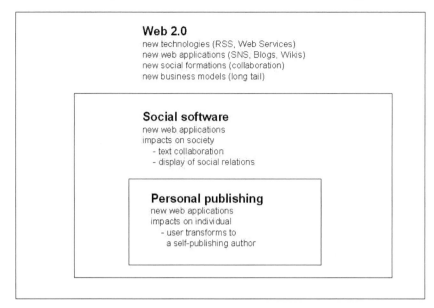

Figure 8.1 Web 2.0, social software and personal publishing.

that users have already become authors in the primary sense of the word: an estimated 57 million weblogs (as of autumn 2006)[5] supports Lanham's notion of a vanishing boundary between "creator and critic" (Lanham 1993: 6). Only a few years ago, publishing on the web was a practice reserved only for the more technically inclined users; Web 2.0-triggered online writing caught on with mainstream web users. Liberated from rigid technical restraints, individual users can now concentrate on the pure content of whatever they intend to publish. However it has to be stressed that as a side effect of such public domain interactivity, every uploaded text, picture, audio or video file can almost instantly be commented on, edited or deleted by other users. Related to this, Bublitz (2008) has shown that in Web 2.0 traditional notions of bilateral interaction gave way to a concept of multilateral interaction:

> [. . .] in Web 2.0-based media formats [. . .] text-building actions can no longer be assigned to individual but only to 'multiple authors' [. . .]. (2008: 255)

It follows that the systematic choices of text resources in *personal publishing* texts are heavily constrained by their social context. Not only in the sense that 'meanings ascribed to language are socially constructed' (Lim 2004: 226), but—more importantly—with regards to a collaboration among various users in the text creation. Though the single-text creation processes are accomplished individually, they are based on 'a common dialog including a number of people' (Hoem and Schwebs 2004: 3). Depending on the individual web application, the impact of such a "common dialog" on text creation can be more or less pronounced. As shown by the continuum presented in Table 8.1, collaborative text-building actions stretch from simple comments of known or unknown users in SNS and blogs to genuinely cooperatively created texts in Wiki webs. At the one extreme, SNS profiles are usually created by a single author, though they include limited possibilities for befriended network members to contribute, e.g. by leaving messages on the pin board (Social Network Sites—Definitions and Characteristic Features). At the other extreme, Wiki webs trigger thoroughly collaborative text-building actions, as they allow anyone who accesses an individual entry to contribute or modify content. In between, blogs prompt single authors or a group of authors (as in group blogs) to create and upload posts. As opposed to SNS, it is not a limited group who is entitled to comment upon entries, but anyone who surfs by.

It follows that on the level of authorship, the term *personal publishing* cannot be taken too literally. The genuine interactivity that is the defining feature of Web 2.0 appears to hinder individual self-contained text building actions: any *personal publishing* text created and uploaded with the help of Web 2.0 applications (social software) triggers collaborative text creation processes at least to some degree. Even SNS that are designed for the self-representation of one single author offer various means for befriended members to create text.[6]

SNS AS A PARTICULAR FORM OF PERSONAL PUBLISHING

In order to explicate some structural and functional continuities of such "user generated texts" diachronically, the next section will elaborate on SNS as one particular form of personal publishing (Social Network Sites—Definitions and Characteristic Features). On the basis of reviewed research on SNS and an illustration of the key features of a particular SNS, non-electronic social network texts, i.e. the poetry album and the

Table 8.1 A Continuum of Web 2.0 Text Collaboration

Social network sites	Blogs	Wikis
Usually one author	One or a few authors	Multiple authors
+ One may post and edit postings	+ One or a few may post and edit postings	+ Anyone may post and edit postings
+ Comments by other SNS members	+ Comments by anyone who surfs by	+ Collaborative text creation of primary texts

◄───►

low collaborative text creation   high collaborative text creation friendship book, are illustrated as functionally related predecessor texts (Functional Predecessors of Social Network Sites).

Social Network Sites—Definitions and Characteristic Features

"Social network sites", also referred to as "social networking services", have stimulated hitherto only minor scientific interest. Two widespread definitions are those by Richter and Koch (2008) and Boyd and Ellison (2007). In Richter and Koch's (2008) terms SNS are about

> [. . .] application systems that offer users functionalities for identity management (1) (i.e. the representation of the own person e.g. in form of a profile) and enable furthermore to keep in touch with other users (2) (and thus the administration of own contacts). (2008: 2)

Likewise Boyd and Ellison (2007) describe SNS as

> [. . .] web-based services that allow individuals to (1) construct a public or semi-public profile within a bounded system, (2) articulate a list of other users with whom they share a connection, and (3) view and traverse their list of connections and those made by others within the system. (2007, online)

As Liu (2007) has shown, four of the largest SNS in the English-speaking world comprise *MySpace*, *Facebook*, *Friendster* and *Orkut*. The samples used in this paper are exclusively drawn from profiles of the SNS *Facebook*, facilitated by the fact that the author is an active member of this network.

At the core of SNS are the so-called 'personal profiles', as they provide a necessary prerequisite to get in touch with other users. Once registered as a SNS member, one is prompted to complete templates with personal questions, such as date of birth, hobbies, favourite books and TV shows etc. In addition to this, more private information can be provided, such as status of relationship and sexual orientation. Having answered these questions the profile is generated automatically and may be published on the Internet with just a few mouse clicks.[7] Figure 8.2 shows a simplified illustration of a representative *Facebook* profile.[8] We can see at one glance the versatility of information presented on such profiles. We find a picture in an identification (ID) photo format, sections with personal details, various means of contacting the owner and—among many other sections—an overview of the user's network friends. As a characteristic feature of the SNS *Facebook*, these standardised modules can be almost endlessly extended by diverse applications, such as the "I-like-module", generating lists of any preferences whatsoever or the "hug-me" module, allowing you to do "more stuff to your friends: hug, slap, tickle, give beer to, throw Britney at and more!"[9]

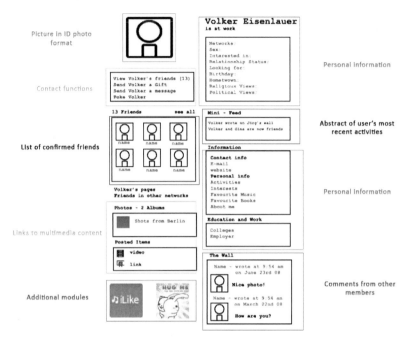

Figure 8.2   Structural features of a *Facebook* profile.

Functional Predecessors of Social Network Sites

On the basis of the introduced key features of SNS, we can now shift the focus to functionally related predecessor texts. As has been shown, SNS central functions include, first, the textual (self) presentation of the individual authors, and, second, the documentation and display of social relations. It follows that a diachronic focus must ask for traditional texts with congruent or at least related text functions.

A text genre that has been utilised for recording social networks since the mid-sixteenth century is the German Posiealbum or "poetry album". Also referred to as 'Stammbuch' (*album*), 'Liber amicorum' or "Denkmal der Freundschaft" (*friendship souvenir*), the poetry album has been passed around students, soldiers and—from the twentieth entury on—primarily among pupils to ask people in their social environment to inscribe dedications (Bodensohn 1968; Angermann 1971; Loesch 2003; Linke 2007). Besides the text function of documenting social relations of a particular person, Linke (2007) emphasises that the individual entries leave inscribers room for self representation.

"Poetry albums" are collections of relational acts that are delivered at someone's request (and/or at someone's suggestion), they are media that target the documentation of a social network and prove the poetry album's owner as a member of a community. [. . .] Thereby the single entries stand for people of such a social network and leave room for self-presentation.(translation by author from Linke 2007)

Comparing Linke's (2007) definition with the key features of SNS, we come across striking similarities (see Table 8.2).

Identity management in SNS encompasses in Richter and Koch's (2008) terms the representation of the self in the form of a profile. In comparison Linke (2007) emphasises that the single entries in poetry albums leave room for self-representation, though she does not elaborate on this. Boyd and Ellison (2007) emphasise the articulation of a list of users with whom the profile owners share a connection as a particular feature of SNS. Correspondingly Linke (2007) describes poetry albums as media that target the documentation of a social network in the form of collections of interpersonal acts. Of course, SNS applications offer certain functional enhancements when compared with poetry albums. In particular, these include mechanisms that support the dynamic administration of contacts—such as creating friends lists—as well as tools that support correspondence with online contacts—such as the 'send message function' or the 'public wall'.

FROM POETRY ALBUMS TO SOCIAL NETWORK SITES

Having identified functional continuities between poetry albums and SNS, A Structural Comparison discusses their analogies on a representational level. Thereby the focus will not be limited to traditional poetry album entries but will include inscriptions in more recent 'friendship books' that

Table 8.2   Key Features of SNS and Poetry Albums

	Social network sites (Boyd and Ellison 2008; Richter and Koch 2008)	Poetry album (Linke 2008)
Self presentation	"[...] the representation of the own person e.g. in form of a profile [...]"	"Thereby the single entries [...] leave room for self-presentation"
Social network record	"web-based services that allow individuals to [...] articulate a list of other users with whom they share a connection"	"[...] media that target the documentation of a social network [...]"

typically get passed from student to student for their inscriptions, just like poetry albums. Beyond a comparison of purely text-internal characteristics, Poetry Albums and Social Network Sites as Text Genre gives information on the socio-cultural contexts and accounts further for the individual communicative embedding and social actions contributing to the overall meanings of traditional and hypertextual genres for documenting friendship. In terms of data, the present study draws on a small corpus of texts, consisting of twenty-five poetry albums, twelve friendship books and 100 SNS profiles.

A Structural Comparison

On a representational level, poetry album inscription and SNS profiles appear, at first glance, to have very little in common (see Figure 8.3a).

A classic poetry album entry consists typically of a verse and iconic attachments, such as drawings, stickers and other decorative material (Angermann 1971; Linke 2007). Linke (2007) lists inscriptions with religious-moral content (more or less) jocular sayings as well as emotional, lyric texts as typical poetry album verses. Bodensohn (1968) emphasises

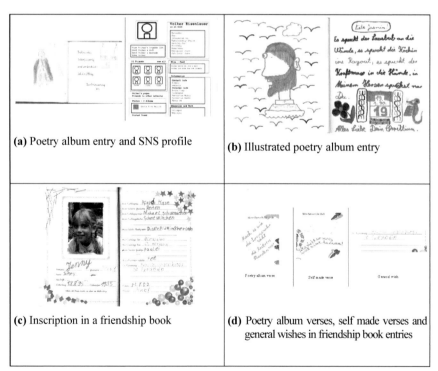

(a) Poetry album entry and SNS profile

(b) Illustrated poetry album entry

(c) Inscription in a friendship book

(d) Poetry album verses, self made verses and general wishes in friendship book entries

Figure 8.3   Poetry albums and friendship books.

the recurrent presence of poetry album verses that are preserved over several generations:

> [In present poetry albums] we find verses and inscriptions again that great-grandmother also collected in her poetry album when she attended boarding school. (translation by author from Bodensohn 1968: 91)

My own data provides evidence for the rather heterogenic nature of album verses, confirming Linke's (2007) broad categories. In accordance with Linke (2007), the data suggests a further distinction between classic inscriptions with meta-communicative comments, such as "Zum Andenken" or "Zur Erinnerung an" ("*To Remember Me*") and more letter-like entries containing an address and a complimentary close. Regarding the pictorial elements of the individual inscriptions, the various drawings, stickers, attached photographs, postcards etc showed a strong tendency to visualise, at least partly, the ideational meanings expressed in the respective verses. In this sense the drawings of the poetry album inscription of Figure 8.3a offer a smiling king and a castle, thus exemplifying parts of the meaning of the verse "*Froh zu sein bedarf es wenig und wer froh ist ist ein König*" / "*Only a few people achieve true happiness and those who do are happy as kings*" (author translation). However, other pictorial elements, such as attached stickers, showed no obvious relation to the album verses and were of a more general kind. Furthermore, there were illustrations that appeared to be utilised for signifying the relationship between inscriber and poetry album owner or visualised a common interest or other common ground aspects, thus carrying predominantly interpersonal meanings. Related to this, the illustration of Figure 8.3b shows indeed no relation to the attached verse but depicts "Ernst Mach", after whom the school was named that both inscriber and poetry album owner were attending.

As shown in Functional Predecessors of Social Network Sites and illustrated by Figure 8.3a, SNS profiles reveal varied personal information about the profile owner: A photograph depicts his or her visual appearance, other sections expose an assortment of other details about the author, such as age, gender, hobbies, state of relationship, sexual orientation etc. As opposed to this, poetry album entries make no explicit references to personal details of the author at least on a linguistic level: except for the author's name and place and date of inscription, there are no hints as to her/his person. Signs reflecting the individuality of the author appear to arise in a more implicit way, e.g. through the choice and style of the pictorial attachments, the specific handwriting style and through the overall text layout. Further, as Linke (2007) has shown, conventional and repeatedly inscribed poetry album verses may occasionally get modified, thus revealing the inscriber through her/his individualised entry. In this respect my data contains the album verse "*Lebe glücklich lebe heiter wie der Spatz am Blitzableiter"/"Live as happily and as optimistically, as a sparrow on a lightning rod"* (author translation) for which Linke (2007) already found evidence in the mid-nineteenth century, in the form of the verse *"Lebe glücklich, lebe froh wie der Mops im Paletot"/"Live happily and cheerfully, like a pug in a sports coat"* (author translation). As she shows, this verse has also undergone various other transformations over the years, e.g. *"Sei heiter und froh, wie die Maus in Mexiko"/"Be happy and cheerful, like a mouse in Mexico"* (author translation), *"Lebe glücklich, lebe froh, wie der König Salomo"/"Live happily and cheerfully, like King Solomon"* (author translation).

Shifting the focus to a more recent form of poetry albums, the so-called 'friendship book', we find some dramatic changes on a representational level. As illustrated by Figure 8.3c, friendship books contain theme question templates very similar to SNS profiles, asking for personal details, such as favourite animal, favourite books and songs, hobbies, career wish etc. Just as in SNS, profiles inscribers are prompted to attach a photograph in an ID photo format. On the other hand, friendship books typically provide templates such as "my verse for you" or "as a friendship souvenir", prompting the author to deliver inscriptions in the style of traditional poetry albums. As my data demonstrates, only a few inscribers reverted to their intertextual knowledge and attached poetry album-like verses. More commonly, inscribers expressed a general wish or a self-made verse in the respective text templates (Figure 8.3d)

Poetry Albums and Social Network Sites as Text Genre

Accounting for the socio-cultural context of poetry albums highlights this type of social network genre as a textual practice carried on particularly in German-speaking societies. Social network texts have a long tradition and were for centuries reserved for adults (cf. album exchanges among university students in the sixteenth century as well as guestbook practices in seventeenth-century aristocratic circles). However, from the late nineteenth century onwards 'inscribing dedications in someone's album' became more and more a domain of schoolchildren (Loesch 2003). To this day, it is still a common practice for German schoolchildren to exchange poetry albums and friendship books, especially among the younger children (ages seven to fourteen).

Reflecting upon the communicative context of poetry albums, Linke (2007) emphasises that the individual entries depend on the cultural practice of "inscribing in someone's album". The author, however, neglects to elaborate on this practice further. In line with Linke's (2007) notion of text genre as a linkage of text patterns with specific cultural practices, the present study aims to fill this gap: drawing on the Systemic Functional understanding of genre as social activity[11], the communicative practices that surround and condition poetry albums and SNS can be described.

Ventola (1987) understands genre as goal-oriented, both verbally and nonverbally realised semiotic systems or social processes, which are established and maintained within a society (1987: 61).

As such, genre has two defining characteristics, which are "purpose" and "structure". While purpose relates to the dominant communicative function, it conditions at the same time a text's structure in terms of stages (Taboada 2004a; Ventola 1987; Hadic-Zabala 2005). Each stage contributes to the overall meanings 'that must be made for the genre to be accomplished successfully' (Eggins 1994: 59).

Applying such a notion of genre to the particular focus of the present study, one can deduce the following: regarding the purpose of poetry albums and SNS, Functional Predecessors of Social Network Sites delineated the articulation of social relations on the one hand and the self-representation of individual inscribers on the other hand as common communicative functions. As has been shown, the individual textual realisations of these functions vary dramatically according to the individual text genre-poetry album, friendship book and SNS. The second key feature of genre, a text's structure in terms of communicative stages, may help to illuminate and facilitate comparison of the particular contexts in which the creation of a poetry album inscription and likewise the adding of friends in SNS is embedded. Thus the following section aims to illuminate the communicative stages that have to be completed for a textual (poetry album) and hypertextual (SNS) documentation of a social network. To specify the communicative stages and their individual functions, I will apply Halliday's (1994 [1985]), see also Halliday and Mathiessen 2004)) dialogic notion of speech act.

Halliday's Dialogic Notion of Speech Acts

In Halliday's (1994 [1985]) sense, "speech acts" ought to more appropriately be renamed "interacts", as they always trigger some kind of reaction: 'it is an exchange in which giving implies receiving, and demanding implies giving in response' (1994: 68). Accordingly, Halliday distinguishes four basic 'interacts' of this kind (Table 8.3): offer information, demand information, offer goods and services and demand goods and services.

The speech act "offer information" is typically expressed by statements; the preferred response is agreement or acknowledgment. It is, however, also possible to disagree or remain noncommittal. The "demand information" speech act is typically articulated in question form and the expected response is an answer, although the listener may disclaim the question, e.g. in *I don't know*. As Halliday (1994 [1985]) has shown, "offer goods and services" implies no typical grammatical category but is most commonly expressed by a range of standard phrases; the preferred response is acceptance, although offers may, of course, be rejected. The "demand goods and services" speech act is typically expressed by some kind of command or

Table 8.3   Halliday's Four Basic Interacts

Speech acts can	Initiation	Expected response	Alternative	Example
Offer information	statement	acknowledgement	contradiction	*He is giving her a drink*
Demand information	question	answer	disclaimer	*What is he giving her?*
Offer goods & services	offer	acceptance	rejection	*Would you like a drink?*
Demand goods & services	command	undertaking	refusal	*Give me a drink!*

directive and the preferred response is an undertaking, although there may be a refusal (see also van Leeuwen 2005, 118).[11]

Schematic Structure of the Action "Inscribing in Someone's Poetry Album"

With regards to the "practice of inscribing in someone's poetry album or friendship book", there can be at least three communicative stages identified, encompassing, ^inscription request ^ inscription confirmation ^ inscription transfer^[12]. From a speech act point of view a "request for an inscription" can be performed by a demand information act, such as *"Would you like to write in my album?"* Likewise, we can imagine an offer information act, as in *"My album still lacks inscriptions"*. Also a demand goods and services act, as in *"Please write an entry!"* would be appropriate. Furthermore, it might also be the inscriber who is asking to write an entry, as in *"Can I write something in your album?"* Correspondingly, there are various speech acts appropriate for the other two communicative stages of inscription confirmations and inscription transfer.

It follows from the above that interlocutors have free choice in the individual wording of their illocutions: questions, statements and even commands could be pronounced at all three communicative stages. Moreover, the choice of the individual speech act appears to reflect the specific contextual and socio-cultural conditions, for example, an institutional or non-institutional frame and their respective roles. In this sense, a student asking for an inscription in her poetry album will address her teacher in a different way than she would her fellow students; she will also ask her best friend in a different manner than she would her older brother.

Schematic Structure of the Action "Friend Adding" in Social Network Sites

In terms comparable to these used for poetry albums, the action of documenting contacts on SNS profiles can be described by the following communicative stages:

ˆcontact identificationˆ contact requestˆ contact confirmationˆ

However, it should be stressed that the actual inscription is not the result of an individual text creation process but from an automatically generated hyperlink that gets listed in the "friend section" of an individual profile, thus linking the profiles of requester and requested. The communicative stages of "friend adding" in SNS are highly multimodal, accordingly the analysis will account for linguistic as well as for pictorial resources

"Friend Adding" from a Linguistic Point of View

The communicative stage of "contact identification" in SNS involves users spotting other users in the system: after joining a SNS and filling out certain templates in order to generate a personal profile (Social Network Sites—Definitions and Characteristic Features), SNS members get prompted to identify others "with whom they have a relationship" (Boyd and Ellison 2007). This may be carried out with the help of search mask parameters asking for information one may already have about the possible contact. Another option is to identify and/or to connect to previously unknown people. It follows that SNS can be used, on the one hand, to maintain previously established "real life"contacts, and, on the other hand, to establish new "virtual ties". However, according to a study by Ellison, Steinfield and Lampe (2007), the SNS *Facebook* is primarily used to socialise with people previously known:

> [Facebook] is used to maintain existing offline relationships or solidify offline connections, as opposed to meeting new people. (quoted in Boyd and Ellison 2007, online)

At the second communicative stage of "contact request", users are required to add the recognised person as a friend. By pushing the button "add friend" the potential new friend receives an automatically generated e-mail asking him/her to confirm the contact (see Figure 8.4a).

The third communicative stage of "contact confirmation" is performed by the person who received the contact request. By clicking on the link underneath

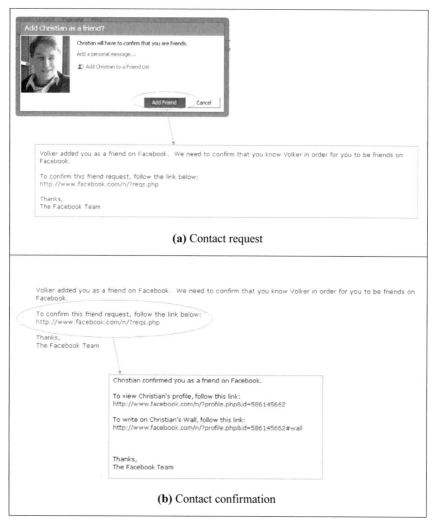

(a) Contact request

(b) Contact confirmation

Figure 8.4   Contact request and confirmation in SNS.

the demand "follow the link below", the system automatically generates a confirmation e-mail and sends it to the requester (see Figure 8.4b).

To account for the complexity of the speech acts involved in "friend adding", I suggest a diagrammatical distinction between speech acts performed by the software system and speech acts intended by the individual user, as illustrated in Table 8.4.

On the level of contact identification, an individual member fills in the parameters of the search mask or clicks on her/his individual details. Thus users "offer some kind of information". In turn the system provides some data

Table 8.4   "Automatized speech acts" in SNS

Interactional Stage	Textual Performance	Speech Act by System	Speech Act by User
Contact Identification	Filling in the parameters of the search mask	**Offer information**	**Offer information**
Contact request	<u>Action</u> Clicking the "add friend" button <u>Lexicogrammatical form</u> Automatically generated e-mail	**Demanding goods and Services** "Follow the link below"	**Demanding information** "Do you want to become my SNS friend?"
Contact confirmation	<u>Action</u> Following the link <u>Lexicogrammatical form</u> Automatically generated e-mail	**Offering information** "C. confirmed you as a friend."	**Offering information** "Yes, I want to be your SNS friend."

on possible contacts and performs an "offer information act" itself. On the level of contact request, the user carries out the speech function (illocution) of "demanding information" that is a form of question asking for validation of a possible social relationship, in the sense of *"do you want to become my SNS friend?"* However on the lexicogrammatical plane, the requester has no influence on the individual wording: the friendship request is carried out by a machine-generated and standardised e-mail performing a "goods and services demand" in requesting the addressee *"to follow the link below"*. The preferred response is the "contact confirmation". Note that the only alternative for the respondent is to ignore the contact request. As opposed to real life contexts, there are no options for disclaimers, as in statements like *"I have to think about it"* or *"I'll tell you tomorrow"*.

It has to be noted that users do have the possibility to add some comments to the individual request, such as *"Hi, great to find you here, how are you?"* Nevertheless, to confirm the request the addressee still has to undertake the action of clicking the hyperlink i.e. responding to an automatically generated speech act.

"Friend Adding" from a Multimodal Point of View

Accounting for the pictorial mode in the process of friend adding, users may easily identify possible acquaintances by their profile pictures. Commonly profile pictures are offered by the system after a search query has been conducted. In terms of the second communicative stage, 'contact request', we find multimodal requests that are listed in addition to the e-mail-based friendship requests on the individual personal profiles. The key features of such multimodal requests include the profile picture and name of the requester, number of common friends, "confirm" and "ignore" buttons, as well as a "send message option" (see Figure 8.5). Apart from the heading "friend requests", there are no linguistic means and no speech acts requesting friendship. However, as Kress and van Leeuwen (1996) have shown, like linguistic representations, images can also either "offer" or "demand":

> If a person represented in an image looks at the viewer, the image realizes a 'demand': the gaze [. . .] demands something from the viewer, demands that the viewer enter into some kind of imaginary relation with him or her. If such a look is not present, the image is an 'offer'. It then 'offers' the represented participants to the viewer as items of information, objects of contemplation, impersonally, as though they were specimens in a display case. (1996: 122)

Applying this model to the profile pictures of the friendship requests reveals 'multimodal acts' arising from a complex interplay between pictorial and verbal information. Some photographs appear to simulate direct contact, while in others no contact is made between the viewer and the represented participant. In Figure 8.5a the direct gaze represents a "demand" for the viewer to enter into a 'parasocial' relationship with the depicted person.

Very different to this, Figure 8.5b represents an "offer". Here the viewer is an invisible onlooker on a scene in which someone is balancing on a traffic fence. Within the system of 'gaze', no contact is made between the viewer and the represented participant. While the picture in figure 8.5(a) addresses the viewer with a 'visual you' and demands her/him to enter into some kind of imaginary relationship with the depicted person, the indirect address of the photograph of figure 8.5(b) is more open to interpretation. It should however be emphasised that the specific meanings of such pictorial 'offer' or 'demand' acts arise out of numerous contextual cues: as shown by the example in Figure 8.6a, a demand act—a visual you—can be performed simultaneously by several people. Unless "Vincent J." is known to the user, it remains unclear who amongst the depicted people owns this SNS profile.

The multimodal act in Figure 8.6b lacks contextualisation: the person is presented against an abstract white background; the colours are limited to black and white, and the distribution of light and shade is rather crude. Thus the visual demand suggests a distance from real-life naturalism and implies—in terms of what we consider true or untrue—a low modality (Kress and van Leeuwen 1996: 159–181). As illustrated by the examples in Figure 8.6c, some multimodal friendship requests of this kind incorporate no picture at all or present photos in which the profile owner is not even

Figure 8.5 Multimodal demand and offer act.

Figure 8.6 Multimodal acts of friendship requests.

presented. The third communicative stage "contact confirmation" is performed by an automatically generated email (see Figure 4b) and involves no pictorial modes.

Results

Contrasting poetry albums, friendship books and SNS, we obtain the following results: the textual structure of poetry album inscriptions builds on conventionalised textual patterns that can be traced back to the mid-sixteenth century. In contrast, in friendship book entries and SNS profiles, the medium, with its pre-ordained templates, determines both the structure and the content of the individual inscriptions. From a macro-point of view, something that all text types have in common is their regress on fixed and formulaic cultural units. Poetry album verses resort to pattern books, for which we find evidence as early as in the sixteenth century, as well as to the author's intertextual knowledge about album verses. The choice of a particular verse is constitutive for writing an entry in someone's poetry album. The individuality and/or the self-representation of the author arises from the choice and a possible modification of an established album verse (see Linke 2007). Further, the pictorial elements of an inscription appear to offer various means for an indirect presentation of the author: notions about the pictorial parts of an inscription seem to be less strict, ranging from attached stickers and postcards to silhouettes and handmade drawings. In contrast, friendship book entries and SNS profiles are utilised to present the authors in a much more direct manner. In doing so, both texts draw on media discourse-related entities to deploy them for the individual positioning of the author, thus functioning, as Liu (2007) has shown, as expressive arenas for taste performance.[13] Related to this, we can contrast the template "This is my favourite book" of a friendship book with a "visual bookshelf" taken from a *Facebook* profile. The friendship book's template provides information about the inscriber's favourite book. It is elicited by the statement "das ist mein Lieblings-buch" (*This is my favourite book*) and constrained by the size of the supplied frame. In contrast to this, *Facebook*'s 'visual bookshelf' gives much more detailed information: about books the owner is currently reading, books she has already read and those she plans to read in future. By virtue of its hypertextual nature, *Facebook*'s 'visual bookshelf' comprises not only explicit statements about the author's literature preferences but also hyperlinks from the displayed titles to discussion boards where one may comment on the individual books or click on a further hyperlink to purchase the specific title via the e-commerce platform "Amazon".

Discussing the wider cultural and communicative context in which the act of inscribing in someone's poetry album and likewise "friend adding" in SNS is embedded reveals the following. Exchanging and/or inscribing in poetry albums and friendship books is a common practice among German schoolchildren, thus documenting social networks within their close social environment. Collecting and documenting contacts on SNS is practiced by a great variety of age groups and is not bound to spatial constraints. Both practices, poetry albums inscriptions and friend adding, involve at least three communicative stages. In the actions surrounding the creation of a poetry album entry, interlocutors have free choice in the individual wording of their illocutions: questions, statements and even commands may be pronounced at all three communicative stages. Thus the individual linguistic choice reflects the interpersonal relationship among the participants and various other contextual conditions. In contrast, the speech acts of "friend adding" in SNS are completely homogenous on a lexicogrammatical level. Wording and sequencing are generated by the software system; thus there is no space for variation. Whether the user addresses a former classmate, an ex-lover, a colleague or his/her best friend, on the level of expression, she or he has no choice but to press the "add friend" button, which again initiates a sequence of standardised speech acts. However, the incorporation of profile pictures appears to counter such linguistic unification: the individual visual act (offer and/or demand pictures) and its multiple components (facial expression, background, colour modulation, dress etc) may modulate the otherwise pre-determined ways of addressing someone in many subtle ways. As shown, a visual "demand act" performed by the direct gaze may combine with a verbal "offer act" expressed in the heading "you have 9 friendship requests". In contrast, we also found "offer acts" on both levels, the pictorial and the verbal (see Figure 8.7).

On the other hand, it must be emphasised that on a pictorial level the specific interpersonal context has no influence on the choice of pictures.

CONCLUSION

The term "personal publishing" is not to be taken literally for two reasons. First, texts created and uploaded with Web 2.0 applications are always embedded in more or less prevalent actions of text collaboration. Second, it has been shown that such texts may initiate various automated communication processes that contribute to the publication of content. It follows that "personal publishing texts" are always assigned to more than one author. Further, text creation actions may be prompted by standardised communicative stages of the individual web application.

The poetry album and the friendship book may be seen as predecessor texts of SNS. All of these texts correspond in articulating a social network. In addition to this, they all offer a means for textual self-representation: while in poetry albums personal details of inscribers may arise only in a more implicit way; friendship books and SNS profiles make personal information explicit.

From a text genre point of view, poetry albums, friendship books and SNS can be described as couplings between cognitive templates (in poetry

Figure 8.7　Interplay of pictorial and verbal speech act.

albums) and/or medial text templates (in friendship books and SNS profiles) within specific cultural practices. The practice of inscribing someone's poetry albums involves at least three communicative stages. Thereby interlocutors are given free choice in the linguistic realisation of their illocutions. As a particular feature, the choice of an individual speech act reflects the specific contextual conditions. In contrast to this, in the three-staged practice of friend adding, the specific social context, that is the individual relationship among interlocutors, remains unreflected on a linguistic and on a pictorial level. Nevertheless, it has to be emphasised that the individual visual act (offer and/or demand pictures) and its multiple components may modulate in many subtle ways the mere linguistic mode of addressing someone.

Having identified structural continuities of poetry albums and SNS in terms of their articulating social networks, a further research aim concerns the question of "self representation" and will specify the particular multimodal means that reveal personal information of the inscribers in poetry albums, friendship books and SNS profiles.

NOTES

1. In accordance with previous research (Boyd 2006, Boyd and Elison 2007), I will use the acronym SNS to refer to social network sites.
2. The German "Poesiealbum" or poetry album gets typically passed around pupils and people in the close social environment are asked to inscribe dedications (see Functional Predecessors of Social Network Sites).
3. Stephen Fry: Web 2.0 (Video interview). http://www.filmdetail.com/archives/2008/03/27/stephen-fry-on-web-20. [19.07.2008]
4. Richter and Koch (2007)
5. http://technorati.com/weblog/2006/11/161.html [03.09.2008]
6. Such a dialectical notion of an individual user actively creating and uploading information about her/his persons, which in turn get commented and contextualised by other users shows some striking similarities with Mead's two phases of the self: "*I*" as the initative part of the self, "*me*" as "the internalization of roles which derive from [. . .] linguistic interaction" (see Wenzel 1990).

7. However, it has to be stressed that in *Facebook* most of the information templates are optional.
8. Note that this schematic illustration is based on the site's old design, before Facebook underwent a relaunch in September 2008.
9. http://www.Facebook.com/apps/application.php?id=2345673396 [20.07.2008]
10. Gruber and Muntigl (2005).
11. Note that such a description of speech acts and their respective linguistic initiations does not account for individual situational conditions.
12. In accordance with Ventola (1987) the communicative stages are written in a linear sequence. The symbol ^ is used to indicate that the stages are ordered with respect to each other.
13. "By composing interest tokens around a theme, profile users craft their 'taste statements'" (Liu 2007: 1).

REFERENCES

Angermann, G. (1971) *Stammbücher und Poesiealben als Spiegel ihrer Zeit*, Münster: Aschendorff.
Bodensohn, A. (1968) *Das Ich in zweiter Person : die Zwiesprache des Poesiealbums*, Frankfurt M. : Dipa-Verlag.
Boyd, D., and Ellison, N. (2007) 'Social Network Sites: Definition, History, and Scholarship.' In *Journal of Computer Mediated Communication*, 13, (1). Available online at <http://jcmc.indiana.edu/vol13/issue1/boyd.ellison.html> (accessed 29 May 2008).
Boyd, D. (2006) 'Friends, Friendsters, and MySpace Top 8: Writing Community into Being on Social Network Sites.' In *First Monday*, 11 (12). Available online at http://www.firstmonday.org/issues/issue11_12/boyd/index.html (accessed 29 May 2008).
Bublitz, W. (2008) "Sailing the islands or watching from the dock": The treacherous simplicity of a metaphor. How we handle 'new (electronic) hypertext' versus 'old (printed) text'." In Gerbig, A., and Mason, O. eds. *Language, People, Numbers: Corpus Linguistics and Society*. Amsterdam: Rodopi: pp. 249–275.
Bucher, H. J. (1998) 'Vom Textdesign zum Hypertext. Gedruckte und elektronischen Zeitungen als nicht-lineare Medien.' In Biere U., und Holly W. (Hrsg.) *Medien im Wandel*. Wiesbaden: Westdeutscher Verlag: pp. 63–102.
Brecht, B. (1932[1967]) 'Radiotheorie.' In Ders. *Gesammelte Werke*, Bd. 18, Frankfurt/Main: Suhrkamp 1967, pp. 119–134.
Eggins, S. (1994) *An Introduction to Systemic Functional Linguistics*, 1st ed, London: Pinter Publishers.
Eisenlauer, V., and Hoffmann C. (2008) 'The metapragmatics of remediated text design.' *Information Design Journal* 16/1: 1–19.
Ellison, N. B., Steinfield, C. and Lampe, C. (2007) 'The Benefits of Facebook "friends"': 'Social capital and college students use of online social network sites.' In *Journal of Computer-Mediated Communication* 12(4). Available online at http://jcmc.indiana.edu/vol12/issue4/ellison.html (accessed 29 May 2009).
Gruber, H., and Muntigl, P. (2005) 'Generic and rhetorical structures of texts: Two sides of the same coin?' *Folia Linguistica* 39(1/2): 75–113.
Hadic-Zabala, L. (2005) 'The genre of on-line personal ads.' In Carter, N. et al. eds. *Working Paper in Linguistics, Proceedings of the 22nd NorthWest Linguistics Conference*. Simon Fraser University, pp. 133–144. Available online

at <http://www.sfu.ca/gradlings/NWLC_Proceedings.htm> (accessed 15 June 2008).

Halliday, M. A. K. (1994 [1985]) *An Introduction to Functional Grammar,* 2nd ed, London: Arnold.

Halliday, M. A. K., and Matthiessen, C. (2004) *An Introduction to Functional Grammar,* 3rd ed, London: Arnold.

Hoem, J., and Schwebs, T. (2004) 'Personal publishing and media literacy'. In *IFIP World. Conference on Computers in Education (WCCE 2005).* Available online at http://infodesign.no/artikler/personal_%20publishing_media_literacy.pdf accessed (2 February 2008).

Kress, G., and van Leeuwen, T. (1996) *Reading Images—The Grammar of Visual Design,* 1st ed, London: Routledge.

Lanham, R. (1993) *The Electronic Word: Democracy, Technology, and the Arts,* Chicago and London: University of Chicago Press

Lim, F. (2004) 'Developing an integrative multisemiotic model.' In O'Halloran, K. ed. *Multimodal Discourse Analysis,* London: Continuum: pp. 220–246.

Linke, A. (2007) 'Der Poesiealbumeintrag.' Unveröffentlichter Vortrag auf der Tagung *Die Macht der Kontexte,* Banz, 13. bis 15. April 2007.

Liu, H. (2007) 'Social network profiles as taste performances,' *Journal of Computer Mediated Communication,* 13, (1). Available online at <http://jcmc.indiana.edu/vol13/issue1/liu.html> (accessed 29 May 2008).

Loesch, P. (2003) *Der Freundschaft Denkmal. Stammbücher und Poesiealben aus fünf Jahrhunderten im Bestand der Sächsischen Landesbibliothek—Staats— und Universitätsbibliothek Dresden.* Dresden: SLUB

Richter, A und Koch, M. (2007) 'Social Software—Status quo und Zukunft' In *Technischer Bericht Nr. 2007–01, Fakultät für Informatik, Universität der Bundeswehr München.* Available online at <http://www.kooperationssysteme.de/uploads/RichterKoch2007.pdf> (accessed 13 July 2008).

Richter, A., und Koch, M. (2008) 'Functions of Social Networking Services.' In *Proceedings of COOP, the 8th International Conference on the Design of Cooperative Systems. Available online at* <http://www.kooperationssysteme.de/wp-content/uploads/coop08_richterkoch_functions_of_social_networking_services_final.pdf> (accessed 01 July 2008).

Storrer, A. (2000) 'Was ist "hyper" am Hypertext?. ' In Kallmeyer, W. (Hrsg.) *Sprache und neue Medien,* Berlin/New York: de Gruyter: pp. 222–249.

Taboada, M. T. (2004a) *Building Coherence and Cohesion: Task-Oriented Dialogue in English and Spanish,* Amsterdam: John Benjamins.

van Leeuwen, T. (2005) *Introducing Social Semiotics,* London: Routledge.

Ventola, E. (1987) *The Structure of Social Interaction: A Systemic Approach to the Semiotics of Service Encounters,* London: Frances Pinter.

Wenzel, H. (1990) *George Herbert* Mead *zur Einführung.* Hamburg: Junius.

WEBSITE REFERENCES

http://www.Facebook.com/apps/application.php?id=2345673396 [20.07.2008]
http://www.filmdetail.com/archives/2008/03/27/stephen-fry-on-web-20/ [19.07.2008]
http://technorati.com/weblog/2006/11/161.html [03.09.2008]

9 Knowledge Communication in Green Corporate Marketing

A Multimodal Discourse Analysis of an *Ecomagination* Video

Carmen Daniela Maier

INTRODUCTION

Today we witness a global growth of environmental awareness that is reflected both in how various social practices take place and in how those social practices are represented in multimodal discourses across various media[1].

Creating convincing multimodal discourses focused on environmental issues proves to be a challenge for many categories of communicators. Science communicators, marketing communicators, researchers and educators are among those who try to foster more environmental awareness, responsibility and pro-environmental behaviour, either through new types of discourses or through renewed versions of already existing ones. For example, the traditional advertising discourse in which new products and their benefits are persuasively presented by marketing communicators has almost disappeared from the advertising materials of many companies. Howlett and Raglon's study of over 500 newspaper and magazine advertisements (2001) confirm that although the use of natural imagery to sell products has been a common phenomenon for decades, the contemporary trend is 'to create corporate images which are environmentally friendly and benign' (Howlett and Raglon 2001: 245).

The new green marketing materials that employ several semiotic modes from moving images to texts and sounds have transformed the scene of marketing communication. Through these materials, companies attempt to share their views, experience and results in order to present their new environmentally friendly products and to position themselves as eco-friendly corporations. The use of several semiotic modes in these green marketing materials tries to respond to the needs and capabilities of contemporary multiliterate audiences[2]. The focus on the combination of several semiotic modes is motivated by the fact that these multiliterate audiences 'can synthesize information distributed across different modes and understand not only the meaning in each mode but also the additional information added through the interaction between modes' (Maier, Kampf and Kastberg 2006: 457). However, as already mentioned, "the greening of the corporation" (Howlett and Raglon

2001: 245) through convincing environmental discourses represents a challenge for many communicators. Many of these materials show that the marketing communicators' ability to design or to coordinate the design of such materials can and should be trained and enhanced.

Obviously, the strategic exploitation of the meaning-making potential of multimodal combinations when creating environmental discourses targeted at multiliterate audiences is of vital importance for all contemporary communicators. The means to address environmental issues can be found in a multimodal approach to the design of environmental discourses. A first step in this process would be a more nuanced understanding of the specific roles of several semiotic modes and of their interplay in effectively communicating various types of knowledge. Such an understanding can be facilitated through adopting a multimodal perspective upon the integration of semiotic modes in environmental discourses.

In this article, my focus is on the analysis of the multimodal discursive strategies that are employed in a green marketing video. Of central interest is the model of analysis through which the multimodal aspect of these discursive strategies can be highlighted. Based on the detailed multimodal discourse analysis of the video, the analytical part of the article attempts to illustrate the empirical strengths of the multimodal approach. The article intends to demonstrate that a multimodal discourse analysis could offer science and marketing communicators an opportunity to develop their strategies for integrating different semiotic modes in their environmental discourses. In order to reflect on the implications of the multimodal perspective as an analytical tool of environmental discourses, the article explores one of the videos included by General Electric (GE) Company in their *Ecomagination* campaign. The video can be accessed in one of the campaign's showcases at http://ge.ecomagination. com/site/index.html#milan.

Although this article focuses on the multimodal analysis of a marketing video, it is also relevant for various types of communicators because it raises vital questions about specific strategies in communicating knowledge when environmental issues are or should be in focus.

THEORETICAL APPROACHES

The ever-growing number of discourses focused on environmental issues has attracted the attention of researchers belonging to various research traditions such as linguistics, philosophy anthropology, natural sciences, social sciences and so on. In addition, the need to combine the exploratory perspectives has become increasingly pressing due to the complexity of contemporary environmental discourses. The environmental issues have also nuanced traditional approaches as researchers in various micro- and macro-environmental discourses had to articulate their work in alternative ways. Ecophilosophy and ecofeminism are just a couple of such approaches through which environmental discourses are critically evaluated (Benton and Short 1999).

When exploring the polyphony of environmental voices, Harré, Brockmeier and Mühlhäusler acknowledge the fact that 'language is not the only medium by means of which environmental issues are made, brought to public attention and so on' (Harré, Brockmeier and Mühlhäusler 1999: 3). However, the majority of interdisciplinary studies are focused on the linguistic aspects of the environmental discourses. At the end of their discussion of the various approaches employed to analyse environmental discourses, Mühlhäuser and Peace conclude that future approaches to environmental discourse should take into consideration the diversity of expressions and they state that:

This requires adopting Halliday's instructions to be critically aware of the instrument of language and its uses. Green approaches to discourse can promote awareness that the language one uses privileges certain perceptions and actions and that expressing matters differently will privilege others. (Mühlhäuser and Peace 2006: 472)

Following their suggestion, in this paper, I adopt a social semiotic approach in order to focus on language and its uses in environmental discourse while extending my exploration beyond this semiotic mode. Kress and van Leeuwen's (e.g. 2001) notion of discourse is at the basis of my analysis of environmental discourse in green marketing materials. They define discourses in Foucault's sense as 'socially constructed knowledges of (some aspect of) reality . . . developed in specific social contexts and in ways which are appropriate to the interests of the social actors in these contexts' (Kress and van Leeuwen 2001: 4). Van Leeuwen emphasises that 'knowledge is selective, and what it selects depends on the interests and purposes of the institutions that have fostered the knowledge' (van Leeuwen, 2005b: 109). He also underlines that in this situation, 'discourses consist of a version of a social practice *plus* ideas about it and attitudes to it' (van Leeuwen 2005b: 106). Additionally, 'discourses not only constitute (selective and transformed) versions of social practices, they also legitimate (or de-legitimate, critique) the practices which they recontextualise' (Machin and van Leeuwen 2007: 61). According to van Leeuwen, there are four basic types of transformation when knowledge about *social actors* (2006), *actions* (1995), *time* (2005a) and *space* is selectively communicated. Reality is changed in a discourse through *inclusion/exclusion, rearrangement, addition* and *substitution* (van Leeuwen 2005: 111). For example, when social actors are included in a discourse, they can be represented as individuals (*individualisation*) or as a group (*aggregation* or *collectivisation*). Furthermore, their identity can be defined in terms of what they do (*functionalisation*) and/or what they are (*identification*). The social actors' reactions can be specified as *affective* or *cognitive*. Social actions can be represented in the discourse through various substitution processes of *activation* and *de-activation*. These processes affect the representation of the social actors because, for example, the processes of *de-activation* 'allow the exclusion of social actors' (van Leeuwen 2008: 30). Certainly, both social actors and their actions can be excluded from a discourse. In the same time, *legitimations* (van Leeuwen 2007) and *purposes* (van Leeuwen 2000a&b)

can be added to the representation of social actions. In my analysis I adopt van Leeuwen's categories and apply them multimodally. Van Leeuwen also demonstrates in parts of his work that 'other semiotic modes can also recontextualize social practices' (van Leeuwen 2008: 22).

My social semiotic approach to the exploration of knowledge communication in environmental discourse is a multimodal one. The main reason for adopting multimodality in this analysis is that it employs a unifying meta-language that can address the meaning making resources of several modes as well as their multilayered relationships. The partiality of modes in creating meaning is a fundamental assumption in multimodality. Consequently, for Kress and Jewitt, all the involved modes carry different aspects of meaning of any event of communication in different ways, and 'each mode is *partial* in relation to the whole of meaning' (Kress and Jewitt, 2003: 3). Kress and van Leeuwen (2001: 3) explain that a multimodal approach can show how meaning produced by a certain semiotic mode can be duplicated, complemented, reinterpreted or even subverted through the simultaneous deployment of several other semiotic modes. O'Halloran emphasises that 'it is not only the culmination of choices made across semiotic resources in their interaction with other resources that makes meaning, but also the temporal and spatial unfolding of those choices' (O'Halloran 2004: 109). The work of researchers in multimodality has repeatedly proven the adaptability of multimodality in accommodating the exploration of a great variety of complex texts from tv commercials (Thibault 2000; Baldry 2005; Baldry and Thibault, 2006) and films (O'Halloran 2004) to architectural design of an opera house (O'Toole 2004), a museum (Hofinger and Ventola 2004), and classroom communication (Kress, Jewitt, Ogborn and Tsatsarelis 2001).

The approach of multimodality is fundamental for the present analysis of communication of knowledge in green corporate materials since it allows me to maintain an explanatory consistency when investigating the types of knowledge that are communicated across semiotic modes. My analysis draws upon and extends these analytical frameworks by examining the interdependencies between semiotic modes in facilitating the communication of some of van Leeuwen's types of knowledge. In this paper, I focus on only two meaning-making resources, which I roughly call the verbal mode and the visual mode. The presentation of the complexity of the whole multimodal range of knowledge types is beyond the scope of this paper. Furthermore, I have assumed that the presentation of the analytical model can also be done on the basis of these two main modes only. Certainly, the present discussion of the roles of the verbal and visual modes can represent a convenient starting point for applying the analytical model to a range of visual and verbal submodes in further research or in designing similar materials.

The benefit of this interdisciplinary framework for various communicators is the set of multimodal descriptions for different categories of selected knowledge. These types are correlated with the meaning-making potential of the visual and verbal modes. In this way, communicators can systematically work with van Leeuwen's categorisation scheme of selected knowledge in order to design or improve their environmental discourses based on the interaction and combination of various semiotic modes.

DATA SELECTION AND TRANSCRIPTION

The data for the present analysis has been extracted from the GE webpage dealing with the *Ecomagination* campaigns. General Electric is one of the companies that try to employ complex environmental discourses in order to present their new environmentally friendly products and to position themselves as a leading eco-friendly corporation. Their environmental discourses are multimodally represented across various media through annual reports, print ads, online ads, TV ads, audio podcasts and so on. Certainly, these representations are supposed to reflect the company's activities, namely the actual enactments of their eco-friendly views and commitments. The *Ecomagination* campaigns are supposed to 'provide awareness for business executives and consumers on the platform while also educating them about GE products and services' (statement existing on the GE homepage). *Ecomagination* campaign showcases incorporate a series of videos, which are given commentary by a voice-over narrator. In this paper, I concentrate upon the *Milan* video (http:// ge.ecomagination.com/site/#milan) and its environmental discourse.

In order to obtain a rigorous segmentation of the video for the written transcription, I have converted the video from a Quicktime Movie Player .mov file to an .avi file with the help of the editing software programme Adobe Premiere. I have decided to fragment the text, not into one second intervals, but into one frame intervals, due to the nature of the multimodal text that I'm dealing with. The degree of detail description in the transcription of the video is motivated by the nature of my exploration, which is focused on determining the role of certain analytical components that can be found even at the level of a single frame. I have worked with a Microsoft Office Table document for the multimodal analysis of the video.[3] With regard to the columns of the table, it must be mentioned that I have selectively introduced in each column of the table only those analytical parameters that are relevant to this specific multimodal analysis.

Table 9.1 exemplifies the multimodal method of transcription to record specific instances of knowledge selection in the *Milan* video. This method of transcription was used for each frame as a basis for the multimodal analysis.

Before I turn to the analysis of the video, it should be mentioned that I have not restricted my multimodal analysis to the video presented in this paper. However, I have chosen to present my analytical model in this paper only on the basis of this example due to a couple of reasons. First of all, the length of this paper does not permit a more detailed presentation of my analytical investigation. Second, the present example provides the data needed for an integrated understanding of the analytical model. My primary goal is to present a model of analysis that can provide the framework for designing new materials and can facilitate further research of multimodal environmental discourses.

Table 9.1   Sample for the Multimodal Transcription of Knowledge Selection in
Milan Video

No.	Frame	Frame attributes	Voice-over commentary	Processes of knowledge selection	
	Time			Visual	Verbal
6.	0:00:30–0:00:33	Medium black-and-white shot Group shot (different age and race) Eye contact with viewers Lack of background	*Eddie, Marvin, Roger, Danny and Jed ...*	Collectivisation relational and physical identification	Individual isation

ANALYSIS OF CATEGORIES AND SELECTION OF KNOWLEDGE

In the following, I will describe the main categories of knowledge about social actors, social actions, time and space. I will also explain how they are selected verbally and visually in the environmental discourse. The multimodal analysis of these categories is structured on the basis of the types and subtypes selection processes mentioned above: exclusion, rearrangement, addition and substitution.

Categories of Social Actors

There are three main categories of social actors in the discourse: the GE employees, Italian citizens and people in general. The ways in which each category of actors is presented and represented in the discourse facilitate the communication of specific knowledge about them.

The GE employees' identity is established linguistically through *functionalisation* and *relational identification*: they are employees, and they are employed by GE. So, their identity is collectively defined in terms of their job through *linguistic collectivisation*: *GE employees*. However, they are also identified through visual and verbal individualisation. The GE employees are visually categorised in terms of race, age and gender in black-and-white close-up, medium and long shots, in which they just look at the viewer and do nothing apart from smiling. There are only two shots in which individual GE employees are working. Their individual identity is also linguistically defined when they are informally nominated by the voice-over narrator: *Allow us to introduce John . . .* The physical identification and naming confirm that the company is interested in communicating specific knowledge about their employees through verbal and visual representations in which they are individualised. The distance between viewer and company becomes smaller when GE employees are individually named and shown in series of shots in which they look at the viewer. This visual direct address not only explicitly acknowledges the viewers as the verbal direct address does, but it also establishes an imaginary contact with the viewers, demanding something from them. The communication of knowledge about GE employees is also influenced by processes of visual addition. The GE employees are visually differentiated from the Italians through the usage of black-and-white shots. This process of differentiation adds a visual emphasis on the representation of the GE employees as a special category of actors, elevating them above the other actors.

If GE employees are represented as people with whom the viewers should engage due to direct gaze, the Italians are visually represented as "items of information" having no gaze connection with the viewers. However, they are shown in daily situations like cooking at home or in a restaurant, so viewers can also relate to them. The Italians are also categorised through visual individualisation in terms of age (adults and children) and sex (men and women). They are also classified in terms of who they are on the basis of citizenship through linguistic *aggregation*: *more than 1 million Italian homes*. In fact, they are not named as a people, but they are identified through another noun, namely "homes". Their citizenship is relegated to the symbolic identification of their homes. By employing an evaluative device, namely the comparative *more than*, the process of knowledge selection is intensified through the strategy of evaluative addition. In addition, their Italian identity is functionally established by showing them engaged in activities a viewer would usually link to Italians: making food with tomatoes and basil, drinking espresso or sewing design clothes.

Both in the case of the GE employees and in the case of the Italians, the actors are verbally presented and visually represented in terms of who they are and/or what they do. The fact that the main process of selecting the knowledge about these actors is visual individualisation clearly facilitates the identification of the viewer with each category. However, by using more close-up shots for the visual representation of the GE employees than for the Italians, the viewers seem to be invited to primarily identify themselves with this category of actors.

The key distinction between these two categories of actors is represented visually by the way in which they are functionally categorised with respect to GE environmental activities. It is evident that the Italians are de-emphasised as they are not linked to the GE activities verbally presented and visually represented in the video. The Italians' identities are defined through their various occupations, but this visual functionalisation is not linked to GE. The GE employees are clearly foregrounded because they are represented as having active roles in the environmental change through their work. Choosing these methods of representation, the selection of knowledge related to social actors contributes both verbally and visually to the allocation of roles, as the GE employees are the active participants, while the Italians are the passive ones. Certainly, the Italians have also active roles in relation to their lives, but they are neither verbally presented nor visually represented as active in relation to environmental practices. In this way, the Italians are represented just as GE's customers or consumers of electricity in general.

This relationship between the two categories of actors is verbally rearranged by the voice-over narrator when, by saying *all of us*, he becomes the bridge between all the categories of actors existing in the discourse. And, as I will demonstrate later on, this relationship is also verbally rearranged in the way in which the actions are presented. A sense of consensus is reached between all social actors through the implicit inclusion of other categories of social actors in the environmental discourse. So, another group of social actors is linguistically established by *us, all of us* and *people*. Nevertheless, this is not a clear-cut category, as in the case of the first appearance of "us", the *us* seems to be the GE company: *Allow us to introduce John . . .* Later on, in *Reminding all of us from the busy streets of Milan to the hills of South Carolina, Earth's most prolific sources of energy are its people*, the viewers and people in general are included. Through this inclusion, although not yet participating in the social practice represented in the environmental discourse, everybody is assigned the same responsibility.

Table 9.2 provides a typology of processes of selection of knowledge about actors in the *Milan* video.

Table 9.2   Processes of Selection of Knowledge about Actors

Categories of actors	Processes of knowledge selection		Examples	
	Verbal	Visual	Verbal	Visual
GE employees	Individualisation (informal nominalization)	Individualisation	*Tuanna*	Close-up shot of GE employee
	Collectivisation Functionalisation Relational identification	Collectivisation	*GE employees*	Group shots of GE employees
		Relational & physical identification		Group shots (different age, gender, race)
		Functionalisation		Working GE employee
Italians	Aggregation	Collectivisation	More than <u>one million Italian homes</u>	Crowd of Italians on street
	Addition		More than one million Italian homes	
		Functionalisation		Working Italian
People	Inclusion		*Allow <u>us</u> to introduce...* *Reminding <u>all of us</u> ...* *Earth's most prolific sources of energy are its <u>people</u>*	

Discourse Schema and the Social Actions

Other vital elements of the environmental discourse existing in the *Milan* video are the actions. The representation model for a chronological sequence of these actions can take the form of the following discourse schema: Initial problem (need of cheap electricity at global level)— Solution (traditional technological solutions at local level)—Problematic outcome (high nitrogen oxide emissions at global level)—Solution (upgrading the technological solutions at local level)—Final outcomes (cheap electricity and collaboration at global level).

This order is definitely edited in that the video concentrates more on verbally communicating knowledge about "the ideas and attitudes" that are attached to the GE actions and the subsequent reactions[4]. Van Leeuwen suggests that 'discourses are never only about what we do, but always also about why we do it' (van Leeuwen, 2005: 104). In order to reveal the "why", the verbal representation of actions and reactions undergoes the following transformations in the present discourse. The knowledge about actions is primarily selected through processes of exclusion. The first part of the scenario is excluded both verbally and visually, although indirectly it is implied that there is a global need for electricity. Certainly, predicators like *upgrading* and *reducing* imply the existence of products that have not been upgraded and that the nitrogen oxide emissions have been higher. However, the selection of knowledge is realised through suppression as there is no visual or verbal trace of the actors involved in the first actions, and the viewer cannot infer with certainty whom they are. By excluding the first part of the scenario, everything starts with GE employees and their present environmentally friendly activities and ends with the main consequence of these activities: *Reminding all of us from the busy streets of Milan to the hills of South Carolina, Earth's most prolific sources of energy are its people.*

Furthermore, by excluding the first part of the scenario, the remaining actions have been foregrounded. They have also been foregrounded through processes of substitution and addition. The substitution processes that are employed in the representation of actions are objectivisation and abstraction. While actions like *extend, generate, do, fuels, opts* are activated, namely represented dynamically, other actions are de-activated. First, two actions are de-activated through processes of objectivisation in *daily efforts* and *global reach* as the actions are presented not as dynamic processes but as qualities. By objectifying these actions, their permanent qualities are highlighted. These two objectified actions are logically related by the action *extend*, which legitimates them by establishing a causal relation between them. *Collaboration* is also a de-activated action represented through a nominalisation that allows the whole social practice to be labeled. Metaphorically represented actions like *fuels* and *to power* highlight the actions' qualities through processes of overdetermination, as they can stand for the generation of both electricity and collaboration. In the case of *Earth's most prolific sources of energy are its people*, the process of substitution is generalisation. When discussing the importance of generalisation, van Leeuwen emphasises the fact that 'texts which are mainly concerned with legitimising or de-legitimising actions and reactions tend to move high up on the generalisation scale, including only the names of episodes, or of whole social practice' (van Leeuwen 2008: 69). The voice-over commentary contains not only representations of actions, but also representations of reactions: the affective reaction *encouraging* and the cognitive reaction *reminding*. Both reactions, combined with the previously discussed de-activated actions, contribute to the verbal elevation of the specific social practice to a higher level of generalisation.

The processes of knowledge selection involved in the verbal representation of actions play important roles in the realisation of legitimations and purposes, transforming the whole environmental discourse. Van Leeuwen distinguishes between legitimations and purposes, stating that for purposes 'to serve as legitimations, an additional feature is required', namely an implicit reference to some moral values (van Leeuwen, 2008: 125). Certainly, the purposes of upgrading the products are to generate electricity and reduce nitrogen oxide emissions. However, the upgrading is legitimated in terms of a discourse of collaboration. This rationalisation foregrounds verbally not the cleaner generation of electricity, but the general commonsense knowledge regarding the importance of human behaviour and way of thinking. Visually, this discourse of collaboration is not represented. Even though there are shots in which both GE employees and Italians separately appear in groups, there is no visual representation of the collaboration between GE employees and Italians, and there are no images in which GE employees and the Italians are together. As already mentioned in the discussion of the categories of actors, the actions in which the GE employees and the Italians are involved in the video's shots establish their identities: GE employees and GE customers. In conclusion, there is an obvious discrepancy between the actions represented verbally and the actions presented visually. This inconsistency weakens the environmental message of the discourse because the selected knowledge from each mode do not enter into a relationship of complementation with each other. The discourse of collaboration from the voice-over commentary is subverted by the video's shots due to the visual separation of the two categories of actors and due to the types of actions that are visually presented.

Table 9.3 provides a typology of processes of selection of knowledge about actions in the *Milan* video.

Table 9.3 Processes of Selection of Knowledge about Actions

Processes of selection of knowledge about actions			Examples
Exclusion	Supression of the discourse first part		
Substitution	Actions	Activation	*Extend, generate, do, fuels, opts*
		De-activation: nominalisation, temporalisation, spatialisation	*Collaboration* *Daily efforts* *Global reach*
		Abstraction: generalisation	*Earth's most prolific sources of energy are its people*
		Overdetermination	*Fuels, to power*
	Reactions	Affective	*Encouraging*
		Cognitive	*Reminding*
Addition	Purposes		*Generate electricity* *Reduce nitrogen oxide emissions by 40%*
	Legitimations	Rationalisation	*Encouraging a level of collaboration for craftsmanship fuels craftsmanship and one community opts to power another Reminding all of us from the busy streets of Milan to the hills of South Carolina, Earth's most prolific sources of energy are its people.*

Time and Space

The aspect of time is crucial in this environmental discourse. Verbally, the action of generating electricity is synchronised with three other actions: reducing nitrogen oxide emissions, encouraging a level of collaboration, and reminding us that Earth's most prolific sources of energy are its people. By selecting the knowledge about time through *synchronisation* of these actions, the company succeeds in making clear that the activity of producing green products with global beneficial effects cannot be separated from a certain way of thinking about the environment and all people's responsibility towards it. The attribute in *daily efforts* and progressive aspect of the present participle form of the verbs *reducing, encouraging and reminding* strengthen the link between the actions, and they also confer a sense of continuity to the whole social practice. These forms also facilitate a shift in focus from single activities towards recurrent activities, behaviour and attitudes.

Visually, the temporal dimension of the social practice is represented in a circular way as the video ends with similar black-and-white shots of GE employees that also appear in the first part of the video. The fact that the black-and-white shots of GE employees are repeated in the video also suggests that city life has been protected and supported by the GE Company for quite a long time. In general, time is weakly presented visually as, apart from the above-mentioned repetition of black-and-white shots, there are no other visual indications of a temporal sequencing of actions. This arbitrariness is definitely linked to the discrepancy between the content of voice-over commentary and the content of video's shots suggested in the discussion of actions. The black-and-white close ups of turbines and GE employees also suggest that the company is in a way set apart from day-to-day life and its status is therefore elevated. Certainly, these close-up shots reinforce the temporal arbitrariness and contribute to the discrepancy between the verbal discourse of collaboration and the visual separation of the actions performed by the two categories of actors.

Another visual aspect that influences the selective communication of knowledge about time in this environmental discourse is the inclusion of medium and extreme close-up shots of turbines, actors, flowers etc. These types of shots affect the way in which discursive time is perceived by the viewer as a close up shot draws the viewer into the discursive space, it gives the possibility to focus, and it also gives the impression that time stands still.

Space is another important element of the present discourse. The ways in which space is presented and represented facilitates the communication of specific knowledge not only about concrete places but also about the role of space in the development of this environmental discourse. Verbally, there are references to three locations: *hills of South Carolina, busy streets of Milan* and *Earth*. The verbal transition realised by circumstances of location, namely "*from . . . to*", suggests that it is not an obvious concern to indicate where the actions are located, but to sustain the above-mentioned discourse of collaboration. By connecting the GE with a natural environment, namely *hills of South Carolina*, the legitimation of their actions is foregrounded.

Visually, these locations are supplemented with images of the actual electric plant in which GE employees work, and images of the working places, homes or other settings of Italians. While the locations of the Italians' workplaces are represented in more detail due to the use of long shots, the places in which the GE employees work are not strongly represented through the visuals. Black-and-white close-up shots of the products, namely the turbines, supplement the scarce visual representation of GE's working place. The choice is motivated by the fact that, as mentioned before, in the identification of Italians the visual functionalisation is foregrounded, while in the case of the GE employees, it is the verbal functionalisation. Furthermore, the black-and-white close-up shots of the turbines give the viewer the possibility to focus on those products and their precision. Also in connection with the selection of knowledge about space, it should be mentioned that, according to van Leeuwen, 'many representations of space and spatial arrangements are directly linked to actions. This may range from body positions, such as standing or sitting, to indications of a location' (van Leeuwen 2008: 91). Visually, the body positions of the actors in the *Milan* video, namely standing GE employees and (mainly) sitting Italians[5], provide another explicit indication of the active and passive roles of the two categories of actors in the actions appearing in the environmental discourse.

Figure 9.1 provides a diagrammatic representation of how knowledge about time and space appears in the video.

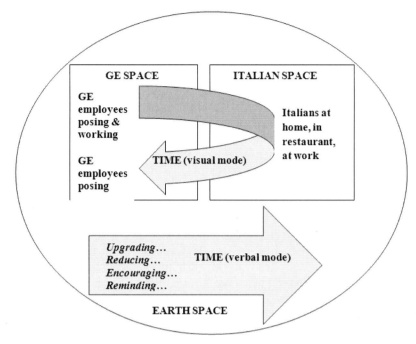

Figure 9.1 Diagram of time-space representation.

CONCLUSIONS

Through a multimodal analysis of the environmental discourse, I have explored how GE presents their new environmentally friendly products and how they try to position themselves as an eco-friendly corporation. I have discussed only a few strategies through which the selection of knowledge about actors, actions, time and space influences the environmental discourse.

The traditional advertising discourse in which new products and their benefits are persuasively presented has been replaced in the *Milan* video by a verbal environmental discourse, in which presenting the company as an eco-friendly one, fostering pro-environmental global awareness and collaboration is more important. The need to shape the public opinion concerning the corporation's environmental impact overshadows verbally the need to advertise specific products. Closing the gap between us (the company) and them (the consumers) is also a vital goal. Consequently, through processes of knowledge selection, the discursive focus is gradually moved from *what* to *why*, from *individual* to *humanity*, from *single activities* to *recurrent behaviour* and from *local action* to *global reaction*.

As I have tried to demonstrate, it is obvious that the verbal and visual modes subvert each other instead of complementing each other in this video. While the commentaries of the voice-over narration emphasise the idea of collaboration, the images isolate the actors from each other in order to foreground the GE employees and their meaningful activities. Furthermore, as actions realised through verbal processes of deactivation and abstraction are more difficult to represent in the visual mode, the visualised actions include only individual actors working with machines and not collaboration with other actors. The lack of collaboration is also suggested through the discrepancy between the visual representations of GE employees and Italians as the GE employees are visualised in series of outstanding black-and-white shots that elevate their status. These visual subversions definitely weaken the overall environmental message of the video. In conclusion, according to the above-mentioned analytical findings, the video's message is less about environmental issues and more about GE being a reliable company that has been around for a long time.

The controversial aspects of environmental discourse from various multimodal texts and contexts definitely need our attention in the future. The interest in the environmental issues will intensify in the years to come, and we, as researchers and educators, have to keep pace with the swift development of renewed persuasive strategies through which knowledge is multimodally communicated in various environmental discourses.

APPENDIX

The voice-over commentary in *Milan* video:

Allow us to introduce John, Eddie, Marvin, Roger, Danny and Jed. Tuanna. Rodney and Lucius. Ammanda. GE employees whose work day begins in Greensville, South Carolina, but whose daily efforts extend a global reach.

In Milan, two GEs H System gas turbines assembled in Greensville generate the electricity to power more than 1 million Italian homes. And by upgrading to GEs DLN 2.6+ Combustion System, do so while reducing nitrogen oxide emissions by 40% cleanly and efficiently.

Encouraging a level of collaboration for craftsmanship fuels craftsmanship, and one community opts to power another. Reminding all of us from the busy streets of Milan to the hills of South Carolina, Earth's most prolific sources of energy are its people.

NOTES

1. A multimodal text is any text in which several meaning-making resources beside language are employed in order to fulfill the communicative purposes of the text (Maier, 2006: 5).
2. According to Maier, Kampf and Kastberg, multimodal literacy represents 'the way in which the audience constructs meaning across the different modes through which content is disseminated' (Maier, Kampf and Kastberg, 2007: 456).
3. For the continuation of the present research in a quantitative analysis, the software programme File Maker Pro could be employed for constructing

relational databases for all the *Ecomagination* videos with the analytical parameters used in the present article. Another possibility could be to use the relational database incorporated in the multimodal concordancer designed by Anthony Baldry (2005). I consider that it can constitute an efficient tool not only for segmenting the videos in analytical components but also for identifying and thus comparing the recurrent patterns in them. The multimodal concordancer also offers the possibility to account for the ways in which the variations in kind or degree of selections in the visual, verbal and other modes have an impact upon the overall structure of the video.

4. The whole voice-over commentary of the video appears in the appendix.
5. There is only one shot with Italians standing in a kitchen.

REFERENCES

Baldry, A. (2005) *A Multimodal Approach to Text Studies in English. The Role of MCA in Multimodal Concordancing and Multimodal Corpus Linguistics.* Campobasso: Palladino Editore.

Baldry, A. and Thibault, P. (2006) *Multimodal Transcription and Text Analysis*, London: Equinox.

Benton, L. M. and Short, J. R. (1999) *Environmental Discourse and Practice*, Oxford: Blackwell Publishers.

Foucalt, M. (1977) *The Archeology of knowledge,* London: Tavistock GE accessed on 23 May 2007 at: http://ge.ecomagination.com/site/index.html *Milan* video accessed on 23 May 2007 at: http://ge.ecomagniation.com/site/index.html#milan

Harré, R., Brockmeier, J. and Mühlhäusler, P. (1999) *Greenspeak. A Study of Environmental Discourse*, London: Sage Publications.

Hofinger, A., and Ventola E. (2004) 'Multimodality in operation: language and picture in a museum.' In Ventola, E., Charles, C. and Kaltenbacher, M. eds. *Perspectives on Multimodality*, Amsterdam: John Benjamins Publishing Company: pp. 193–211.

Howlett, M., and Raglon, R. S. (2001) 'Constructing the environmental spectacle: green advertisements and the greening of the corporate image.' In Mühlhäusler, P., and Fill, A. eds. *The Ecolinguistics Reader*, London: Cassell: pp. 245–258.

Kress, G., and van Leeuwen, T. (2001) *Multimodal Discourse: The Modes and Media of Contemporary Communication*, London: Arnold.

Kress, G., and Jewitt, C., eds. (2003) *Multimodal Literacy*, New York: Peter Lang.

Kress, G., Jewitt, C., Ogborn, J. and Tsatsarelis, C. (2001) *Multimodal Teaching and Learning: The Rhetorics of the Science Classroom*, London: Continuum.

Machin, D., and van Leeuwen, T. (2007) *Global Media Discourse. A Critical Introduction*, London: Routledge.

Maier, C. D. (2006) 'The Promotional Genre of Film Trailers: Persuasive Structures in a Multimodal Form', unpublished PhD thesis. Aarhus School of Business (ASB), University of Aarhus.

Maier, C. D., Kampf, C. and Kastberg, P. (2007) 'Multimodal analysis—an integrative approach for specialized visualizing on the web', *Journal of Technical Writing and Communication* 37(4): 453–478.

Mühlhäuser, P., and Peace, A. (2006) 'Environmental discourses'. *Annual Review of Anthropology* 35: 457–479.

O'Halloran, K. L. (2004) 'Visual semiosis in film.' In O'Halloran, K. L. ed. *Multimodal Discourse Analysis. Systemic Functional Perspectives*, London: Continuum: pp. 109–131.

O'Toole, M. (2004) 'Opera Ludentes: the Sydney Opera House at work and play.' In O'Halloran, K. L. ed. *Multimodal Discourse Analysis. Systemic Functional Perspectives*, London: Continuum: pp. 11–28.

Thibault, P. (2000) 'The multimodal transcription of a television advertisement: theory and practice.' In Baldry, A. ed. *Multimodality and Multimediality in the Distance Learning Age*, Campobasso: Palladino Editore: pp. 311–385.

van Leeuwen, T. (2008) *Discourse and Practice. New Tools for Critical Discourse Analysis*, New York: Oxford University Press.

———— (2007) 'Legitimation in discourse and communication.' *Discourse and Communication* 1(1): 91–112.

———— (2005a) 'Time in discourse.' *Linguistics and the Human Sciences* 1(1): 125–145.

———— (2005b) *Introducing Social Semiotics*, London: Routledge.

———— (2000a) 'The construction of purpose in discourse.' In Sarangi, S., and Coulthard M. eds. *Discourse and Social Life*, London: Longman: pp. 66–82.

———— (2000b) 'Visual racism.' Reisigl, M., and Wodak, R. eds. *The Semiotics of Racism: Approaches in Critical Discourse Analysis*, Vienna: Passagen Verlag: pp. 330–350.

———— (1996) 'The representation of social actors.' In Caldas-Coulthard, C. R., and Coulthard M. eds. *Texts and Practices: Reading in Critical Discourse Analysis*, London: Routledge: pp. 32–70.

———— (1995) 'Representing social actions.' *Discourse and Society* 6(1): 81–106.

10 The Implications of Multimodality for Media Literacy

Sun Sun Lim, Elmie Nekmat
and Siti Nurharnani Nahar

INTRODUCTION

With the advent of Web 2.0, the media consumer is endowed with the ability to consume, produce and disseminate media messages that often involve multimodal representations, which incorporate text, images and sound. Consequently, in both receptive and expressive modes of communication, multimodal representation demands that media consumers have knowledge and competencies in a wide range of aspects—textual understanding, visual and aural literacy, genre identification, critical analysis, legal know-how, ICT skills, industry insights and more. While multimodal representation in itself poses significant media literacy challenges to the media consumer, this chapter argues that several concomitant trends in the mediascape further compound the severity of these challenges: the growing ease of manipulability of media content, the rise in media genre-hybridisation and the increasing proliferation of user-generated media content. The chapter then considers why and how media literacy needs to be reassessed in a mediascape increasingly marked by multimodality. Finally, it concludes by identifying which literacies are most critical in our current mediascape and makes several recommendations for research and policy formulation.

MULTIMODAL REPRESENTATION—SHIFTS IN THE MEDIASCAPE

The mediascape has seen a discernible shift in semiotic modes of representation towards a growing dominance of visual images. While unimodal text-only documents have certainly not faded into oblivion, their importance has waned as media continues to evolve with enhanced capacities for holding and displaying texts in various modes, containing graphics, pictures, layout techniques and more (Goodman 1996). Over the past century, there has been a broad move from the supremacy of writing and the written word to the dominance of the image in different media technologies (Jewitt and Kress 2003). These technologies, also known as 'technologies of literacy' (Warschauer 2003: 115), had notably shifted from the printing press, which privileged the written word, i.e. text, over all other semiotic modes (Kaplan 1995). Kress argues that in the current media environment, images are assuming increasing importance such that images lead over text and the screen takes precedence over books (2003). Kress states that the screen is a "visual entity" (2003: 65) and text that appears on screen is similarly treated as an image and follows the same principles of visual design. As a result, written text, which appears with images plays a secondary role with regard to conveying meaning. Arguably, this trend arose from the popularity of film and television, resulting in the format of print media such as newspapers, magazines and books being altered, such that visual images have become, and continue to be, increasingly prominent (Kress and van Leeuwen 1996). Multimodal representation is therefore not entirely novel in this information age but is a reflection of the intensifying use of multiple communication modes in media, particularly that of visuals. Notably though, while television, film and printed texts have long been marrying textual and visual content, the advent of information technology has made multimodal communication much more prevalent (Warschauer 2003). On top of combining text, photos, videos, audio and graphics in a single presentation, the decentralised nature of information production further aids the proliferation of this multimodal communication phenomenon. In sum, multimodal representation is by no means a new phenomenon, but one that has evolved in its intensity, scale and complexity with the introduction of new information and communication technologies.

MULTIMODALITY AND CONCOMITANT TRENDS

While multimodal representation in itself poses significant media literacy challenges to the media consumer, several concomitant trends in the mediascape further compound the severity of these challenges: the growing ease of manipulability of media content, the rise in media genre-hybridisation and the increasing proliferation of user-generated media content. Each point will be discussed and illustrated as in the following section.

Multimodality and the Manipulability of Media

With the advent of digitisation, media and information have become extremely easy to modify and manipulate. As Feldman (1997) argues, compared to analogue media where the process of reshaping information can often be "difficult, slow and untidy", digital media on the other hand allows users to infinitely and easily alter information "at a stroke" (4). This affordance of advanced digital tools has significant implications for all stages of information representation: from the moment it is created and captured in digital form, to its dissemination, on to audiences' engagement with the information and beyond.

While media content of different modes can be easily modified and altered, in light of the significance of images in today's mediascape, let us consider the implications of the ease of manipulating images. Digital graphics are presently used in creating interactive user interfaces, virtual reality, animation, as well as reconstructing three dimensional objects from their "2D projectional presentations" (Groß, 1994: 2). The digitisation of graphics enables us to handle images in unprecedented ways, including the restoration of old and damaged photographs and the seamless recombination and morphing of snippets of different images. Such affordances have been adopted with enthusiasm and exploited by artists and media producers in surprising and creative ways. However, the ability to modify digital images has also opened an avenue for misinformation and deception.

This concern is not unwarranted considering that doctored images are being disseminated even by established and reputable media organisations such as Reuters and the *Los Angeles Times*. A 2006 Reuters photograph of smoke rising from buildings in Beirut was attacked by American bloggers for having been doctored (British Broadcasting Corporation (BBC) News 2006). Upon investigation, it was found that Adnan Hajj, the Reuters photographer, had distorted the photograph to include more smoke and damage. In another example, Brian Walski created a new photograph by manipulating two photographs that he had taken for the Los Angeles Times (van Riper 2003). In the first photograph, a US soldier was pictured with his gun pointed horizontally while in the second photograph, the soldier's gun was lowered when a man with a baby stood near him. By combining both photos, the altered image made it appear as though the soldier was pointing his gun directly at the man with the baby, presumably to heighten the photograph's dramatic effect and to enhance its human interest value.

Such egregious practices, even by professionals from renowned news organisations, are a stark reminder that today's media consumer needs to be even more critical and sceptical than ever in their consumption of media content. In these two cases, the visual literacy skills of the consumer are tested as they need to appreciate the telltale signs of digitally doctored photographs. Yet the sophistication of today's graphic applications produces such flawless results that the visual literacy skills of even shrewd media consumers may be easily defeated. In such a mediascape, media consumers have the unenviable responsibility of being constantly questioning and discerning about their media sources, regardless of how established and reputable those sources might be. Quality indicators that used to serve media consumers well are of diminished value into today's media environment.

Quite apart from the manipulability of media itself, the access to media content can also be manipulated, especially online. The prominence of online information can also be directed such that some content is replicated repeatedly, while others remain obscure and difficult to access. Given that the World Wide Web is a seemingly infinite mass of information, media consumers have no option but to locate information online using search engines. The ways in which search engine results are ordered depend on a combination of factors, including the design of search engines algorithms, the search engine's revenue stream and business model and the original source of the content (Hargittai 2004). Commercial interests are behind the most popular Web sites, which users frequently visit to get their online content (Hargittai 2004). The order of search engine results becomes significant because most users are unwilling to explore results beyond the third page (iProspect 2008). In 2008 the percentage decreased to 9% as compared to 2006 (12%), 2004 (17%) and 2002 (22%).

Hence, media consumers are in some sense at the mercy of search engines. Search engines and directories systematically exclude certain sites in favour of others, either by design or by accident (Introna and Nissenbaum 2000). For example, Google has been observed to exclude certain sites from its searches—compared to google.com, 113 sites were excluded, in whole or in part, from the French google.fr and German google.de (Zittrain and Edelman 2002). In this regard, the discerning media consumer is one who understands how media industry practices and pressures may result in the omission of particular content and the amplification of others, and that the information which they derive from online sources can be fraught with bias. However, it would be fair to say that such esoteric knowledge about how search engines work would be beyond the average media consumer.

Multimodality and Genre-Hybridisation

Practices within the media industry are leaning towards the hybridisation of different media forms. The classical distinctions between documentaries, news, information, entertainment, dramas, comedies, editorials and advertisements have become blurred. There has been a growing trend towards eclecticism, where 'a cultural text creatively mixes, blends, or recombines pre-existing and relatively discrete cultural forms, formulas and techniques' (Ott 2007: 58). Such media production practices result in texts, which can be particularly challenging for media consumers, as their conventional frames for understanding media content may be inadequate or even inappropriate. As Campbell and Freed (1993) opined, 'television is certainly a fertile breeding ground for genre confusion. Categories once chiselled in granite melt in a swirl of crossover jargon: docudrama, infotainment, infomercial, dramedy'(77). Similarly, with print media, such as newspapers and magazines, expanding into online platforms with new channels for interacting with readers, the classical categories of reportage, opinion-editorials and letters from readers have been partially displaced by hybrid forms such as readers' blogs and opinion forums, 'first-person' citizen journalist reports replete with amateur photos etc.

The combination of genre hybridisation and multimodality has given birth to even more boundary-crossing media types. The rising sophistication of computer animation and production techniques has facilitated the creation of multimodal content of an extremely high quality, such that genre-hybridisation in television and films has broken new ground. An excellent example is the British television programme *Prehistoric Park*, which features the well-known British wildlife documentary host Nigel Marven playing himself. In this programme, Marven (with the help of a time-travel device) is tasked with finding extinct animals from prehistoric eras and bringing them back to the present day for exhibition in the Prehistoric Park. The prehistoric animals are rendered in computer-generated imagery and animatronics, and they interact with the human actors and natural landscapes in a lifelike fashion. Marven is often shown spying on the prehistoric creatures in their 'natural' habitats and touching them when they are taken into captivity.

While the characters in the show are thus multimodal in nature, the style of the show is multi-genre and defies classification. Marven appears in his usual guise of the reputable wildlife expert who addresses viewers directly, as though they were watching a documentary. The wildlife scenes are set in actual physical locations and bear the patina of a scientifically based nature programme, thus appearing highly realistic. However, *Prehistoric Park* is mostly fictional and more closely resembles a drama with the typical elements of emotions, humour, suspense and even tragedy. This blend of multimodality and genre-hybridisation sends mixed signals to viewers, as 'traditional' production techniques are both obverted and subverted. A sampling of viewers' comments on clips of the show excerpted on youtube.com reveals the confusion that some viewers experience—from "it's my favourite *documentary* tv show (emphasis mine)", to "But it looks so real to me, is this real!?", "so you mean everything in this is real?" and "im (sic) watching this on tv right now, IS THIS REAL OR FAKE !?!??!?!?!" (Sidewaysnic, n.d.). As these comments exemplify, the potent combination of multimodality and genre-hybridisation can significantly test consumers' media literacy skills.

Multimodality and the Proliferation of User-Generated Content

Information technology now provides media consumers with the means to create, replicate and disseminate media content. With the spread of affordable media production hardware and software, and the emergence of a slew of content sharing sites on the Internet, the growth of user-generated content has been significant. Previously, the high costs of information production and dissemination served as barriers and restricted the number of content providers to only those with adequate authority and capital (Metzger 2007). Today, as long as one has the technical know-how and access to the technology, one can easily become an author. We should bear in mind of course, that the extent to which individuals can and do avail of such self-authoring opportunities differs according to motivations, skills and interests.

In short, media consumers are now able to produce their own forms of representation, both uni- and multimodal. This proliferation of user-generated content compounds the subjectivity of the information, which they create as each different mode offers the potential for different "representational and communicational action by their users" (Kress 2003, 5). The average media consumer is now concurrently in possession of the resources of representation, the resources of production and the resources of dissemination. These distinct resources require specific competencies not only in their use but also in the design of information, i.e. in the consumer's receptive and expressive modes (Kress 2003). In other words, it is more important than ever for the average consumer to understand the role of the designer with regards to the meaning-potentials of the resources which they now enjoy. This is further complicated by the interplays between the 'semiotic resources' (i.e. mode) and the 'material substance' (i.e. medium; Kress and van Leeuwen 2001, 215: 41), which provide various potentialities, but also present complexities in the representation of information.

Critical reflexivity is also required in view of the synergies and potential for convergence amongst different forms of digital media such as computers, mobile phones, cameras, palmtops and many more. The increasing portability of these media tools, coupled with their enhanced capacity to hold different modes of information greatly increases one's ability not only to produce but also to communicate information through various modes and resources. Inevitably, media consumers' exposure to multimodal forms of communication will only increase. Therefore, possessing the competencies to comprehend how the various modes and 'material resources' affect the representational potential of information not only requires critical reflectivity of the context in which the information was produced but also reflexivity in one's own production of information.

REASSESSING MEDIA LITERACY

Media literacy can be defined as the ability to 'decode, evaluate, analyse and produce messages' in a variety of forms (Aufderheide 1993: 1). While this pithy definition adequately captures the multi-faceted nature of media literacy, the way in which media literacy is defined depends not only on the entity defining it but, more significantly, should change to suit the evolution of the media landscape (Potter 2004). Indeed, in light of the trends discussed in the previous section, a reassessment of the concept of media literacy is timely. In this regard, what are the implications of multimodality for media literacy, especially when it comes to one's critical analysis and evaluation of media content? Several scholars have identified several media literacy imperatives arising from the increasingly complex nature of multimodal representation.

The Need for Multimodal Literacy and Multiple Literacies

Accompanying the proliferation of multimodal representation in today's media landscape have been shifts in how meanings are created and understood (Jewitt and Kress 2003; Lankshear and Knobel 2003). With the widespread deployment of different modalities, media and materials, each with its own logic and affordances, media consumers' meaning-making processes are getting more complex than ever. Understandably, scholars concerned about the effects of multimodality have focused on understanding the different ways in which meaning can be created and communicated in the world today (Kress and van Leeuwen 1996; Baldry 2000; O' Halloran 2004). They have focused, *inter alia*, on the 'semiotic affordances of image, of writing and of speech and of multimodal texts' (Jewitt and Kress 2003: 166) and on how 'intra and inter-semioses' arising from the interaction within and between two or more semiotic modes empower or disempower creators and receivers of multimodal texts (O' Halloran 2004: 224).

The multimodally literate media consumer is primarily viewed as one who 1) displays a systematic understanding of how texts make meanings and how these meanings can be conveyed by different communicative forms such as language, image, sound, gesture etc; 2) possesses the competency to integrate textual analysis with an appreciation of how audiences engage with the texts under scrutiny; and 3) has the capacity to integrate textual analysis with an understanding of the political, economic and social contexts in which the texts are produced and consumed (Burn and Parker 2003: 3–4). As compared to multimodal literacies that emphasise the ability to critically decipher the meaning-making potential of semiotic resources, media literacy; focuses on the skills to access, consume, assess and produce content (Livingstone 2004), with a shift "towards a concern with critique, reflection and judgement" (Martin 2006; 18). The ability to critically analyse symbolic texts thus lies at the intersection of multimodal literacy and media literacy; and a robust definition of media literacy that serves today's mediascape has to take into account multimodality and incorporate multimodal literacy. Clearly, the range of literacies that comprise media literacy has widened. There have been calls for 'new literacies' and 'multiple literacies' for understanding 'post-typographic' forms of social practices in the consumption and production of media content (Lankshear and Knobel 2003: 16–17). It is only with the possession of multiple literacies that individuals can participate in our highly mediatised information society in an efficacious manner (Kellner 2002). A few key literacies are discussed in the subsequent sections.

Reading and Navigating the Multimodal and Hypertextual Environment

While the current multimodal and hypertextual media environment seems to exemplify a 'brave new world' in media representations, the basic principles of critical literacy, which applied to traditional print and mass-media contexts are still relevant today. For example, the ability to critically appraise the heterogeneity of sources, competing authorities, non-linear or visual forms of representation are not skills which are specific to the multi-modal media environment but have long been required for consuming text (Livingstone 2003). However, Luke (2000: 70) does refine the definition of particular literacies, which will enhance one's navigation of hypertextual environments and evaluation of online information. They are 1) possessing the adequate meta-knowledge of how ideas and information 'bits' are structured in different media genres and how they affect people's reading and uses of information; 2) displaying mastery of the technical and analytical skills with which to negotiate those representational systems in diverse contexts; and 3) having the capacity to understand and relate these systems and skills as operating within relations and interests of power within and across social institutions.

Jewitt and Kress (2003: 73) also identified salient distinctions between the unimodal, text environment and the multimodal, hypertextual one. They argue that the former tends to have horizontal and linear content while the latter 'immerses one in an intertextual and multimodal universe of visual, audio, symbolic and linguistic meaning systems', which are laterally connected, thus making reading and navigation more challenging. Readers are engaged in a multimodal reading of texts, and have the added burden of navigating through multi-layered and multi-coded animation, symbols, linguistic text, photos etc at the same time. In such an environment, having a contextualised knowledge of the ideas carried by different pieces of information will no longer suffice. Instead, media consumers are required to understand the relations amongst these ideas and how these ideas are affected by their representation through the different modes.

Furthermore, one also has to be aware of the effects resulting from the process of following a hyperlink from one webpage to another, with each different page embedded with different modes of representation. For example, reading about the large number of whales being driven up to shore elicits a different response as compared to seeing images of the whales on the shoreline. This process potentially affects not only their cognitive, but also their emotive states, affecting their ability to make sound judgments about the credibility of the information, which they presented. The ability to read and navigate the multimodal and hypertextual media environment is thus a key component of the aforementioned 'multiple literacies' required in today's mediascape.

Recognising the Limitations of Foundational Knowledge Structures

The critical evaluation of media content rests on an extensive body of knowledge pertaining to the broader social, cultural, economic, political, and historical contexts in which media content is produced (Bazalgette 1997). Apart from such contextual knowledge, Potter (2004) posits a more comprehensive set of foundational knowledge structures that a media literate person needs to possess for the critical evaluation of information. They are knowledge of 1) media content 2) media effects, 3) media industry, 4) the real-world, and 5) self (Potter 2004). These knowledge structures enable media users to approach problem-solving and meaning-making with a greater variety of tools. However, the robustness of these knowledge structures is increasingly challenged by the multimodal nature of online communication, as well as the three concomitant trends discussed above, i.e. the manipulability of media, media genre-hybridisation and the emergence of user-generated content. Compared to traditional publishing, content posted on the Internet may not be filtered through professional gatekeepers, and not all Web sites specify traditional authority indicators such as author's identity or affiliated association. There are no common standards for posting information online, and digital information may be easily changed, misused, plagiarised or created anonymously under false pretences (Fritch and Cromwell 2001, 2002; Metzger, Flanagin, Eyal, Lemus and McCann 2003). In addition, since user-generated content can and often is presented in a format similar to that of established media organisations, Burbules (1998: 109) argues that there is a "levelling effect" where all information becomes equally easy to access, thus contributing to the perception that all authors offer the same level of credibility to Internet consumers.

In such circumstances, how relevant is one's knowledge of media effects or media industries when evaluating information sources? For example, is it sufficient to claim that information presented by a trustworthy online news agency is more reliable than an independent source, which posts photographs of a similar event on a blog and even includes embedded video footage of the actual event? In this instance, the modes of representation might actually be more revealing indicators of information reliability than knowledge about the media producer or media industry as a whole. Furthermore, the increasingly hazy divisions between media producers and consumers makes it difficult to establish valid and reliable criteria for ascertaining the quality, ideology, market influences or professional production values of online content.

One emerging grey area is the incorporation of user-generated content by mainstream media organisations seeking to ride the wave of citizen journalism. Viewers and readers are encouraged to contribute content which then becomes embedded within the company's proprietary material. For example, readers' and viewers' contributions are regularly showcased in Korea's *OhMyNews*, Singapore's *Straits Times*'s *STOMP* and Cable News Network's (CNN) *iReporter*, whereas BBC News online currently picks up more Internet traffic from micro-blogging site *Twitter* than it sends there (Hitwise 2008). Yet these organisations also issue disclaimers to absolve themselves from errors and inaccuracies in these contributions from their audiences, clearly signalling that incorporation of user-generated content is not tantamount to editorial endorsement.

In such a media milieu, the keystone of critical media literacy, i.e. the knowledge of the operations and consequences of media producers as prime quality indicators, is no longer as valid as it used to be (Livingstone 2004). Hence, while media consumers need to maintain and grow their media-related knowledge structures, another literacy which they must possess is the ability to recognise the limitations of these structures, and to deploy them in a reflexive manner that suits the ever-changing contextual demands.

Enhancing Visual Literacy

The growing dominance of visuals as a form of representation also necessitates an increased focus on what it means to 'read' images from the media. Kress (2003: 65) stresses the importance of understanding the logic of new reading paths, where the image 'dominates the semiotic organization of the screen'. Other scholars and experts on visual literacy have also emphasised the importance of understanding the effects of 'representational conventions' of visual images used in media for the creation and sharing of meanings (Messaris 1998: 70). Arguably, visual representations have the potential to imbue information with an aura of reliability and a veneer of truthfulness. Hence, visually literate media consumers are also those who can interpret the content of visual images, examine their social impact and evaluate the purpose, audience and ownership of visuals (Bamford 2003). Besides the new logics of reading required in the highly visual media environment and the critical reflection skills needed for the contextual appraisal of visual images, the competency to ascertain the authenticity and reliability of visual images in media is especially vital in today's multimodal environment. Therefore, visual literacy is yet another literacy in the repertoire of literacies, which today's media consumers should possess.

CONCLUSION AND RECOMMENDATIONS

The nature, intensity and scale of multimodality in today's media content pose interesting and potentially daunting challenges for consumers' media literacy skills. The multimodal environment necessitates that consumers be even more critical in evaluating media content information now, more than ever, since the onus of information credibility no longer rests mainly on traditional gatekeepers. Associated trends, such as the growing ease of manipulability of media content, the rise in media genre-hybridisation and the increasing proliferation of user-generated media content also serve to heighten the magnitude of these media literacy challenges. In this regard, what can media organisations, public agencies and individuals themselves do to confront these challenges or, at the very least, to ameliorate their effects?

Media organisations should take the initiative to provide evidence of reflexivity on their part. In particular, they should be more transparent about their media production processes and policies. Media consumers may then have a set of 'environmental standards of media practice' (Silverstone 2007: 176) on which to base their own judgments. Media organisations can also seek to introduce their own quality indicators, which serve as guidelines on how media content can be read, understood and criticised. A good example is online encyclopaedia *Wikipedia*, which practices collaborative writing and editing of articles by volunteers who source, format, rewrite and link articles. All *Wikipedia* content must strive to adhere to the policies of *Neutral Point of View, Verifiability* and *No Original Research* (Ayers, Matthews, and Yates 2008: 200). Hence, entries must be objective, have their claims supported with reliable sources and be based on content previously published by third parties. Entries that do not meet these benchmarks are flagged with standard message templates to warn readers of the inadequacy of the content. More information providers would do well to emulate *Wikipedia's* establishment of transparent standards and its user-friendly style of communicating them.

Similarly, search engines should explain more clearly how their search results are derived and clearly differentiate sponsored hits so that consumers can be more well-informed in their use of search engine results (Machill 2004). *Google* has been a trailblazer in this regard, where sponsored links are clearly demarcated. Measures, such as those taken by *Wikipedia* and *Google,* will help to raise public confidence in media organisations and the content, which they provide. As media organisations seek to pursue market share and industry recognition, introducing such measures need not be onerous but can be acts of enlightened self-interest. However, it should also be cautioned that these measures and reliability indicators are double edged as media consumers may go into 'auto-pilot' mode and make snap judgments about information credibility on the basis of these assurances.

Policy interventions are also urgently required to help people keep pace with ever-changing media trends so that they can continue to function well in a highly mediatised society. On a public policy level, there is a need to prioritise which components of media literacy need to be most urgently inculcated so that citizens can avail of new media opportunities to maximise benefits and minimise harms. Training in multimodality needs to be built into the formal school curriculum from an early age. To assume that young media consumers, popularly referred to as the digital natives, are well-versed in multimodal content would be a mistake. They may be highly attuned to the functional aspects of the multimodal, multi-media environment. However, their ability to consume media in a critical and discerning fashion may be wanting, as several studies suggest (see, for example, Hobbs and Frost 2003; Livingstone and Bober 2004; Shenton 2004). Hence, it is critical that training in media literacy, and multimodal literacy be incorporated into the formal curriculum as early as possible, particularly since these children would already have grown up in an environment where multimodal representation is a given.

Furthermore, multimodal media literacy training should focus on technical competencies and critical discernment *concurrently*, rather than in isolation, for better results (Potter 2008). To this end, Kalantzis and Cope (2000) proposed a 'pedagogy of multiliteracies' to instil an appreciation for the multimodal media environment, comprising 1) situated practice—working from a base of the student's personal interests and life experience; 2) overt instruction—comparing and contrasting different patterns and conventions of meaning in varied cultural settings; 3) critical framing—critiquing and contextualising information and messages; and 4) transformed practice—transferral of learning from one context to another, and putting theory to practice (239–242). Such a holistic, life-centred approach better reflects the realities of the current media environment where multimodality is ubiquitous.

As for the media literacy skills that need to be imparted to prepare individuals for the multimodal environment, special attention must be paid to critical literacy in both receptive and expressive modes so that people can be discerning media consumers as well as producers. In Singapore for example, the trend is towards the imparting of functional literacy skills e.g. teaching people how to blog, with less attention being paid to critical literacy dimensions, e.g. helping people to understand the impact of blogging (Lim and Nekmat 2009). In this regard, programmes tailored to inculcate critical 'prosumption' of media content need to emphasise that the semiotic democracy and multimedia affordances that come with the production of media content have personal and societal impact, as well as legal implications.

In light of the fact that the mediascape is in a constant state of flux, media literacy education must not end with the formal school years. Continuing adult education is also essential so that working adults can keep abreast of the latest media trends which may well impact on their self-efficacy, workplace productivity and sense of well-being. To this end, media literacy programmes targeted at adults should capitalise on trends in informal learning (see, for example, Drotner 2008). For example, fostering a core group of technology evangelists or ambassadors who engage in peer-to-peer teaching would be one approach. Public resources should also be enhanced for self-instruction and independent learning in the acquisition of media literacy skills. Online portals, public information booths and community libraries can be key nodes for disseminating such resources. Ultimately, policy makers need to realise that the repertoire of media literacy skills which individuals require will constantly increase in number and change in composition. Media literacy programmes must therefore be tailored accordingly and refreshed constantly in today's rapidly progressing multimodal and multimedia landscape.

What then of media consumers themselves? Above all, they need to come to terms with the mercurial nature of the mediascape and recognise that heuristics for understanding and assessing media content are being rapidly superseded. While the instinct to surrender helplessly to these apparently inexorable trends is great, media consumers should still seek to equip themselves with the competencies to critically and profitably access, consume and produce media content. Indeed, it can never be sufficiently stressed that the responsibility ultimately lies with media consumers to be conscious of the limitless possibilities and potential pitfalls in our multimodal media environment.

REFERENCES

Aufderheide, P. (1993) *Media Literacy: A Report of the National Leadership Conference on Media Literacy*, Aspen, Colorado: Aspen Institute.

Ayers, P., Matthews, C. and Yates, B. (2008) *How Wikipedia Works and How You Can Be Part of It*, San Francisco, California: No Starch Press.

Baldry, A. P. (2000) *Multimodality and Multimediality in the Distance Learning Age: Papers in English Linguistics*, Campobasso, Italy: Palladino Editore.

Bamford, A. (2003) *The Visual Literacy White Paper*. UK: Adobe Systems Incorporated. Available online at <http://www.adobe.com/education/digkids/resources/visual_literacy.html> (accessed 22 November 2008).

Bazalgette, C. (1997) An agenda for the second phase of media literacy development. In Kubey, R. W. ed. *Media Literacy in the Information Age: Current Perspectives, Information and Behaviour*, New Brunswick, New Jersey: Transaction: pp. 69–78.

BBC News. (2006) 'Reuters drops Beirut photographer'. BBC News, August 08. <http://news.bbc.co.uk/2/hi/middle_east/5254838.stm> (accessed 29 August 29 2008).

Burbules, N. C. (1998) 'Rhetorics of the Web: hyperreading and critical literacy', In Snyder, I. ed. *Page to Screen: Taking Literacy into the Electronic Era*, London: Routledge: pp. 102–122.

Burn, A., and Parker, D. (2003) *Analysing Media Texts*, London: Continuum International Publishing.

Campbell, R. and Freed, R. (1993) 'We know it when we see it': Postmodernism and Television. *Television Quarterly* 26: 75–87.

Drotner, K., Jensen, H.S. and Schroder, K.C. (2008) *Informal Learning and Digital Media*, Newcastle, UK: Cambridge Scholars.

Feldman, T. (1997) *An Introduction to Digital Media,* New York: Routledge.

Fritch, J. W., and Cromwell, R. L. (2002) 'Delving deeper into evaluation: Exploring cognitive authority on the Internet.' Reference Services Review 30 (3): 242–254.

———— (2001) 'Evaluating Internet resources: Identity, affiliation, and cognitive authority in a networked world', *Journal of the American Society for Information Science and Technology* 52(6): 499–507.

Goodman, S. (1996) 'Visual English.' In Goodman S., and Graddol, D. eds. *Redesigning English: New Texts, New Identities*, London: Routledge: pp. 38–72.

Groß, M. (1994) *Visual Computing: The Integration of Computer Graphics, Visual Perception and Imaging*. Berlin: Springer-Verlag.

Hargittai, E. (2004) The changing online landscape: from free-for-all to commercial gatekeeping. In Day, P., and Shuler, D. eds. *Community Practice in the Network Society: Local Actions/Global Interaction*, New York: Routledge: pp. 66–76.

Hitwise (2008) *Hitwise UK Social Networking Update*, Online. Available HTTP: <http://sg.hitwise.com/press-center/   hitwiseHS2004/uk-facebook-22072208.php> (accessed 3 December 2008).

Hobbs, R., and Frost, R. (2003) 'Measuring the acquisition of media-literacy skills.' *Reading Research Quarterly* 38(3): 330–355.

Introna, L. D., and Nissenbaum, H. (2000) 'Shaping the Web: Why the Politics of SearchEngines Matters.' *The Information Society* 16: 169–185.

iProspect (2008) *Blended Search Results Study* Online. Available HTTP: <http://www.iprospect.com/premiumPDFs/ researchstudy_apr2008_blendedsearchresults.pdf > (accessed 28 September 2008).

Jewitt, C., and Kress, G. (2003) *Multimodal Literacy*, London: Peter Lang.

Kalantzis, M., and Cope, B. (2000) 'A multiliteracies pedagogy: A pedagogical supplement.' In Kalantzis M., and Cope B. eds. *Multiliteracies: Literacy Learning and the Design of Social Futures*, New York: Routledge: pp. 239–248.

Kaplan, N. (1995) *E-literacies. Computer-mediated Communication Magazine* 2 (3): 3–35.

Kellner, D. (2002) 'Technological revolution, multiple literacies, and the restructuring of education.' In Snyder, I. ed. *Silicon Literacies*, London: Routlege: pp. 154–169.

Kress, G. (2003) *Literacy in the New Media Age*, New York: Routledge.

Kress, G., and van Leeuwen, T. (2001) *Multimodal Discourse: The Modes and Media of Contemporary Communication*, London: Arnold Publishers.

———— (1996) *Reading Images: The Grammar of Visual Design*, London: Routledge.

Lankshear, C., and Knobel, M. (2003) *New Literacies: Changing Knowledge and Classroom Learning*, Philadelphia: Open University Press.

Lim, S. S., and Nekmat, E. (2009) 'Media Education in Singapore—New media, new literacies?' In Cheung, C. K. ed. *Media Education in Asia*, Netherlands: Springer: pp. 185–198.

Livingstone, S. (2003) *The Changing Nature and Uses of Media Literacy*, European Medi@Culture-Online. Available HTTP: <http://www.lse.ac.uk/collections/media@lse/pdf/Media@lseEWP4_july03.pdf> (accessed 27 September 2008).

———— (2004) 'Media Literacy and the Challenge of New Information and Communication Technologies.' *The Communication Review* 7(1): 3–14.

Livingstone, S., and Bober, M. (2004) *UK children go online: surveying the experiences of young people and their parents*. Monograph. July. Online. Available HTTP: <http://eprints.lse.ac.uk/395/> (accessed 6 July 2008).

Luke, C. (2000) 'Cyber-schooling and technological change.' In Cope, B. and Kalantzis, M. eds. *Multiliteracies: Literacy Learning and the Design of Social Futures*, New York: Routledge: pp. 69–91.

Machill, M., Neuberger, C., Schweiger, W. and Wirth, W. (2004) 'Navigating the Internet: a study of German language search engines.' *European Journal of Communication* 19: 321–347.

Martin, A. (2006) 'Literacies for the digital age: A preview of part 1.' In Martin, A., and Madigan, D. eds. *Digital Literacies for Learning*, London, Ridgmount: Facet Publishing: pp. 3–26.

Messaris, P. (1998) 'Visual aspects of media literacy.' *Journal of Communication* 48, (1): 70–80.

Metzger, M. J. (2007) 'Making sense of credibility on the Web: models for evaluating online information and recommendations for future research', *Journal of the American Society for Information Science and Technology* 58 (13): 2078–2091.

Metzger, M. J., Flanagin, A. J., Eyal, K., Lemus, D. R. and McCann, R. M. (2003) 'Credibility for the 21st century: integrating perspectives on source, message, and media credibility in the contemporary media environment.' *Communication Yearbook* 27 (1): 293–335.

O'Halloran, K. L., ed. (2004) *Multimodal Discourse Analysis*, New York: Continuum.

Ott, B. L. (2007) *The Small Screen: How Television Equips Us to Live in the Information Age*, London: Blackwell.

Potter, W. J. (2004) *Theory of Media Literacy: A Cognitive Approach*, Thousand Oaks: CA: Sage Publications Inc.

————— (2008) *Media Literacy* 4th ed. Los Angeles: Sage Publications.

SidewaysNic, "Prehistoric Park," YouTube video, 2:26, from a performance televised by Animal Planet, added May 22, 2007, http://www.youtube.com/watch?v=hp-XPlj67As.

Shenton, A. K. (2004) 'Research into young people's information-seeking: perspectives and methods', *ASLIB Proceedings* 56, no. 4: 243–254.

Silverstone, R. (2007) *Media and Morality: On the Rise of the Mediapolis*, London: Polity.

van Riper, F. (2003) "Manipulating Truth, Losing Credibility". *The Washington Post*, April 09. Available online at <http://www.washingtonpost.com/wp-srv/photo/essays/vanRiper/030409.htm> (accessed 19 September 2008).

Warschauer, M. (2003) *Technology and Social Inclusion: Rethinking the Digital Divide*, London, England: The MIT Press.

Zittrain, J., and Edelman, B. (2002) *Localized Google search result exclusions: statement of issues and call for data*. Berkman Center for Internet and Society, Harvard Law School, October 26. Available online at <http://cyber.law.harvard.edu/filtering/google/> (accessed 29 September 2008).

11 The Changing Pedagogic Landscape of Subject English in UK Classrooms

Carey Jewitt

INTRODUCTION

The pedagogic landscape of subject English classrooms in the UK is changing as a consequence of the use of technologies. The changing representational and communicational facilities made available via technologies are of particular importance for changing forms of knowledge and how these are mobilised and circulated. This paper investigates these changes with a specific attention on how image and writing feature in the English classroom and their emergent effect on pedagogic practice and curricular knowledge.

To help contextualise the analysis of multimodal contemporary school English the paper starts with a brief discussion of how multimodal perspectives have been applied to school English and the social conditions that underpin the contemporary production of English. The Interactive Whiteboard (IWB) is then used as an exemplar technology through which the pedagogic space of contemporary school English can be examined. The IWB is chosen as a technology because it is indicative of how changes in representational and communicational forms can effect knowledge and practice in the English classroom. Throughout the paper technology mediated practices in school English are scrutinised through illustrative case-study examples of English teaching collected in 2000[1] and in 2005[2] to explore the role of writing and image in the production of English.

SCHOOL ENGLISH THROUGH A MULTIMODAL LENS

Multimodal research has been undertaken that shows the complex ways in which image, gesture, gaze, interaction with objects, body posture and writing and speech interact in the 'everyday' classroom production of school subject knowledge (Jewitt, 2008). For example, building on earlier work on multimodality in school Science (Kress et al. 2001), the Production of School English Project (SEP; Kress et al. 2005) developed a multimodal research methodology to examine school English. The SEP analysed the multimodal forms of school English that resulted from the interaction of the stipulated curriculum policy with the social conditions of the environment in which English was actually produced. It mapped the modal and semiotic resources used by English teachers and students, how and when these were used, and for what purposes. Mode refers to regular set of organising principles and resources (e.g. image, music and gesture are modes) that is an outcome of the cultural shaping of a material. Each mode consists of a set of semiotic resources, which have meaning potential, based on their past uses, and affordances based on their possible uses.

The analysis highlighted how students and teachers co-produce notions of ability, resistance and identity in the classroom through their non-verbal interaction. The classroom displays, artefacts, and the embodied practices of teacher and students were orchestrated to realise versions of English as a school subject. The research showed that teaching English as well as the work of literacy and learning is beyond language alone and demands interpretation of a range of modes, the semiotic resources these make available and the relationships between them.

How modes and semiotic resources feature and are orchestrated in the production of school knowledge is shaped by the social, cultural and historical context. The Three Continents Project[3] (see Battacharly et al. 2007) extended the SEP approach to explore the post-colonial construction of school English in Delhi, Johannesburg and London from a multimodal perspective. The project focuses on how subject English articulates national policies on language, identity and power. It showed that the extent to which students body posture, movement, gesture, gaze and talk are drawn into the production of school English in these different cities is regulated in significantly different ways. These differences speak to particular curriculum notions of English and literacy (as well as citizenship) that are residues and re-makings of the post-colonial construction of English.

Multimodal research has shown the significance of the role of image, and its relationship with writing for the construction of knowledge in textbooks and other learning resources (e.g. Moss 2003; Bezemer and Kress 2008; Walsh 2003). This research has highlighted, among other things, the implications of multimodal design for how students navigate digital and print materials through the creation of reading pathways that rely on pictures, colour and other graphical elements, and layout. Recent work by Bezemer and Kress (2008), for instance, examines contemporary curriculum materials for school English and investigates the gains and losses of different multimodal ensembles for learning (this work is discussed in more detail later in the paper).

The complex multimodal work of becoming literate has been foregrounded by multimodal research through the investigation of students' production of multimodal texts, models and digital multimedia materials in the English classroom (Kress 2003; Kenner 2004; Bearne 2003; Burn and Parker 2003; Pahl and Rowsell 2006; Stein 2007). Multimodal studies of literacy practices have served to highlight the importance of various aspects of English not accounted for within a linguistic approach. These aspects include the spatial organisation and framing of writing on the page, the directionality, shape, size and angle of a script (Kenner 2004), as well as the embodied dimensions of writing (Lancaster 2001), the interaction between image, graphical marks and writing (Pahl 1999), and the role of voice and the body (Franks 2003). These and other studies show the benefits of approaching literacy, writing and reading as multimodal activities (Bearne and Wolstencroft 2007).

The construction of learner identities is another key theme within multimodal studies of literacy and English. Leander and Frank (2006), for example, conducted research on the use of image in the everyday 'digital literacies' of young people with a specific focus on social practices of identity in online and offline contexts. Walsh's study of young people's literacy practices in an English class in New York (Walsh 2007) focused on the development of Web sites suggests that a multimodal account can change what counts as literacy work. While Stein (2007) and Newfield et al. (2005) have shown the relation between identity, literacy and multimodal meaning making through their research with students living in informal settlements in South Africa who used two-dimensional (2D) drawings, writing, three-dimensional (3D) figures, spoken dialogues and performance to create narratives of identity and culture in the school classroom.

As this brief overview suggests multimodality can be applied to investigate many aspects of school English and literacy, including classroom interaction, pedagogic practice and policy, learning and literacy practices, the production of artefacts and issues of identity and culture.

CONTEMPORARY SOCIAL CONDITIONS FOR SCHOOL ENGLISH

Contemporary societies are increasingly theorised as global, fluid and networked (Castells 2001). The emerging knowledge economy is characterised by the accelerated transnational flows of people, information, ideology and materials, and communicational contexts where knowledge is highly situated, visual and multimodal, rapidly changing and more diverse than ever before.

The exploration of the English classroom presented in this paper is underpinned by four thematic social trends that seem directly relevant to forms of literacy and school English: first, the reconfiguration of representational and communicational resources and shapes of knowledge; second, the fluid reconfiguration, indeed some might argue collapsing, boundary between everyday and specialised knowledge; third, the blurring, changing roles between users of knowledge and the producers of knowledge; and fourth, the modularisation of knowledge and attention into bite-size chunks. These contemporary social conditions continuously reconfigure and redesign the communicational landscape to change the texts, practices and the manner in which people learn, the conditions for learning and our ideas about knowledge (Saljo 2004).

Multimodality asks how the use of the facilities of a specific technology—'old' or 'new'—configure image, word and other modes in distinct ways and asks what are the effects for the production of English. These questions provide the starting point for the exploration of the re-mediation of the pedagogic space of subject English by IWB technology presented in the remainder of this paper. More specifically, questions can be asked across sites of school English that have the potential to illuminate the consequences of social change. Such as, how do the representational and communicational facilities made available in the contemporary English classroom effect what English is? For instance, what modes are available, how are they used and for what purposes? What sites of display are introduced into the classroom and how are these become drawn into practices? Do these change the position of teacher and students in the classroom, and if so, what is the effect? What kinds of texts enter the English classroom? How are these mobilised and circulated, by whom and how are these fragmented and connected? What practices are these texts and modal resources a part of? Before addressing these questions through the analysis, the data that underpins this exploration is introduced.

ILLUSTRATIVE CASE-STUDY DATA-SETS

This paper draws on two data-sets of in-depth case studies of the teaching of school English to explore indicative emergent trends in the contemporary English classroom.

The first data set consists of nine in-depth case studies of the teaching of school English in Inner-London schools in 2000 from the Production of School English Project conducted by Kress, Jewitt, Jones and colleagues (Kress et al. 2005). The case studies were conducted in nine London schools selected on the basis that the English department was well established, with classes primarily focused on teaching the curriculum rather than managing student behaviour and that the schools had a high level of student diversity with respect to ethnicity, language and social class. Data included a half-term period of classroom observation of the delivery of a curriculum topic at year Nine (ages 14–15), video recording of lessons, collection of the texts used and produced during these lesson and interviews with the teachers observed and focus group interviews with students. This chapter draws on the analysis of the case studies to provide a comparative background and to support reflection on change.

The second data set the paper draws on nine in-depth case studies of the teaching of school English with IWBs from the (Moss et al. 2007). Each of the schools was selected on the basis that the core subject department was fully equipped with IWBs and that the department was pedagogically robust. Data was collected from Year Nine teaching groups. Data collection in each phase consisted of a week-long period of structured observation of the delivery of a curriculum topic in the core subject area equipped with IWBs, video recording of two lessons from each teaching group, collection of IWB texts used during these lesson sequences and interviews with the head of the subject department, and the teachers observed. In addition, the research team conducted focus group interviews with pupils and administered a pupil survey. For the purpose of this chapter the focus is on the analysis of illustrative examples to generate analytical dimensions and questions concerning the changing relationship of image and writing in the contemporary English classroom.

The analytical discussion uses a multimodal (and historical) perspective to look across the two data sets in order to explore indicative trends emerging for literacy and school English against the backdrop of change in the technologised pedagogic space of the English classroom.

TECHNOLOGY AND THE PEDAGOGIC SPACE
OF THE ENGLISH CLASSROOM

In 2000, at the time of SEP, the majority of families in the UK were not connected to broadband, children's mobile phone usage was costly and low, digital cameras and camcorders were expensive and not widely available to the majority, Google had only been established for just over a year and YouTube and Flickr had yet to be developed. Although some specialist schools and Media/English departments were equipped with digital cameras and editing equipment this was not the case for the majority of English teachers. Technology in the English department classrooms SEP visited and observed was a television, a video player, sometimes an Overhead Projector and occasionally a computer on the teacher's desk (usually silently beaming out stars from a black-and-white screen saver). In short there was little technology in the classroom, and what was available were discrete separate media platforms. Student use of technology was restricted to occasional class trips to the computer suite to word process completed written work for presentation or to research a topic on the school Intranet. The SEP experience of technology in the English classroom in 2000 echoes the findings of broader studies (e.g the ImpaCT2 study, Harrison et al. 2001).

Nearly a decade on, mobile technologies, Web 2.0 and broadband Internet[4] among other technological developments have had a significant effect on the social communicational landscape the majority (though not all) of young people inhabit in the UK. The digital pedagogic space of the English classroom has also changed (albeit to different degrees and at uneven rates). A key factor in this is the use of Interactive Whiteboards (IWBs) in secondary school English. It is difficult to establish the current number of IWBs in secondary schools; there are estimated to be an average of sixteen in an average UK secondary school (BESA 2006), with over 4000 IWBs in London secondary schools and nearly a half of English lessons in London schools being taught using one (Moss et al. 2007).

The IWB provides a touch-sensitive multimodal digital hub in the classroom—a portal to the Internet—a technology that epitomises convergence (Moss et al. 2007). Substantial government funding in 2004/2005 supported the provision of IWBs into core subjects, including English. This policy initiative can be seen as one response that articulates and mediates the changing social conditions outlined earlier. Education policy and commercial discourses that underpin the adoption and expansion of IWBs are informed by the need to make curriculum and school experience relevant, a desire to increase student engagement through interactivity, as well as the pressures of examination and the promise of speed (Jewitt, Moss and Cardini 2007).

SITES OF DISPLAY AND CONFIGURATIONS OF SPACE IN THE ENGLISH CLASSROOM

The introduction of IWB technology to UK secondary schools has had an effect on the sites of display of the English classroom and how the classroom is configured.

In 2000, at the time of SEP, it was common for English teachers not to have a desk, although some had a desk at the front or to the side of the classroom.[5] During the lessons we observed English teachers adopted a wide range of teaching positions in the classroom. The technical requirements of IWBs remediate and regulate this diversity. An IWB needs to be accompanied by a desk for the computer it is connected to, and this needs to be placed at the front-side of the classroom. The once-roaming English teacher now needs to return to this desk (i.e. to the front of class) to operate the computer. Schools that have invested in wireless peripherals such as slates (which enable the IWB to be operated from any point in the classroom) have unlocked the teacher from the front of the classroom and offer new possibilities for the design and control of pedagogic space. The IWB can have a homogenising effect on the classroom, in that it reduces the differences in the design and use of space between school subjects such as English and Science.

These social and pedagogic effects are shaped by the requirements of the technology as well as decisions that stem from the difficulty of embedding new technologies in existing teaching practice. For instance, several schools that participated in the IWB project removed all blackboards and non-interactive whiteboards from their classrooms to 'force' teachers to use the IWB. In addition, technicians who fit the IWB now have a new normative effect on the classroom, wanting to know '[w]here is the teacher's wall'.

Sites of display are not only media, they are sites of social engagement in which social interactions are subsumed to prior social conditions (Scollon and Wong-Scollon 2003). It is therefore important to note that the IWB was initially designed as a presentational tool for business. This provenance is embedded in its presentational facilities. The technology often requires the classroom lights to be dimmed or the curtains to be drawn to reduce glare and enhance images. In response students frequently take up audience mode in what becomes a pseudo-cinematic experience while the teacher performs virtually tied to the front of the classroom by the need to move through a series of slides. The IWB can also add to the diversity and complexity of the classroom with respect to sites of display, as it can create two different spaces—the IWB, a flipchart or (non-interactive) Whiteboard.

These sites have different material and social affordances. Time, for instance, is configured quite differently: the IWB offers a sequence of screens that are used through a lesson (each of which can be saved) while the (non-interactive) Whiteboard offers one 'screen', which can have a permanence in a lesson but is in the longer term temporary. Furthermore the relationship between the IWB, a textbook or worksheet, individual computers and students' textbooks needs to be considered: in particular, the question of how does this increasingly complex and rich semiotic landscape effect the practices of interpreting information and making connections across these 'sites of display'.

Thinking of screens as artefacts that produce social occasions and make particular social interactions possible (Jones, 2005; Scollon and Wong-Scollon, 2003) draws attention to what teachers and students in the English classroom actually *do* with sites of display.

WRITING AND TYPOGRAPHY IN THE CONTEMPORARY CLASSROOM

As noted above, IWB technology reorganises classroom time and space. One effect of this is to remediate writing as a mode in the English classroom: changing what writing is, how it features in the lesson and how it is configured with other modes.

Perhaps a historical comparison is useful in making this point. Writing featured in the learning materials, class work and course work observed in SEP (in 2000). However there was a general avoidance of extended writing, and teachers' expressed concerns about the student's competence in writing and their sense of its lack of salience to their students. This trend appears to have gained strength in the contemporary English classroom; writing persists but in short bursts of activity including the annotation of texts, the filling in of a missing word, the collecting up of thoughts written on post-it notes, brainstorming and mind-maps. The facilities of the IWB do not easily support coherent and extensive writing.

Written, prepared PowerPoint slides and writing in real time in the class-room are, this paper suggests, emerging as two discreet forms of writing within pedagogic practice with an IWB, further mediated by the choice of typographic fonts. Many teachers prepare PowerPoint presentations for the classroom. As these texts (or texts on the Internet) are presented to the whole class, teachers annotate them by hand (e.g. to highlight examples of persuasive writing). Increasingly, handwriting (and handwritten style fonts) take on the quality of immediacy and responsiveness that fonts associated with type does not. For example, throughout a lesson on Macbeth's solilo-quy the teacher used a series of PowerPoint slides to display the text—Mac-beth's Soliloquy. The text was discussed and annotated by the teacher in real time. In this and other instances in which a typed text was annotated distinct kinds of activity and distributions of 'authorship' were realised through the contrast of typographic fonts (summarised in Table 11.1).

The work of the teacher is represented in type writing and the scribing of the collective work/voice of the class in the handwriting. The typed writ-ing refers to a matter of evidence (e.g. this is Macbeth's Soliloquy), and the handwriting attends to responses, interpretations and meaning. (A teach-er's choice of a font such as Apple Chancery—which mimics handwriting—can be seen as an attempt to diffuse this distinction and collapse the time scales of preparation and delivery)[6]. Thus an association is built between type writing and canonical English on the one hand and handwriting and interpretation on the other. Type writing becomes seen as authority and handwriting as the personal and individual. These two distinct forms of writing and uses of font in the English classroom maintain the permanent fixedness of the canon against the ephemeral and temporary character of interpretation. In this way the teacher's choice of mode, form of writing, and selection of font are key for the production of English. How these forms of writing are configured in relation to each other is then a clue to the work that is expected of the student.

Table 11.1   Comparison of Features of Typed Writing and Handwriting on the IWB in the UK Subject English Classroom

Comparative features	Typed written	Handwriting
Writing tool	Keyboard	Hand and stylus
Time	Prepared	Real-time
	Permanent/Fixed/Recorded	Temporary/Ephemeral
Location	Out of classroom/Lesson	In classroom/Lesson
Authorship	Teacher	Teacher scribing students
	Authority	Personal/Individual
Focus	Evidence/ Canonical text	Interpretation/ Response

VISUAL AND MULTIMODAL STARTING POINTS FOR ENGLISH

Increasingly it is image that provides the starting point for an English lesson. Teachers often show a clip of digital video (often via U-Tube)[7], display an image to offer a route into a concept—often downloaded from the Internet—use PowerPoint presentations to make their argument, visually annotate a text, or connect to a webpage. The use of image is also prevalent in students' work in the English classroom, with the use of clipart, digital photographs—taken by the student or downloaded from the Internet—and the design of PowerPoint presentations both in class and out of school for homework.

While subject English has always had a relationship with image, the specific ways in which writing, image and other non-linguistic modes feature in the classroom appears to be changing in ways that are significant: introducing a poem via an image on the IWB, for example, or using images to explore symbolism or narrative. In a lesson on Macbeth, a teacher displayed a photograph downloaded from the Internet from the Royal Shakespeare Company (RSC) archive, showing Macbeth and Lady Macbeth on the IWB to explore the notion of tragedy. He asked the students to suggest who the two characters are, what they might be saying to one another and how they might be feeling. The students wrote their responses on post-it notes that were collected by the teacher and stuck on the IWB as they were read aloud. These visual starting points offered relatively open ways into the production of school English that are connected with the students' experiences of imagery, and in the case of Macbeth the drama of soap opera were woven back into the lesson. The concept of tragedy was slowly built up by the use of image to prompt discussion.

VISUAL TEXTS AND RESOURCES

The ease and availability of images from the Internet and elsewhere is, this paper argues, supporting a re-making of the relationships between image and writing[8]. The classical relationships between image and word is discussed as either: 'anchorage' (Barthes 1977) in which the writing helps to tie down the meaning of the image by helping the reader choose what is to be noticed; 'reinforcement' through repetition in which image and word do 'the same' thing; or 'elaboration' in which image and word extend the meaning of one another. However, these classifications no longer capture the full struggle between word and image in the contemporary context.

Recent work by Bezemer and Kress (2008), for instance, examines contemporary curriculum materials for school English and investigates the gains and losses of different multimodal ensembles for learning. It sets out to provide an account of the changes to the design of these learning resources and of their epistemological and social-pedagogic significance.

Through investigation of the relationship between image, writing, action and layout they show that image and layout are increasingly meshed in the construction of content. This is exemplified by their survey of a sample 300 pages of textbooks from across 1930s, 1980s and 2000 that found that the average number of images per page in English textbooks has increased exponentially (by more than 3000%). Their analysis also shows that the quality and function of image or animation in English textbooks is in a state of change. Image and word frequently attend to discrete aspects of meaning with images or as object of reflection. Increasingly concepts are introduced, established and analysed visually, and writing is brought into new relationships with, or even exchanged for, visual and multimodal forms of representation (Jewitt 2002, 2006).

The IWB enables connection to a wide range of texts, sources and so on. The use of links and hyperlinks to connect out to Channel 4 TV, advertising companies, holiday Web sites, YouTube and other video sites connects different domains directly into the English classroom—including texts from the everyday lives of students, commercial texts and popular media culture. In addition, previously discrete texts for study (e.g. novels, poems etc) have now been made available online. In the process printed text is repackaged with image, animation and sound, digitally annotated, fragmented and connected via hyperlinks to author biographies and other historically and socially relevant knowledge—to become part of a larger web of texts. This diversifies the kinds of texts that enter and circulate across the English classroom, and serves to connect English with the technologies and experiences that students engage with out of school.

One effect of this is to create connections across previously distinct boundaries of education and other spaces, such as the commercial sector—making 'third spaces'—and pedagogising the everyday. This expands the frame of the classroom (although not always in ways that may be positive) as well as what is legitimated and not legitimated as part of the construction of curriculum knowledge and further remakes the authority of texts and unsettles the boundaries and forms of knowledge. This has implications for what is to be learnt (i.e. what English is), as well as literacy practices such as reading and writing, pedagogic practices and the subjectivity of students. In short, it changes the semiotic landscape of the English classroom, even though these changes vary across an uneven terrain.

VISUAL DISCURSIVE SPACES

The IWB can be used to open up visual discursive spaces and in doing so support the reconfiguration of notions of authority. This example of an English lesson on the use of image and sounds in poetry is taken from the IWB data. The poem used in the lesson is, *The Blessing* by Imtiaz Dharker, which is studied for examination in the module 'Poems from Other Cultures'. The teacher's starting point for the analysis of the poem is an illustration that accompanies the poem—a drawing of children dancing and playing around a burst water pipe.

The discussion of the image by teacher and students centred on the question of what does it show and what might the poem be about. The class brainstormed the title of the poem, and the teacher produced a spider-diagram on the IWB to filter and organise their comments. She then showed a series of photographs on the IWB of objects related to the poem, including a congregation and a seedpod. The students were asked to match these images to the words and given the task of matching to lines in the poem. Later in the lesson the teacher displayed a poem made by a student that she had scanned and made digital; this was then discussed and annotated.

The resources and experiences that the teacher draws on in this interaction are different than if she were to start this discussion with the poem as a written text. This reveals, this paper argues, a shift in authority, a connection with a variety of experiences and knowledge outside of the canon. In doing so it offers new ways into the poem (and new connections for English as a subject). What also matters here for English is that the canonical text—the poem—is itself disappearing—becoming visual and fragmented (although these new fragments are perhaps being woven into a richer cloth of experience).

Anchoring Meaning

As the above example demonstrates, the visual is no longer an adjunct illustration to writing; rather, image and word are integrated and image is presented as a first step in accessing the effect of language, with image often coming first. The teacher presents the visual and visual imagery in language as having a *factual* basis from which students can understand the meaning of a poem. The matching exercise presents the reading of poetry as a visual and linguistic process—a multimodal process. Through her use of the texts the teacher reshapes the imagery of language as the relationship of word and image in a text. The imaginative work of language and imagery that in the past teachers would have required students to analyse through speech is now mediated via the multimodal potentials of new technologies to be materialised in a visual representation. In short, what English is, what is to be learnt and how it is to be learnt—the practices of text making, writing and reading—are reshaped by the legitimated availability of image and other modes in the English classroom. In addition, what is involved in and demanded of the learner is altered.

The move to the visual provides different anchors for meaning. The SEP data includes this same teacher (described above using an IWB to teaching a poem) in 2000 using an overhead projector (OHP) to teach a poem. There are several marked differences that suggest an emerging trend or shift in meaning that is key for thinking about subject English in the contemporary classroom. The teacher uses image as a starting point for the poem—rather than writing. Rather than using the Oxford English Dictionary (OED), the teacher uses images to define the words she considers difficult for her students (e.g. congregation, cracked seedpod) rather than the OED. The teacher displays the poem in fragments broken up across the IWB screens—words, lines and the poem title slowly leading to the poem spread across several screens. This resonates with the teacher's use of the poem in the 2000 data and yet it differs in important ways: in the 2000 lesson, she displayed the whole poem on an OHP transparency, which then got slowly carved up through the process of interrogation.

Finally, the teacher worked with the whole class and the students interacted with the meaning of the poem on the IWB from the start of the lesson, for example matching image and word and answering questions. This contrasts with the teacher's use of the poem in 2000 when a strong boundary was made between reading the poem and analysing it. This boundary was realised in how the poem was presented and how the classroom work was organised. First, the teacher (and the students) read the whole poem aloud (without discussion). Second, half way through the lesson the students were organised into small groups and given a photocopy of a section of the poem to interpret, and each group fed-back their ideas later in the lesson. In the contemporary context the boundaries between the work of reading and analysing, and the work of teacher and student were remade.

Modularisation

Digital texts often interrupt, fragment and unsettle 'traditional' genres of textbooks, students' texts, worksheets and other types of learning resources that circulate in the English classroom. A key aspect of this is the modularisation of knowledge, which can be seen as a gradual move affecting all media (Manovich 2005). The textbook form, for instance, is changing with respect to how information is organised into bite-size panels—chunks of information related through the mode of layout. Teachers regularly open an English lesson with the use of video clips (from YouTube, the BBC learning zone and other online video resources)—malleable and flexible episodes—to be inserted into teacher discourse. In the move from page to screen in the adaptation of a book to the screen (e.g. to a CD-Rom or web resource) information is reorganised into new 'chunks' across screens (Jewitt 2002, 2006).

For example, one written page may be distributed across four screen pages—in which each paragraph becomes separated from the others—and placed alongside image. This serves to break up and simultaneously remake the original narrative by building new connections and relationships through the re-organisation of the text. This modularisation of information can also be seen in teachers' design of learning resources: for example, teachers' the use of images from the Internet, manipulated and rearranged alongside written or audio elements taken from a variety of sources or more the subtle breaking up of a text across IWB screens (e.g. the poem in the case above).

This modularisation process is, this paper argues, a pervasive response to broad social conditions: a material realisation of the management of information and attention across the curriculum that echoes a managerial discourse of effectiveness. This bite-size modularity also resonates with the pressures and concerns of schools, such as examination, and concerns about students' attention spans and engagement. In addition it marks a more general move to deliver content across a range of media formats, including mobile phones. This reshaping of knowledge into small units structures *how* young people and teachers engage with curriculum knowledge in the English classroom.

Hybrid Textual Spaces

New digital spaces for display and collaboration can be created through the use of IWBs in combination with visualisers and scanners (Moss et al. 2007; Mavers. 2008). Several teachers in the IWB case studies used scanners to enhance the presentational and interactive potential of the IWB. These technologies enable teachers to scan a student text and display it easily and immediately on the IWB. This enables student work to be shared and become the focus of discussion. Further students work once digitised can be manipulated and annotated. For example, in the poetry lesson discussed earlier the teacher scanned and displayed a poem made by a student. This was then discussed and annotated by the teacher in response to students' comments.

Through this process a new kind of shared text is created, which, this paper argues, can effect the configurations of authorship and authority in the classroom (the features of this text are summarised in Table 11.2).

The teacher without an IWB could ask a student to read aloud their text, however, this would not display the text in its entirety to the class. Speech could not present the layout of the text, any accompanying images nor the use of fonts and headings. Only some texts can be shared by reading them aloud. Reading a text aloud is also a transduction of the original text and therefore a transformation and partial. When a student text is digitised and displayed on the IWB, it is (to some extent) no longer a student text, nor is it a teacher text. Rather it is a co-constructed text—a kind of hybrid text—and as such it creates and occupies a third space in the classroom.

The displayed student text moves from a student's exercise book—a personal semi-private space—to the IWB, a shared public space. It moves from a student space into a teacher space in the classroom and in doing so it remakes the space of the board. This also serves to re-orientate the relations of teacher and student to the production of knowledge in the classroom (although the teacher remains in control of what gets onto the board). As the

Table 11.2   Comparison of the Features of a Student Text in Their Exercise Book and Displayed on an IWB

Comparative features	Student text in exercise book	Student text displayed on an IWB
Authorship	Individual (Student)	Collaborative (students and teacher)
Location	Exercise book	IWB screen
Size	A4	Enlarged to fit screen
Medium	Paper	Digital
Potential to manipulate	None	Can be resized etc
Space	Semi-private/ Personal	Public
Audience	Teacher	Whole class and teacher
Practices the text is inserted into (and enacted through)	Possibly 'read aloud' Discussion Marking and grading by teacher	Display Discussion Annotation by class Marking and grading by teacher

text is annotated the authorship of the student is overlaid with the comments and ideas of others, transforming the individual text to a collaborative text. This text is further transformed by the discourse space it is inserted into and the practices that it becomes embedded within (ie. previously the students work would have been read primarily by the teacher and graded). The move of student texts to the IWB therefore has implications for authorship and pedagogic practices and relations in the English classroom.

Changing Practices

Some new practices are emerging in the English classroom as a consequence of the changes in landscape of the UK subject English classroom: specifically, as a consequence of the changes described in this paper in how image and writing feature in lessons, changing notions of authorship and shifts in the authority of the text (and teacher). These include an emergent pedagogic use of the distinction between typed writing and handwriting; visual forms of annotation employing colour and visual symbols; new forms of display of student texts and artefacts; the embedding of video and audio files in classroom discourse; and visual argumentation and discursive processes.

The discursive organisation and regulation of the classroom is, as this paper has shown, re-shaped (to different degrees) by the introduction and use of IWBs. In addition teachers are involved in the design of pedagogic resources for the IWB. Making teaching resources is a key practice for UK teachers, and this activity persists in the digital environment of the contemporary classroom.[9] Teachers' design of digital IWB resources is key to the production of school English: how teachers select, adapt and arrange modes, design interactivity and set pace in the digital materials they make and the ways they bring these into action in the classroom plays a central role in shaping what English is.

Teachers are expert in the production of worksheets and there is a long history of the production of print-based resources. Few traditions, established practices, expertise and stable genres for digital pedagogic resources however are currently available to teachers.[10] This raises important issues for how teachers harness the multimodal potentials and facilities of the IWB to teaching (see Jewitt, Moss and Cardini 2007 for a fuller discussion). The increasing use of multimodal texts in the English classroom also has an effect on the repertoire of practices that students are required to engage in, raising questions of what is to be attended to, and fundamental questions for what it means to read and write in a multimodal landscape (Jewitt 2005; Marsh 2005; Kress 2003).

Regulation of Time

The use of IWB technologies reconfigures the time, space, rhythm and flow of lessons, as discussed earlier regarding the preparation of PowerPoint texts and the modularisation of curriculum knowledge. Time as pace is realised through the resources (texts) used on the IWB. The amount of information that can be held on the space of the screen is less than can be held on a blackboard; thus, each breaks information up differently. In addition the narrative trail left across a series of blackboards is removed when a teacher moves through a sequence of IWB slides. This shifts control of the narrative trail of a lesson from students to teacher (a control that can be exasperated by a presentational use of PowerPoint).

The flow that is possible with an IWB enables teachers to move between texts and formats easily and quickly: from PowerPoint to Digital video clip, to the Internet and back again. There is little lesson 'down time' or 'wastage'. This has some positive effects. It also raises questions for how time is regulated and managed in teachers' pedagogic design of digital resources, including what can be left open, what needs to be closed and how can space for thinking be designed into a text.

CONCLUSION

This paper has shown how the changing pedagogic landscape of subject English classrooms in the UK is being reshaped as a consequence of social and technological change. Through the use of the IWB as an exemplar technology, it has highlighted the significance of these changes for the teaching and learning of subject English. In particular it has shown the effects of the changing representational and communicational facilities made available via technologies, on forms of knowledge and how these are mobilised and circulated in the contemporary landscape of school English. The paper has paid particular attention to how image and writing feature in the contemporary English classroom. Specifically, it has used illustrative case study examples to explore the changing role of writing, and it has been suggested that two modal forms of writing (typed and handwritten) are emerging with distinct pedagogic functions.

The paper argues that increasingly image provides the starting point for subject English, and highlighted the new role for the visual in school English with respect to how visual resources feature in the classroom and the discursive spaces these are employed to create. Further, the paper has attempted to show the changing relationship between images and writing in the English classroom, for instance, how the visual is emerging as a resource to anchor meaning. The effects of the modularisation of knowledge and the regulation of time on the production of school English were also briefly discussed and explored via the examples presented in the paper.

Throughout, the paper contextualised the exploration of IWB use in English within a discussion of how multimodal perspectives have been applied to school English. It also attempted to place this exploration within the broader social conditions that underpin the contemporary production of English, such as modularisation, managerial discourses within education regarding the regulation of time and a historical sense of the change in technologies available to school English in the UK over the past decade.

The re-visualisation of the pedagogic space of the classroom described in this paper is indicative of the emerging changing roles for writing and image in the English classroom rather than a rejection of writing. To this extent school English can be taken as one example that is indicative of a broader paradigm shift happening more generally in the contemporary communicational landscape. This thereby demonstrates the interconnectedness of the social and cultural context of school English, technologies in the classroom, and the production of curriculum knowledge.

NOTES

1. This data is drawn from 'The Production of School English Project' (*ESRC ref*: R000238463) undertaken by G. Kress, C. Jewitt, K. Jones, J. Bourne, A. Franks, J. Hardcastle and E. Reid.
2. This data is drawn from 'Interactive Whiteboards, Pedagogy and Pupil Performance Evaluation' project data undertaken by G. Moss, C. Jewitt, A. Cardini, Armstrong and F. Castle (funded by Department for Education and Skills [DEFS]).
3. The Three Continents Project is an ongoing collaboration between Carey Jewitt, Pippa Stein, Denise Newfield, Yvonne Reid, Rimli Battacharly and Snehlatta Gupta (funded initially by Association of Common Wealth Universities).
4. The UK government National statistics show 61% of households were connected to the Internet in 2007, an increase of 36% since 2002 http://www.statistics.gov.uk/CCI/nugget.asp?ID=8 (accessed 5.08.08).

5. This contrasts with the Science Classroom where teachers' desks were at the front of the classroom, and there was a distinct separation in the layout of the room between 'teacher space' and 'student space' (see Kress et al 2001).
6. I am grateful to Jackie Marsh, Sheffield University, for drawing the issue of font choice to my attention in her comment on an earlier version of this paper.
7. I am grateful to John Yandell, Institute of Education, for this observation made of Beginner Teachers work in London Schools.
8. The relationship between image and writing is historically situated, with the visual imagery of Medieval times as complex as now but differently articulated as related to the social conditions.
9. Over 70% of London teachers make their own digital resources for use with the IWB (Moss et al, 2007).
10. Although a range of online resource banks aimed at teachers using IWBs exist, the range is limited, and quality is not regulated

REFERENCES

Barthes, R. (1977) *Image, Music, Text*, London: Fontana.
Battacharly, R., Gupta, S., Jewitt, C., Newfield, D., Reid, Y. and Stein, P. (2007) The Policy-Practice Nexus in English Classrooms in Delhi, Johannesburg and London: Teachers and the Textual Cycle in Special, *TESOL Quarterly*, Autumn 2007.
Bearne, E. (2003) 'Rethinking literacy: communication, representation and text.' *Literacy* 37(3): 98–103
Bearne, E., and Wolstencroft, H. (2007) *Visual Approaches to Teaching Writing*, London: Paul Chapman Publishing and UKLA.
BESA (2006) ICT in UK State Schools 2006—summary report, London: BESA Available online at <http://www.besa.org.uk/besa/documents/grab/BESA_ICT_2006_summary.pdf> accessed 14 January 2008.
Bezemer, J., and Kress, G. (2008) 'Writing in multimodal texts: a social semiotic account of designs for learning.' *Written Communication* 25(2) (Special Issue on Writing and New Media): pp. 166–195.
Burn, A., and Parker, D. (2003) 'Tiger's big plan: multimodality and moving image.' In Jewitt, C., and Kress, G. eds. *Multimodal Literacy*, New York: Peter Lang: pp. 56–72.
Castells, M. (2001) *The Internet Galaxy*, Oxford: Oxford University press.
Dharker, I. (1989) 'The Blessing' in *Purdah*. Oxford: Oxford University Press.
Harrison, C., Fisher, T., Haw, K., Lewin, C., McFarlance, A., Mavers, D., Scrimshaw, P. and Somekh, B. (2001) *ImpaCT2*, London: Department for Education and Skills.
Franks, A. (2003) 'Palmer's kiss: Shakespeare, school drama and semiotics.' In Jewitt, C., and Kress, G. eds. *Multimodal Literacy*, New York: Peter Lang: 3: pp. 155–172.
Jewitt, C. (2008) 'Multimodal Classroom Research (2008).' *AERA Review of Research in Education*, Vol 32: 241–267.
——— (2006) *Technology, Literacy, and Learning: A Multimodal Approach*, London: Routledge.
——— (2005) 'Multimodal 'reading' and 'writing' on screen.' *Discourse: Studies in the Cultural Politics of Education* (special edition 'Digital childhood and youth: new texts, new literacies') 26(3): 315–332.
——— (2002) 'The move from page to screen: the multimodal reshaping of school English.' *Journal of Visual Communication* 1(2): 171–196.

Jewitt, C., Moss, G. and Cardini, A. (2007) 'Pace, interactivity and multimodality in teacher design of texts for IWBs.' *Learning, Media and Technology Autumn* 32(3): 302–318.

Jones, R. (2005) 'You show me yours, I'll show you mine.' *Visual Communication* 4(1): 69–92.

Kenner, C. (2004) *Becoming Biliterate: Young Children Learning Different Writing Systems*, Stoke on Trent: Trentham Books.

Kress, G. (2003) *Literacy in the New Media Age*, London: Routledge.

Kress, G., Jewitt, C., Bourne, J., Franks, A., Hardcastle, J., Jones, K. and Reid, E. (2005) *English in Urban Classrooms: A Multimodal Perspective on Teaching and Learning*, London: Routledge Farmer.

Kress, G., Jewitt, C., Ogborn, J. and Tsatsarelis, C. (2001) *Multimodal Teaching and Learning*, London: Continuum Press.

Leander, K., and Frank, A. (2006) 'The aesthetic production and distribution of image/subjects among online youth.' *E-Learning* 3(2): 185–206.

Lancaster, L. (2001) 'Staring at the page: the functions of Gaze in a young child's interpretation of symbolic forms.' *Journal of Early Childhood Literacy* 1(2): 131–152.

Manovich, L. (2005) 'Remixability and modularity.' Available online at <http://www.manovich.net> (accessed 14 January 2008)

Marsh, J., ed. (2005) *Popular Culture, New Media and Digital Literacy in Early Childhood*, London: Routledge/Falmer.

Mavers, D. (2008) 'The visualizer as a pedagogic site' Presented at Pedagogies for Interactive Technologies: IWBs and Visualizers Seminar, WLE Centre for Excellence, Institute of Education, London, February 2009.

Moss, G. (2003) 'Putting the text back into practice: Junior age fiction as objects of design.' In Jewitt, C., and Kress, G. eds. *Multimodal Literacy*, New York, Peter Lang: pp. 73–87.

Moss, G., Jewitt, C., Levacic, R., Armstrong, V. Cardini, A., and Castle, F. (2007) *The Interactive Whiteboards, Pedagogy and Pupil Performance Evaluation* (Research report 816), London: Department for Education and Skills.

Newfield, D., Andrew, D., Stein, P. and Maungedzo, R. (2005) 'No number can describe how good it was: assessment issues in the multimodal classroom.' *Assessment in Education: Principles, Policy and Practice* 10(1): 61–81.

Office of National Statistics (2010). UK Government National Statistics http://www.statistics.gov.uk/CCI/nugget.asp?ID=8 accessed 5 August 2010.

Pahl, K. (1999) *Transformations: Children's Meaning Making in Nursery Education*, Stoke on Trent: Trentham Books.

Pahl, K., and Rowsell, J., eds. (2006) *Travel Notes from the New Literacy Studies: Instances of Practice*, Clevedon: Multilingual Matters Ltd.

Saljo, R. (2004) 'Learning and technologies, people and tools in co-ordinated activities' *International Journal of Educational Research* 41: 489–494.

Scollon, R., and Wong-Scollon, S. (2003) *Discourses in Place,* London: Routledge.

Stein, P. (2007) *Multimodal Pedagogies in Diverse Classrooms: Representation, Rights and Resources*, London: Routledge.

Walsh, C. (2007) 'Creativity as capital in the literacy classroom: youth as multimodal designers.' *Literacy* 41(2): 79–85.

Walsh, M. (2003) 'Reading' pictures: what do they reveal? Young children's reading of visual texts. *Literacy* 37(3): 123–130

12 Picture Books for Young Children of Different Ages

The Changing Relationships between Images and Words

Peter Wignell

INTRODUCTION

In this chapter I examine the relationship between written text and images in children's picture books aimed at young children of different age groups. The objectives of this examination are first to identify any systematic pattern or patterns of change in the relationship between text and images as the age of the children the books are aimed at increases and second, to consider the implications of any pattern of change with particular regard to how picture books help initiate young children into literate practice.

For many children initiation into literate practices comes from multi-semiotic texts: children's picture books. There is a wealth of research on adult/child reading practice both in the home and in early childhood schooling, such as Brice Heath (1983), Wells (1985), Meek (1988), Williams (1995, 1998), Torr (2004, 2007), Unsworth and Chan (2008), Unsworth (2006a) and Unsworth (2006b) and on various aspects of the semiotics of images and on the relationships between images and words in different text types, for example, Royce (1998), Martinec and Salway (2005), Liu and O'Halloran (2009), Lim (2006) and in children's picture books Lim (2002), Painter, (2007) and Wignell (2008). However, there is little, if anything, on changes in the relationship between words and images as the age of the intended audience increases. Or as Meek (1988: 5) states: '. . . books are, as the saying goes, taken as read in discussions about reading teaching.' This chapter attempts to at least partly bridge that gap.

Discussion of the linguistic text in the examples used is based on Systemic Functional Linguistics (Halliday 1985a, 1985b, 1994, 2004; Martin 1984, 1997: Martin and Rose 2003). Discussion of the images in the example texts is based on O'Toole's *The Language of Displayed Art* (1994/2010) and on Kress and van Leeuwen's *Reading Images: The Grammar of Visual Design* (1996). Following Halliday (1978, 1985), both O'Toole and Kress and van Leeuwen use a metafunctional approach to the analysis of images. Halliday proposes that meaning can be categorised into three metafunctions: the interpersonal metafunction, the ideational metafunction and the textual metafunction. These metafunctions are realised simultaneously. Interpersonally a text encodes roles and attitudes, creating a relationship between addressor and addressee. Simultaneously, these roles, relationships and attitudes are established ideationally with regard to some content or idea being talked about, depicted or enacted. Also simultaneously the textual metafunction organises and coordinates the meanings created by the other two to create text that links coherently to co-text and context. However, O'Toole labels his functional categories *modal, representational* and *compositional,* but states that these functions equate with Halliday's *interpersonal, ideational* and *textual* metafunctions (O'Toole 1994: 5). In the discussion that follows I have opted to use the terms *interpersonal, ideational* and *textual.* Where there is slippage the terms in the pairs *modal* and *interpersonal, representational* and *ideational* and *compositional* and *textual* can be taken as being synonymous.

The data for this study comes mostly from my young daughter's library. She has just over 300 books given to her by her parents, relatives and friends. I also used samples of books shown on Web sites, which sell, promote and/or discuss children's books. As a starting point for classification, I used categories based on age appropriateness on children's book websites. For example Huggies Book Club has more than a thousand books categorised for ages between birth and five years. The description of each book typically features both the cover and a sample page or pages. I did not take their categorisation as absolute but I used it as a guide. Some books overlap age categories and appear in adjacent age categories. In this chapter I have restricted my discussion to fiction/story books.

CHANGES IN THE RELATIONSHIP BETWEEN IMAGES AND WRITTEN TEXT ACCORDING TO AGE

I will now discuss a series of samples from picture books for children of different ages in order of ascending age. The age categories I am using are newborn to six months, six months to twelve months, twelve months to twenty-four months, twenty-four months to thirty-six months, thirty-six months to sixty months. I have selected for discussion typical examples of books suggested for each age group.

Books for Very Young Children (Zero to Six Months)

There are very few picture books that consist of pictures only. Kress and van Leeuwen suggest, in their discussion of Dick Bruna's *On My Walk* (Bruna 1988), that in this particular book the presence of images only allows for the 'story' to be told with many different wordings (Kress and van Leeuwen 1996: 26–31). They suggest that 'the 'readings' that parents produce when they read *On My Walk* with their children may all be different, yet these different readings will necessarily have common elements, deriving from their common basis—the elements included in the image and the way these elements are compositionally brought together (Kress and van Leeuwen 1996: 27). In short, while there are quite a few different wordings possible, the number is not infinite. The number of potential wordings is constrained to a degree by the images. So what we have is an oral text, or rather, multiple oral texts, all of which depend on images in order to make sense in the context of the book reading.

This is one possibility. Another can be found in an example like the *Baby Touch Cot Book* (Land 2007), shown in Figure 12.1a below. The 'book' is printed on soft cloth and folds out into a strip of panels. Each panel offers a different sensory experience: texture, sounds, reflection and surprise (through use of a flap). The colours are bright and fully saturated. There is a left-to-right scanning path shown by the curved parallel lines running semi-diagonally across all panels for the length of the strip. The left-to-right orientation is also indicated by the direction the animals are facing. The ladybird, the bird, the snail and the bee all have their heads/eyes facing to the right: they are looking where they are going.

The images do not tell a 'story' as such. However, all panels are linked through the scanning path, and they are all images of things familiar in a garden (and in countless other picture books): ladybird, bird, snail, dragonfly, bee, and flowers. Although a particular narrative is not necessarily indicated by the sequence and content of the panels, it would, following Kress and van Leeuwen (1996), be possible to use the images to tell a number of stories in different words and in different genres. The primary focus, however, is interpersonal: on physical and visual engagement with the text.

Although the primary focus is interpersonal, the textual metafunction is also important. The composition of the images in a long strip with a curved scanning path and the head on the right-hand end of almost all the animals orients children to the left to right orientation of written English. Once a child has learned to recognise objects and beings in images, she or he can do two things: use the images to get the 'book' right side up and use the knowledge that, generally, where the head goes the body follows to work out direction of movement. This left-to-right orientation would also be facilitated interpersonally by the adult reader using a finger to point or trace the direction of the scanning path.

In books for very young children, when words are introduced, they tend to be low in number and dependent on the images. That is, the image provides the context to understand the words in. The words don't make sense without the images. The examples displayed in Figure 12.1b from *Bouncy Lamb* (Church 1999) show a selection of panels. The panels are connected only through repetition. Each panel/page consists of a central image and words above and below the image. The words consist in each case of a name: *Bouncy Lamb*, *Hungry Horse*, *Cuddly Cat* at the top of the page above the image and linked to the image by juxtaposition and a command in imperative mood: *stroke*

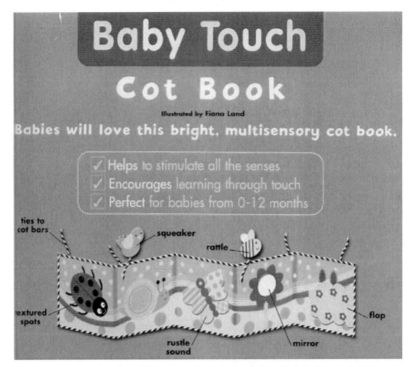

(a) Promotional figure for *Baby Touch Cot Book* (Land, 2007).

(b) *Bouncy Lamb*, two panels (Church, 1999).

Figure 12.1 Newborn to six months.

her head, flick his tail, rub her tum at the bottom of the page underneath the image. The images contain textures to encourage interaction. Hungry Horse's tail is made of wool and can be grabbed and pulled, and Cuddly Cat has a furry tummy. The name of the animal appears to function similarly to Barthes' principle of anchorage, where the written text accompanying the image

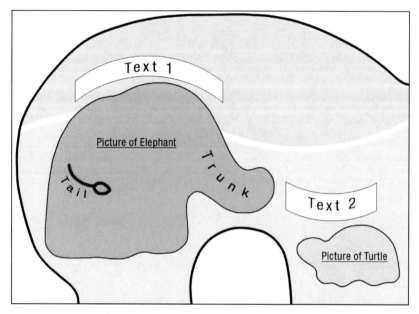

(c)   Panel from *Big Elephant and Little Elephant* (Barker, 1998).

Figure 12.1   Newborn to six months.

helps identify one meaning where without it many interpretations would be possible (Barthes 1977: 38–41). That is, without the name, the picture is a stylised generic picture of a horse. With the name added, it is a picture of a particular, individual horse. There appears, however, to be a kind of reverse anchorage as well where the image gives contextual meaning to the words. For example, *Hungry Horse* and *Cuddly Cat* do not make sense without the images as support. The commands function to draw the adult reader's attention to the textures in the images and invite/command the adult to show the child how to interact physically with the book. Colours are solid, bright and fully saturated. The book is printed on cloth, facilitating engagement through both hands and mouth because it is both soft and not dangerous. The interpersonal metafunction is foregrounded.

There is no narrative structure to the text. Each panel is self-contained and is more or less a repetition of the same thing: the name of an animal, its picture and an instruction to engage with some texture attached to the picture. There is potential for an adult reader to start to build for a child the principle that you start reading at the top of the page and work your way down (working from left to right if you are reading English and many other languages). While the image is central and interpersonally the most salient thing on the page, there is potential for an adult to point out the words, first above and then below the image and then use the instruction to reorient the child to the texture on the image.

In the example from *Big Elephant and Little Elephant* (Barker 1998) in Figure 12.1c the words are linked directly to images by reference. The first clause (*This is Little Elephant*) introduces the main participant. Little Elephant is introduced as a specific individual with a name, not as 'a little elephant'. The image is necessary to retrieve the identity of Little Elephant. The words make little sense without the image.

The colours were originally saturated and bright, although the image below shows fading from the effects of multiple washings. The book is printed on cloth in the shape of an elephant. A Little Elephant, which makes a squeaky sound when squeezed, is attached by string and fits in the gap between the legs of the big elephant so that, when closed, the book is literally Big Elephant and Little Elephant.

When the book is opened, a left-to-right and top-down reading path is immediately indicated. Little Elephant's head/eyes face forwards to the right, as do his trunk and tail, and the words, printed above the characters, are curved and follow the white line dividing land from sky across the upper middle of the page. The first sentence on the page is higher than the second. In addition to this in *Big Elephant and Little Elephant* an embryonic narrative structure (orientation ^ complication(s) ^ resolution) is beginning to emerge (See Martin and Plum 1997; Labov and Waletzky 1967). Little Elephant is introduced and wants to play with all the other animals he meets on his walk (orientation), but none of them wants to play with him (complications) until he meets Big Elephant, who wants to play (resolution). The initial attraction is interpersonal: a book shaped like a brightly coloured toy that makes noises is interpersonally engaging. In addition the textual and ideational metafunctions build on this interpersonal engagement through the scanning/reading path and the storyline integrated with and dependent on the images.

Books for Children from Six Months to Twelve Months

Books for children from six- to twelve-months-old are both similar to and different from books for children from birth to six months. First, while many books for the younger age group are printed either on cloth or board (mainly cloth), books for this age group tend to be printed either on board or on high-quality thick, glossy paper. Images tend to be stylised and 'cartoonish'. Colours tend to be bright and saturated as shown in Figure 12.2a. In this example the words also both complement and depend on the image to make sense. The words *Yum, yum! Nice gingerbread, Maisy* do not make much sense without the image. Likewise, the words add information to the image. Without the words we don't know that the characters are eating gingerbread or that the gingerbread is tasty. The connection between the words and the gingerbread is presumed rather than made explicit. For example, if it said: *Maisy and her friends were eating gingerbread* . . . the connection between words and images would be explicit.

Yum, yum!
Nice gingerbread,
Maisy.

(a)   Double page spread from *At Home with Maisy* (Cousins, 2002).

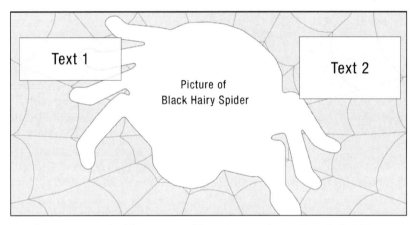

(b)   'Surprise; double page panel from *I'm not Scary* (Campbell, 2007).

Figure 12.2   Six months to twelve months.

Textures and flaps concealing surprises are also common. The example in Figure 12.2b is the final panel in a book called *I'm not Scary* (Campbell 2007). All of the preceding panels contain images highlighted by bright, shiny colours and textures of familiar small and benign garden creatures. The final panel contains a surprise. When you turn the page from the preceding panel a big, black spider pops up out of the pages. The words . . . *horrible hairy spider!* and '*I am scary! Touch me if you dare!*' both in Text 1 and Text 2 boxes, respectively, reinforce the surprise and invite engagement. In the preceding pages, the words were all along the lines of 'I'm not scary. Touch me.' These build expectation. The spider jumping out of the page runs counter to this expectation. The command: *Touch me if you dare!* invites direct physical engagement with the book. These commands, however, must be directed at the adult who is reading the book with the child because children this age cannot read. Although the book does not have a narrative storyline, the final panel introduces a complication of sorts through counter-expectation.

Books for Children from Twelve to Twenty-four Months

Cornelius P Mud, Are You Ready for Bed (Salzburg 2007) shown in Figure 12.3a represents a book at the early end of the twelve- to twenty-four-month age range. It still shares many similarities with books for children six- to twelve-months-old but also illustrates some differences. It uses bright colours and a cartoonish pig and has very few words, but the relationship between the words and the image is quite complex. Compositionally, it is interesting in that on the left-to-right diagonal, it starts with a question: *Have you brushed your teeth?* The reader's line of sight is then drawn down and to the right by the scrubbing brush, which in Text 1 box is oriented diagonally, through the pig's foamy mouth to the answer to the question: *Yes!*, in Text 2 box reinforcing a top-down and left-to-right reading path. The relationship between images and words is more complex here than in the texts for younger children. Moving across and down the diagonal, the words pose a question, which is then answered in the image by the frothy brush and the frothy mouth. The answer is then restated in words. This pattern of question, image and answer is repeated throughout the book. The complications are in the images. Although the answer, in words, to the questions is *Yes!*, the

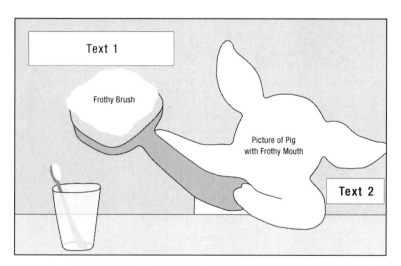

(a) Double page spread from *Cornelius P Mud, Are you Ready for Bed?* (Salzberg, 2007).

Figure 12.3 Twelve months to twenty-four months.

image shows that *Yes!* is on the right track but not entirely the right answer. The complexity comes from the tension between words and images.

The story has the beginnings of a narrative structure with each question, image and answer episode functioning as a complication, which is realised through the slight discrepancy between image and words. The resolution comes when the answer to the question: *Are you ready for bed?* is *No!*. Cornelius needs a hug before he is ready to go to sleep.

At the upper end of the twelve- to-twenty-four-month age group, there is a tendency for words and images to be complementary. Ideationally both 'tell' more or less the same story. Both could exist separately. The story makes sense without the images and you could use just the images to tell a story similar to the one in the book. Ideationally the images also tell the story. However, the images do more than simply tell the same story as the words. Interpersonally the images amplify the words.

Rascal the Dragon (Jennings 2004) shown in Figure 12.3b has a clear narrative structure. It tells the story of a boy, Ben, who wants to adopt a pet dragon. There are a number of complications where Ben's father resists Ben's attempts to adopt a number of dragons, but the narrative is resolved when Ben's father finally relents and Ben is allowed to adopt Rascal the Dragon as a pet. Figure 12.3b shows a typical example of the book's format. Each double-page spread shows one episode of the story. The images and the text are related through intersemiotic complementarity, where 'the visual and verbal modes semantically complement each other to produce a single textual phenomenon' (Royce 1998: 26). While words and images both tell, more or less, the same story, they also do more than that. The relationship is 'synergistic in nature' (Royce 1998: 27). The words both complement and constrain the interpretation of the images. For instance,

'I wish Sniff was mine,' said Ben.   'No,' said Dad. 'He smells.'
'Isn't he good?'

(b)   Double page spread from *Rascal the Dragon* (Jennings, 2004. Lea, illus).

Figure 12.3   Twelve months to twenty-four months.

without the words the reader wouldn't know that the boy's name was Ben, the smelly dragon's name was Sniff or that the man is Ben's father.

The images, as well as representing the story experientially, also amplify aspects of it interpersonally (see Martin and Rose 2003: 37–43). Without the images the reader would not know quite how smelly Sniff was. The figure of the father in the image on the left-hand page adds amplitude to the words *No, said Dad. He smells.* The father's body position, turning and leaning away from Sniff and his gestures of his raised left hand pushing away from his body and his right hand clamping on his nose indicate considerable distaste. The train of flies behind Sniff's head and the stink-mist lines coming from Sniff's body also indicate a none-too-pleasant aroma in the air. These run counter to Ben's wide-eyed enthusiastic expression and his pointing finger. The different depiction of the stance of the figures of both Ben and his father in the image can be taken as a cue to add different emphasis when speaking their parts. The depiction of Sniff is a clue that he/she really does smell but that Ben wants a dragon so much that he is oblivious to it.

Books for Children from Twenty-Four to Thirty-Six months

Figures 12.4a and 12.4b show further changes from earlier books. One thing that stands out is that there are now more words per page than previously.

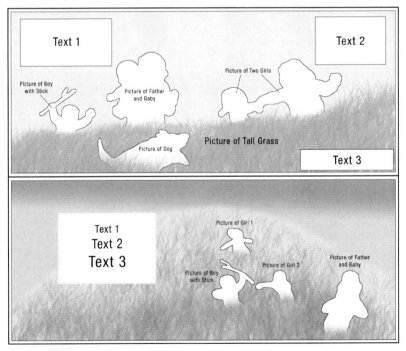

(a)   Two double page spreads from *We're Going on a Bear Hunt* (Rosen and Oxenbury, 1989).

Figure 12.4 Twenty-four months to thirty-six months.

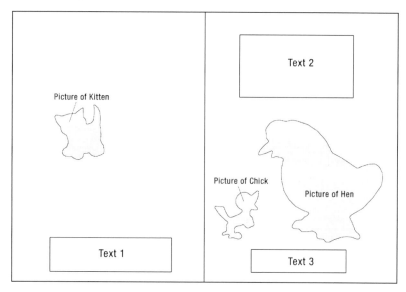

(b)   Double page spread from *Are You My Mother?* (Eastman, 1960).

Figure 12.4   Twenty-four months to thirty-six months.

Both texts have a well-developed narrative structure: the words tell more of the story. The images still complement the words but they are starting to tell less of the story. The interpretation of the images is starting to become more constrained by the words than previously.

In the images the colours are more muted, less interpersonally engaging, than previously. In Figure 12.4a the images in the chorus are in mono-chrome. I take this to indicate that the story, rather than the image, is becoming the main spur for engagement with the book.

Books for Children from Thirty-Six to Sixty Months

In books for the thirty-six to sixty-month age group (Figures 12.5a and 12.5b), the number of words has increased considerably over the previous age group. The words do more and more of the work. The images now depend on, or illustrate, the words. The images stop replicating the whole story but only illustrate selected scenes. The words provide anchorage (Barthes 1977: 38–41) for the images: they tell the reader what the picture is a picture of. While the images illustrate only selected scenes they do contain a lot of detail from those scenes. They tend to be more subdued but more detailed than the images in books for younger children. The story makes sense without the pictures, but a reader using only the images would find it difficult to tell a similar story to the one told by the words in the book. The images remain muted and are interspersed throughout the text rather than foregrounded.

The further north we travelled, the hotter it became. We stood in the shallows at Monkey Mia to see the dolphins.

'Too crowded,' said Dad.

'I liked it better when it was just us and the whales.'

That afternoon, Mum and Billy and I had a picnic in the dunes, then fell asleep like a pride of lions. Later when we went for a dip, a dolphin came up close and swam right between us.

Mum made me wear my hat all the time. 'Hats and sunscreen,' she'd say every time we stopped. 'This sun will burn you to a crisp.'

We went snorkelling at Turquoise Bay. A gentle current carried us over the coral reef, as though the ocean was giving us a tour. There were so many fish, like sparkling jewels. My favourites were the tiny blue angels.

(a)   Double page spread from *Are We There Yet?* (Lester 2005).

Figure 12.5   Thirty-six months to sixty months.

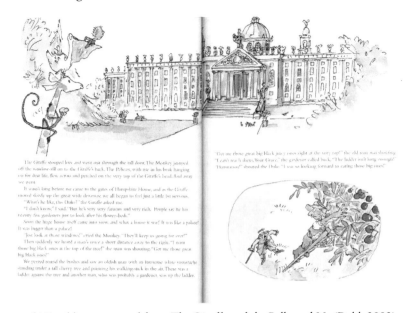

(b) Double page spread from *The Giraffe and the Pelly and Me* (Dahl, 2003)

Figure 12.5   Thirty-six months to sixty months.

In Books for Older Children

In books suggested for children from about the ages of five or six onwards, pictures have all but disappeared. Any images found will only be at chapter headings or small monochrome images in the text. In books for 'tweens' and early teens there are almost no images. Covers, however, are still highly interpersonal. This is one thing that remains constant across books for different age groups: the covers are almost all highly interpersonally engaging, which makes sense since you have to engage with the book in order to select it from among its competitors.

FINDINGS AND IMPLICATIONS

Changes in the Nature of Images as Age of 'Readers' Increases

Figure 12.6 is a compilation of images used as examples in this chapter. It shows a trend towards a progressive decrease in interpersonal prominence of images as books are aimed at children of increasing age. The first line shows images from books for children aged from birth to six months. All of the images foreground the interpersonal. They use strong, bright, fully saturated colours and stylised, cartoonish figures. Many incorporate textures, flaps and pop-ups to encourage direct physical

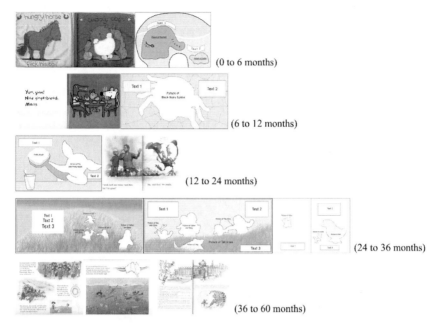

Figure 12.6   Figures from books for children of different ages, showing decrease in interpersonal orientation with increasing age.

engagement with the book. The second line shows images from the six- to twelve-month age range. The colours are still bright and saturated and the figures are also stylised and cartoonish. The number of words has increased. In the third line (twelve to twenty-four months), the first image is from the early end of the age range and in terms of brightness and saturation is similar to those in the first two lines. The second image is from the older end of the age range and has more pastel tones. The figures are stylised but less cartoonish and the number of words has increased and the story in words parallels the story in images.

In the fourth line (twenty-four to thirty-six months), the colours of the images are more muted (one panel is in monochrome). The figures are still stylised, but representationally they are closer to 'true-to-life' than those in books aimed at children from twelve- to twenty-four months. The images are also more detailed and ideationally run parallel to the parts of the story they illustrate. The number of words per page has also increased.

In the fifth line (thirty-six to sixty months) the images are similar to those in the line above but share the page space with more words. The images are interspersed with the words and represent particular parts of a scene rather than paralleling the whole scene. Although each image represents less of the story, each image is also more detailed than the images in the previous two age groups.

In summary, images in books for children in the youngest age groups foreground the interpersonal metafunction. They are bright, colourful, often tactile and relatively simply composed, with the main figure occupying centre stage. One function of this is to promote both visual and physical engagement with the book. With increasing age the emphasis on the interpersonal decreases. Corresponding to this decrease, the images increase in complexity both compositionally and representationally. The interpersonal is still there but not quite as foregrounded as, over time, words take over from images and textures as the principal semiotic system utilised.

Changes in the Relationship Between Images and Words as Age of 'Readers' Increases

If we consider the relationship between images and words in terms of a scale of abstraction or context dependency (Halliday 1985b; Martin 1984, 1997), we find several patterns and trends. I emphasise that these are tendencies, not absolutes. They also overlap age categories and are perhaps best viewed as a scale.

First, in books for the youngest children, two tendencies appear. The first is for the words to depend on the images. That is, without the images the words do not stand alone or make sense by themselves. The words are highly context-dependent and the images provide the context for the words to make sense in. A second tendency is that many books contain explicit and congruent instructions/commands (in imperative mood) for readers to engage with the book. This engagement is directed at the adult who is reading the book to the child so that the adult can direct the child's attention towards the most highly charged interpersonal elements of the book. It includes attractors such as colour, texture, sounds and hidden surprises. In some books for this age range the beginnings of narrative structure appear.

The next step is that, in books aimed at children aged between twelve months to twenty-four months, the relationship between images and words starts to change. The words and images now tend to complement each other: the words and images tell more or less the same story. As well as complementing each other the images can also provide amplification of interpersonal aspects of the story and the words constrain the interpretation of the images. Images now tend to work across metafunctions. They work interpersonally to invite engagement and to help the reader to isolate which parts of the written story to amplify. They work ideationally to help tell the story and they work textually (compositionally) to help direct the reader's scanning path. Narrative structure is generally quite well developed.

In the next step the relationship changes again so that the images come to depend on the words. The words become the main source of meaning, and the images illustrate selected aspects of the story and/or refer to specific words in story, but they no longer duplicate the story. The detail in the images seems to increase as well. One effect of the increase in detail is that the images now no longer have a single element to engage the reader. So, as well as the direction of dependency changing the degree of interpersonal focus in the images also decreases and the ideational focus increases.

In summary, we find a pattern where, initially, the words depend on the images. That is, the images provide the context for the words to make sense in. However, this pattern first changes so that the words and images run more or less parallel to each other and are mutually dependent, mutually constraining and mutually reinforcing. The initial pattern then reverses, with images coming to depend on the words. The words now provide the context for the images to make sense in. The final step is that images disappear altogether, apart from on interpersonally charged book covers.

Implications

The pattern of change in the relationship between words and images discussed above seems to represent a good apprenticeship into reading written text. It shows a steady movement from meanings in language that are context dependent to meanings that are context independent. It also, in 'story' books, progressively builds up narratives, allowing, over time, the words to do more of the work. I suggest that this is what children's picture books have evolved to do and that without regular and repeated exposure to these books the task of becoming literate at school becomes much more difficult.

There seems to be no doubt that being read to and having books performed for them a lot should give children a walk-up start when it comes to literacy at school, even it is as little as just getting the book the right way up. Even something as seemingly basic as getting the book the right way up gives a child an advantage over a child who gets it the wrong way round. Once children can recognise what is in the pictures they almost always orient the pictures the right way up, by default they also orient the print the right way up too. Give a very young child a book without pictures, and the results are much more random.

On the other hand, while this pattern seems a good initiation into written ways of meaning it is not necessarily such a good apprenticeship into reading multisemiotic texts as, with age, the texts become more monomodal. This runs counter to the pattern in the world at large where the texts we encounter all around us in daily life are becoming increasingly multisemiotic in more and more complex ways. Perhaps there is room in the world of children's books to explore ways of continuing the multisemiotic flavour they start out with.

As a final point, in very early literacy learning, the interpersonal provides the impetus which leads the way into the textual and ideational. The child's initial response to books and to parts of books is interpersonal and their response to being read to is to the interpersonal aspects put into the oral text by the adult reader. The adult's oral text is influenced by how the adult reader 'reads' the images. The 'right' emphasis cues the child to what to respond to. This then draws attention to specific parts of the written text which orients the child to writing as well as to images.

REFERENCES

Barker, S., illus. (1998) *Big Elephant and Little Elephant*. London: Campbell Books.
Barthes, R. (1977) 'Rhetoric of the Image.' *Image, Music, Text*, London, Fontana: pp. 32–51.
Brice Heath, S. (1983) *Ways with Words: Language, Life and Work in Communities and Classrooms*, Cambridge: Cambridge University Press.
Campbell, R. (2007) *I'm not Scary*, London: Campbell Books.
Church, J., illus. (1999) *Touch and Feel Bouncy Lamb*, London: Ladybird.
Cousins, L. (2002) *At Home with Maisy*, London:Walker Books.
Dahl, R. (2003) *The Giraffe and Pelly and Me*, London: Johnathan Cape.
Eastman, P. D. (1960) *Are You My Mother?*, London: Random House.
Halliday, M. A. K. (1985a) *Introduction to Functional Grammar*, London: Edward Arnold.
—— (1985b) 'Context of Situation.' In Halliday, M. A. K., and Hasan, R. eds. *Language, Text and Context*, Geelong: Deakin University Press.
Huggies Book Club http://www.huggiesbookclub.com.au last accessed 13 April 2009.
Kress, G., and van Leeuwen, T. (1996) *Reading Images: The Grammar of Visual Design*, 1st ed, London: Routledge.
Jennings, P., Lea, B., illus. (2004) *Rascal the Dragon*, Camberwell: Puffin.
Labov, W., and Waletzky, J. (1967) 'Narrative analysis: Oral versions of personal experience.' In Helm, J. ed. *Essays on the Verbal and Visual Arts*, Seattle, : University of Washington Press: pp. 12–44.
Land, F., illus. (2007) *Baby Touch Cot Book*, London: Ladybird.
Lester, A. (2005) *Are We There Yet*, London: Penguin.
Lim, F V. (2006) 'The Visual Semantics Stratum: Making Meaning in Sequential Images.' In Royce, T., and Bowcher, W. eds. *New Directions in the Analysis of Multimodal Discourse*, New Jersey: Lawrence Erlbaum Associates: pp. 195–214.
—— (2002) 'The Analysis of Language and Visual Images—An Integrative Multisemiotic Approach', Master of Arts (English Language) thesis, National University of Singapore.
Liu, Y., and O'Halloran K. L. (2009) 'Intersemiotic Texture: Analyzing Cohesive Devices between Language and Images'. *Social Semiotics* 19(4):367–388.
Martin, J. R. (1997) 'Analysing Genre: functional parameters.' In Christie, F., and Martin, J. R. eds. *Genres and Institutions: social processes in the workplace and school*, London: Cassell.
—— (1984) *Language, Register and Genre*, Geelong: Deakin University Press.
Martin, J. R., and Rose, D. (2003) *Working with Discourse*, London: Continuum.
Martin, J. R., and Plum G. A. (1997) 'Construing Experience: Some Story Genres.' *Journal of Narrative and Life History* 7 (1–4): pp. 299–308.
Martinec, R., and Salway, A. (2005) 'A System for Image-Text Relations in new (and old) media.' *Visual Communication* 4(3): London: Sage: 337–371.
Meek, M. (1988) *How Texts Teach What Readers Learn*, Stroud: The Thimble Press.

O'Toole, M. (1994) *The Language of Displayed Art*, 1st ed, London: Leicester University Press.

—— (2010) *The Language of Displayed Art*, 2nd ed, London and New York: Routledge.

Painter, C. (2007) 'Children's Picture Book Narratives: Reading Sequences of Images.' In McCabe, A., O'Donnell, M. and Whittaker, R. eds. *Advances in Language and Education*, London: Continuum (manuscript copy).

Rosen, M. and Oxenbury, H. (1989) *We're Going on a Bear Hunt*, London:Walker Books.

Royce, T. G. (1998) 'Synergy on the page: Exploring intersemiotic complementarity in page-based multimodal text', in *JASFL Occasional Papers* 1(1): 25–49.

Salzburg, B. (2007) *Cornelius P Mud, Are You Ready for Bed?*, Somerville: Candlewick Press.

Torr, J. (2007) 'The pleasure of recognition: Intertextuality in the talk of preschoolers during shared reading with mothers and teachers.' Early Years: An International Journal of Research and Development 27(1): 77–93.

—— (2004) 'Talking about picture books: The influence of maternal education on four-year-old children's talk with mothers and preschool teachers.' *Journal of Early Childhood Literacy*, 4(2): 181–210.

Unsworth, L., and Chan, E. (2008) 'Assessing integrative reading of images and text in group reading comprehension tests.' Curriculum Perspectives 28(3): 71–76.

Unsworth, L. (2006a) 'Multiliteracies and a metalanguage of image/text relations: Implications for teaching English as a first or additional language in the 21st century.' In Cadman, K., and O'Regan, K. eds. *Tales out of school: Identity and English language teaching*, Special edition of TESOL in Context. Series S(1) pp. 147–162.

—— (2006b) 'Towards a metalanguage for multiliteracies education: Describing the meaning-making resources of language-image interaction.' English Teaching: Practice and Critique 5(1): 55–76.

Wells, C. G. (1985) 'Pre-school literacy-related activities and success in school.' In Olson, D. R., Torrance, N. and Hildyard, A. eds. *Literacy, Language and Learning: the Nature and Consequences of Reading and Writing*, Cambridge: Cambridge University Press.

Wignell, P. (2008) 'How am I supposed to know how to read this? Intertextual and intratextual cues and clues to how to 'perform' books for young children.' In Wu, C., Matthiessen, M. I. M. and Herke, M. eds. *Voices Around the World: Proceedings of ISFC 35*, Sydney: Macquarie University.

Williams, G. (1995) 'Joint Book-reading and Literacy pedagogy: a socio-semantic examination.' Volume 1. CORE. 19(3). Fiche 2 B01-Fiche 6 B01.

—— (1998) 'Children entering Literate Worlds: perspectives from the study of literate practices.' In Christie, F. and Misson, R. eds. *Literacy and Schooling*, London: Routledge: pp. 18–46.

13 Semiotisation Processes of Space

From Drawing Our Homes to Styling Them

Eija Ventola

INTRODUCTION

The British show the value of their homes by the saying 'My home is my castle'. A home, indeed, is a safe space to be in, to eat, drink and sleep, to be happy and relaxed with the family, friends or alone. When we move into an empty house/flat, we quickly fill it with our own 'things' which represent our life histories. For various reasons, such as that most of us cannot afford to buy everything new when we move in, our 'old things' get mixed with some 'new ones' and the mix will have to fit our semiotic 'living practices'. Only rarely after moving in do we think about reordering the furniture, but perhaps sometimes shift one piece to an adjacent room, or replace an older piece with a new one, without any systematic interior design plans. We usually do not analyse how our homes emerge as semiotic processes, how they are designed and built to realise particular semiotic social practices of living, how we ourselves sometimes change those practices, what such changes involve and what their overall results are. We do not have the tools to perform such an analysis. We leave that to the professionals, urban planners, architects, constructors, interior decorators or 'stylists' as they are also informally called, all of whom are trained to plan, design and build our homes and to do systematic changes in the interiors of our homes.

Yet, these professionals work at various times on our homes, and thus, perhaps, also lack a full, systematic view on the semiotic processes through which our homes come about. Karlsson (2004: 253) points out that as 'the practice of building' transformed into 'knowledge about the practice of building', when the disciplines of architecture and construction were developed, the experts' experience of the building practice got diminished (good architects do not necessarily make good carpenters). Each professional tends to look at our homes only from the point of view of their own expertise, thus not offering us a full semiotic view of how our homes came about, what they mean to us, and how they enable our semiotic social practices in them (whether cooking, entertaining, being entertained etc.). This paper suggests ways of doing such a semiotic analysis, so that we can better conceptualise those processes that enable us to live in our homes 'as if they were castles'. We need to consider and theorise about the systems and structures involved and the dynamic change issues when discussing 'the life of a home' *and* 'a life in a home', particularly in the sense of semiotic and discourse functionality of a home.

In this paper, the next section introduces the theoretical background, and Data and Methods presents the data—my flat. The Exterior and Interior Rank Scales discusses the flat/home from the point of view of urban planning and architectural design. 'Before' and 'After-Views of Living Room–Kitchen explains some interior design perspectives and some dynamic changes that were realised by an interior stylist. In Discussion the changes are evaluated, and the last section concludes the paper by making some suggestions for further research.

THEORETICAL BACKGROUND

The theoretical bases for this paper are the multisemiotic views that have been developed within the systemic-functional approach to functionalism in the contexts of culture and contexts of situation and the multimodal theories largely influenced by them; and in particular the work of Michael O'Toole (1994/2010, 2004). These allow us to see even city planning and the architectural design of a multi-storey house and a flat multifunctionally, by analysing, first, how the flat relates to the city, the suburb and the building where the home is located and, second, by relating these meanings to those that are realised within the flat when it becomes 'a home'.

Buildings 'signify their functional uses'; they address their viewers and operate harmoniously (or not) in their environment. O'Toole (1994: 85, 87) suggests and claims that in this way architecture is similar to language. He links the Hallidayan metafunctional orientation of *experiential, interpersonal* and *textual* meanings that language realises and parallels them with the same kind of metafunctional meanings realised by architecture. He proposes a rank scale of units for analysing the buildings and their meanings: BUILDING, FLOOR, ROOM and ELEMENT. At each rank, various systems that map out the different choices operate simultaneously to realise these metafunctionally oriented meanings (see O'Toole 1994: 86; 2004: 12–13). For instance, at the rank of BUILDING Practical Function or Orientation to Light would be examples of *experiential* systems, Size, Façade or Colour of *interpersonal* systems and Relation to City, Rhythm or Textures examples of *textual* systems. The functions and the rank scale will also be made use of in this paper later, when some of these systems and their exponents will be highlighted in the analysis of the flat/home. The job that the three metafunctions, the units on the rank scale, and the systems at each rank do is 'teasing out the systems of choice which are available to the architects, engineers and builders at different ranks of unit' (O'Toole 2004: 26). O'Toole (1994) demonstrates the application of the theory with his analyses of a promotional brochure of a design home in Perth, *The Verdelho*, with Aalto's *Enzo-Gutzeit* office block in Helsinki and with Le Corbusier's pilgrimage chapel in France. He (2004) has also analysed the Sydney Opera House by the Danish architect, Utzon. O'Toole's framework has further been applied by Alias (2004) to analysing the meanings at Orchard Road and the Marriott Hotel in Singapore. That analysis also briefly discusses Singapore and its planning, and these interpretations will also be useful to the current paper. This framework enables us to relate the semiotics of architecture to the discursive functionality of designed spaces (for examples of other applications of this integrated theory of language and other semiotics, including three-dimensional space (3D), see e.g. articles in O'Halloran 2004; Ventola et al. 2004; Jones and Ventola 2008; Stenglin 2008, 2009).

When analysing my flat/home, how I live in it and in which kind of discourses I engage, I necessarily have to analyse my activities and discourses in the flat *multisemiotically* (if not even *multisystemiotically*)—how they are shaped by the semiotic spaces in which they take place, with semiotics modelled as networks of systemic options for choice. I also have to consider the city planners', architects'/interior designers', constructors' work as well as my own role in the initial shaping of 'my home' and finally the interior decorator/stylist's role in giving the home its latest 'face-lift'.

DATA AND METHODS

The data are the documents collected about the flat, e.g. the sales brochure of the flat, the architectural plans and my draft changes of them, my own and my tenants' and neighbours' experiences in living in the building where the flat is situated, my personal experience in participating in a TV-programme in Finland called 'Pientä pintaremonttia' (a liberal translation as 'Fixing it up slightly')—an interior decoration/styling programme—2007–2008, and the documentation that was produced and collected as the styling process took place (correspondence, images, film clips and texts, the web pages of the programme and of the real estate agency involved in the programme). This paper focuses on the processes of the semiotisation of the flat/home. The analyses of the TV-programme and how that was produced cannot be done in this paper for reasons of space, although the making of the programme also contributes to the contents of paper.

The methods used for the analyses are based on those introduced in the literature presented in Theoretical Background. Following systemic-functional principles and O'Toole (1994, 2004), we can use the general principle of 'constituency' for the analysis and establish the necessary rank scale of the units that can functionally be seen to play a role as wholes in the structuring (so that the structures of the higher rank are seen 'to consist of' the units of the lower rank and vice versa, cf. comparison with the rank scale in grammar). At each rank, functionally recognisable units are 'points of origins of system networks' (Matthiessen and Halliday 1997); the choices of features of the system networks then define how the elements are realised as structures.

We are still far from presenting 'full grammars' of architectural/interior design/styling, as the ranks and the units discussed in the multisemiotic literature dealing with architectural design have not yet been extensively elaborated. In this context, there is no room to delve on the problems, although a few will be pointed out. O'Toole (1994: 86), for example, presents a 'chart' where the rank scale is BUILDING, FLOOR, ROOM, ELEMENT. Each unit should be an entry point to system networks that define the choices of features that then determine the structural realisation. O'Toole (2004) introduces 'a building complex', without much theoretical discussion of its status in the rank scale (an additional rank to the rank scale?), but exemplifying it as the Sydney Opera House complex housing (e.g. the concert house, the theatre, the Bennelong Restaurant etc.), and although he discusses the possible choices involved, he does not present networks, either. But he emphasises the value of a rank scale and as an example points out how at the ROOM-rank a drink bar and a box office in the Opera house require different Elements to realise them experientially (e.g. chairs, counters, equipment etc., see O'Toole 2004: 17). Alias (2004: 58–63) suggests that Singapore and the Marriott Hotel can be analysed by the following rank scale: AREA (Rank 1)—ROADS/MTR (Rank 2.1)—OPEN SPACE (Rank 2.2)—BUILDING (Rank 2.3), and BUILDING has the units of Building, Floor, Room, Element. Adding the rank of AREA is useful, but the discussion of the rank scale is very brief:

> A 'rank' or a 'unit' links each of these built forms [in Singapore] to the other. Major roads link one area or a 'unit' to another . . . Within an area, there are roads and open spaces, which will eventually lead to buildings where there may be different levels or storeys, with different rooms for different functions. Depending on its function, each room may have a different layout or decor . . . Each unit operates or functions in relation to another, usually a neighbouring one, and its general surroundings or environment. (Alias 2004: 60–61)

In brief, we are still far away from stating everything systematically in examples like these (even for language the representation of the systems and structures has taken a long time and still needs work), and the space in this paper does not allow extensive theoretical elaborations, either. For the moment, we can take the ranks, units and functions as 'tools', which enable us to take a step forward to developing an understanding of how various semiotics work together (cf. Martinec 2005 for a discussion of rank-based approaches). The more we know, the sooner we are in the position of making more precise descriptions. One suggestion made in this paper will be that we separate the exterior and interior rank scales influencing the shaping of a flat/home, and here the major focus will be on interior rank of BUILDING, the units Floor, Flat and Rooms and Elements. No system networks will be provided here either, but perhaps these analyses will eventually help us towards being able to draw them.

Further, we have to make sure that in the analysis we also consider the dynamic point of view and not just the synoptic view that networks provide for us (for discussion of dynamic/synoptic, see Ventola 1987; Martin 1992). This will become clear as the analysis of the flat/home proceeds. The dynamicity of the semiotic systems in our example case begins with some constructional changes even before 1994 when the first inhabitant (me) moves in. Since then the interior decoration of the flat has gone through many transformations, as each set of tenants to whom the flat was rented out (1995–2004) had their own preferences of interior decoration. The analysis reported here involves only my own interior decoration when I moved back into the flat in 2004, and, for reasons of space, only part of it—the living room and the kitchen—will be discussed in detail. The focus will primarily be on my own semiotic perceptions of this major living space and its transformations by a professional interior decorator as part of the TV show mentioned.

THE EXTERIOR AND INTERIOR RANK SCALES

The flat/home will first be located as part of the exterior rank scale and then as part of an internal rank scale.

World—Country—City/County—Centre/Suburb— The Flat as a Part of the Urban Universe and as a Result of Urban Planning and Zoning

In the 'exterior' rank scale proposed here, THE WORLD consists of COUNTRIES, which consist of CITIES and non-urban COUNTIES, and further their CENTRES and SUBURBS (cf. group/phrase). Urban planning (see reference, Urban planning 2009) and Zoning, are the semiotisation processes, activated and realised by professionals, that influence our lives and discourses in the cities/counties and centres/suburbs. Ruskeasuo (translation 'brown swamp'), a residential suburb 4,5 km from Helsinki city centre, was initially 'zoned' as an inexpensive spacious housing area but has now become valuable and valued as 'a green, garden suburb'. Its 'zoning' (STREETS that cut through the suburb, PARKS and RECREATIONAL AREAS, OPEN SPACES and the arrangement of these and various kinds of residential and commercial BUILDINGS as co-units at the rank of suburb) has been praised as one of the best 1950s suburbs in Helsinki (see reference Ruskeasuo 2009). Here the focus will be on one residential building in Ruskeasuo where the flat/home is situated, Paraistentie 16. The exterior features of this building will first be discussed, and then the interior features as part of the interior rank scale (Buildings—Floors—Flats—Rooms—Elements as a Result of Architectural Design).

The shape of the BUILDINGS is the result of another semiotisation process, Architectural Design, realising functional, aesthetic etc. meanings. Paraistentie 16 was built in 1994 and resembles so-called 'Point Houses' (typically three-storey high and thus requiring no lift). This 'genre' of houses, typical of the 1950's, has one entry with a staircase in the middle of the house, and it is designed to allow maximal light into the flats by having windows to all directions (see reference Pistetalo 2009). Why was Paraistentie 16 built to resemble point houses? This 'genre' choice harmonises the building with the 1950s point houses in the area and contrasts it functionally with the red brick student-housing opposite and next to it (residential vs. student). Figure 13.1 presents the Front and the Back of Paraistentie 16 A, and the discussion that follows highlights the most prominent external metafunctional features of the building, which make the architectural design of this building operational with the realisations of the other buildings belonging to this genre in this suburb.

The first major system which O'Toole (1994: 86) suggests to be realising experiential meanings in the exterior of the BUILDING is its Practical function, here residential. Both the front and the back of the building indicate that Paraistentie 16 is a multi-storey building, designed to accommodate many people/families living in it, as can be seen from the many windows and the balconies. Thus we also need to consider the unit, FLOOR. Further experiential systems in O'Toole's (1994) framework are systems of Orientation to Light/Wind/Earth to Service (water, power, services etc.). Here perhaps it is only necessary to refer to the way 'Point Houses' were designed to give light to all flats. The windows are not as big as they were in the

| The Front in winter; North-East View | The Back in summer; South-West View |

Figure 13.1 Two views of Paraistentie 16 (the flat analysed is on the third floor on the left, ground floor being the first floor).

1970s, yet the architect has obviously attempted to provide the best light to all sides of the building.

The major systems realising the interpersonal function in O'Toole's (1994) framework to be considered here are Size, Verticality, Façade, Cladding, Colour, Modernity, Orientation to Road / Neighbours / Entrant and Intertextuality. In Size and Verticality Paraistentie 16 represents median choices; it does not stand out from its surroundings, and it is certainly not planned as a landmark of any kind, quite the contrary. In terms of Façade, Cladding, Colour and Modernity the building gives an interpersonally friendly impression of a modern residential house; the colour of the bricks that clad the building is a modest, light yellow. The protruding balconies give the residents further possibility of enjoying light. In Orientation to Road/ Neighbours/Entrant the building is somewhat protected; one has to enter the building by following a path going past the vertical row of balconies in the front.

The third function, sometimes called textual function or texture by O'Toole (1994, 2004; and for paintings compositional), is realised in the ways Paraistentie 16 fits the surroundings in Relation to city/road/adjacent buildings, Proportions, Rhythms, Textural qualities. In relation to the city, the building is a suburban building with public transport close by (the bus and tram stop close by). It 'coheres' best with the low-level point houses of the 1950s in the area but differs from them interpersonally through modernity and in texture, not perhaps so much in its proportions as in the rhythms that the corners of the building, the rows of windows and balconies give it. It also differs in textural surface material from the traditional point houses, because its cover is of light, smooth, yellowish brick, whereas the other, older point houses in the area have a rough, much brighter yellow mortar covering.

Buildings—Floors—Flats—Rooms—Elements as a Result of Architectural Design

In designing a building, an architect places the BUILDING into its surroundings and plans not only its external looks, the parameters for meaning-making of the whole residential multi-storey building but also the relevant interior meanings in the ways FLOORS, FLATS, STORAGE PLACES, STAIRCASES and also in Finland SAUNA areas are located within the building and construed.

Usually buildings are built according to a 'synoptic' plan, but as Karlsson (2004) also points out, there is a considerable amount of 'dynamism' going on in the construction of buildings. In Paraistentie 16, the dynamism was realised both on the floors and in the rooms of my flat. The third FLOOR where the flat is located was first intended as the top residential floor. But soon, the contractors applied for extending flats to the attic floor where a sauna and storage compartments were planned; new plans included two flats and a sauna. A further dynamic reshaping was introduced by me when I started my negotiations with the contractors about purchasing a flat in the Paraistentie 16. I was originally interested in buying the two flats planned for the attic and wanted to join them into one big flat. But the contractor rejected my offer and made me a counter-offer of joining two flats on the third floor together, a three-room flat (65 m^2) a bed-sitter (27 m^2) and building a private sauna for me; thus I ended up buying a four-room flat (92 m^2; see Figure 13.3 below), and the third floor ended having four flat entries instead of five (as on the first and second floors). The plan to join the two flats together was largely drawn by me as a 'lay architect' but was finalised and redrawn professionally by an architect.

The interiors of FLATS and ROOMS are usually the sphere of interior designers and interior home decorators/stylists (see 'Before' and 'After Views' of Living Room–Kitchen), but in Finland architects may to a certain degree function as interior designers as they not only design the order of ROOMS but also the placing, style and brand of some of the ELEMENTS in the rooms: kitchen cupboards, workbench tops, fridges, washbasins, toilets etc., wardrobes in other rooms and sometimes even some home decorations like sofas, arm chairs, sofa tables etc. (usually interior architects). What interests us here is how the original design of my flat was planned as ROOMS and ELEMENTS and how a certain 'dynamism' affected these architectural interior design plans.

Usually flat interiors are standardised by architects, but the buyer may create certain meanings into the flat by making small changes for which s/he is willing to pay. But in the case of my flat/home, the changes were bigger as the original architectural structural plan for *Zoning* was changed when the wall between the two smaller flats was knocked down (it had already been built when I purchased the flat). Further, the choice of not building the half-wall separating the kitchen from the living room area was a choice that I also insisted upon to create a more open space, as well as the double glass doors leading to the third bedroom (the earlier bed-sitter area>TV/guestroom), and a sauna was added to the earlier bed-sitter-bathroom and a bathtub replaced a shower in the other bathroom. For constructional reasons, a column had to be left in the new living room floor area, and I added a few wardrobes and also changed the places of the ones that had been planned, plus, of course, the flat now had two balconies.

So all in all, the flat represented 'somewhat more luxurious living' for me in 1994 when I first moved in. In 'Before' and 'After Views' of Living Room–Kitchen, then, I shall take the first steps to account metafunctionally for my layperson's architectural interior decoration choices as well as my layperson's 'home decoration/styling choices'. As the space is limited, the analysis has to be restricted to the major living area of the flat—the living room, and the kitchen—and the elements in them. My layperson's choices will be contrasted to professional home decorator/stylist's choices.

'Before' and 'After Views' of Living Room–Kitchen

The flat, Paraistentie 16 A 14, has been decorated by me twice, first when I moved in 1994 and then in 2004 when I moved back, having rented the flat out while working abroad. Many of my 'styling' choices the second time round followed my first home styling in the flat. This second styling will be analysed here, and the semiotisation processes involved in this activity gives us the 'Before-view', familiar to us from various kinds of 'alterations' and 'makeover' TV shows and magazine articles. The contrasting semiotisation view, the 'After-view', explains the changes made by a professional interior decorator/stylist who as part of a home decoration TV programme mentioned earlier designed a 'styling face-lift' for my flat/home. Her budget for the 'face-lift' was not huge—2000€–2500€— but more than the 300—, which an average Finnish household spent on home decoration in 2006 (see Kaskinen 2008). The changes have to be considered with this limitation in mind; the purpose of the styling was to boost the sale of the flat which was to be carried out by a real estate agency also sponsoring and co-operating in the TV programme. For reasons of space, the discussion will be limited to comparing the metafunctional changes before and after the changes and considering how the metafunctional meanings create 'hotspots' "where specific functional meanings overlap, interplay or conflict to produce more complex, sometimes contradictory interpretations" (O'Toole 2004: 26).

The Before View of the Living Room–Kitchen Area

The living room–kitchen area is shown from the before-view perspective in Figure 13.2 and the discussion that follows exemplifies the metafunctional choices made in home decoration.

The structural change whereby the wall between the original bed-sitter and the three-room flat was knocked down played a vital role in the

| Living Room – Kitchen before | Living Room before |

Figure 13.2   Two before-views of the living room–kitchen.

composition of the flat, and this compositional change also allowed me to bring certain experiential and interpersonal meanings together. The enlarged living room area allowed more floor space in the living area, excellent for *interpersonal* purposes, as will be discussed shortly (see Stenglin 2008 for an approach to the interpersonal in 3D spaces). The change left a white column for constructional reasons in the middle of the living room space. A further structural compositional change was getting rid of a half-wall, envisaged originally by the architect, between the living room and the kitchen. This *zoning,* allowed free movement from living room to the kitchen and vice versa. The only zone that indicates the boundary between the living room and the kitchen is the tiled floor area. In the kitchen, some unity was structurally created by uniting the workbench area. Instead of a full, vertical cupboard at the end of the workbench by the kitchen window, I wanted to have an extended workbench area, and thus the full cupboard was replaced by a lower and an upper cupboard (with the microwave) so that the kitchen workbench could be extended from wall to wall.

Experientially, the living room usually gathers the family together—frequently the most important element in the room is the TV. My living room was also designed for watching TV (outlets both for the TV and radio). Yet, my conceptualisation of the living room did not include TV; rather, the most prominent elements that governed the floor space by the big window were the two new sofas—one three-person and the other two-person, a smallish, round wooden (birch) old table between them, an old arm chair but refurbished with the same material as the sofas, a white Ikea table (recycled from a friend)—all organised to form a 'group'. Further decoration items were some cushions on the sofa, a Chinese lantern type of lamp, some carpets (woven by my mother), Finnish design items (candle holders, Aalto vase on the window shelf), and various items from my travels around the world, e.g. a Chinese wall-hanging, a wooden Brazilian parrot hanging from the ceiling. These elements seemed to represent a mixture of my experiences of my life in Finland and abroad. A further item in the living room area was an old, multipurpose, old, wooden (pine) Lundia bookshelf, behind the three-seater sofa but pushed against the wall so that one could pass between the sofa and the bookshelf. It was multifunctional: 'a bar' (glasses and bottles), a telephone/fax shelf on one shelf (cf. an office function), and books, mostly art and history (something to browse in a living room).

Between the living room area and the kitchen area was another Lundia shelf, which also was multifunctional: it was a 'music entertainment centre' containing the stereo equipment and compact discs (CDs) and cassettes, but also books, further decorative items from my travels, and some drawers and shelves which contained kitchen items (finer cutlery, serviettes, candles in the drawers and trays and place mats on the shelves). The kitchen elements were either fixed Elements like the fridge, stove, cupboards, workbench (explained already), a white shelf system that I had had made to keep various items like cookery books, piles of clean towels and all the knickknacks that one tends to collect, a tiled floor and non-fixed Elements like the kitchen table and the chairs. Like the Lundia shelves, the kitchen table and chairs (both birch) have been with me since the mid-1980s when I first moved to Helsinki, and they have travelled with me from one place to another. My kitchen table was rectangular and had two short sides and two long sides. Although the kitchen elements are naturally functionally differentiated from the living room elements, when we take into consideration my interpersonal purposes in the living room—kitchen area, we can start seeing how this space started to make cohesive sense and create significant metafunctional hotspots—at least to me as a 'layperson home decorator'.

The original reason for knocking down the wall between the two flats was also the light—in its *interpersonal* function—the original three-room flat did not have enough light for me—and light is very important in a Nordic country; with the structural changes the open space and the double glass doors into the third bedroom now allowed light from the Western side of the building and gave perspective extending from the kitchen through the living room into the TV/guest room (third bedroom). As an entertainer of my guests and as a discourse analyst, my main idea for styling the space was 'flowing discourse' and 'organising entertainment'. The welcoming living room opens up as you enter into the flat (there is no zone between the entrance and the living room except for the floor tiling, the same as in the kitchen). The two new sofas were set facing each other and the positioning of the arm chair complemented the sofas—the purpose being that the people have interesting discussions with each other, sharing a small coffee table between them (for glasses and nibbles). The music and drinks were close by on the 'bar-bookshelf' behind the arm chair and the 'music centre-shelf', and there was even enough space for dancing in the living room area. But no TV.

The colours of the sofas were soft, beige and white, echoed with the brown and white in the carpets. The brown was thus intended to link up with the brownish wooden surfaces, pine for the bookshelves and birch for the floor, the round living room table and the kitchen table and chairs. The wood gave both rooms a certain Scandinavian, rustic impression. The kitchen table and chairs carry a relatively close resemblance to one Ikea table called, Björkudden, which Björkvall (2009: 6–7) says is designed to express 'detachment' created when the guests have to turn their heads to face the person sitting next to one and to indicate 'hierarchical difference', with the host and hostess sitting at the shorter ends of the rectangular table. I did position the table sometimes in the way just described when the number of guests did not exceed four but pushed the table close to the window, leaving me at the end as a hostess. But mostly when I entertained, rather than a 'sit-down dinner', I turned the table sideways, pushed it close to the window, lengthened it by two extra boards to increase the table-top space, and on that surface all the food was laid in Scandinavian buffet fashion.

So where are the metafunctional 'hotspots' of this layperson's styling? The first one seems to be in how the positioning of the guests was designed in entertainment situations, that being the principle 'driving force' behind the choices. The STANDING and the SITTING were conceptualised compositionally, especially for the SITTING with the sofas set opposite each other (easy face-to-face contact) and the armchair completing the sofa arrangement (at the other end there was no seating as it would have blocked the way to the balcony). Guests could easily move between STANDING and SITTING, and with their cocktail/wine glasses they could also easily move to the balcony (for pleasure, if the weather allowed, or to smoke). I usually positioned myself in the arm chair rather than the sofas. This gave me easy access to the next hotspots, BAR and MUSIC-centres, and as the hostess I could provide the guests with drinks or fill-ups and regulate the music on my way to the kitchen and back. The rectangular table in its buffet-position functioned as the fourth hotspot, providing the guests with FOOD. The happily conversing people in the interactive circle of the sofas, or standing, could easily detach themselves and move to the kitchen area to get food from the kitchen buffet table. The combined living room–kitchen realised functionality—creating a space where talking, eating, drinking and providing entertainment were facilitated.

Although the overall impression to me was very functional, to a professional outsider, the invited interior decorator, the stylist, it represented haphazardly realised choices—mixing old personal history in Elements with the new, and mixing various materials and colours (see van Leeuwen, this volume, for a discussion of functionalism).

After-View of the Living Room—Kitchen

The purpose of professional styling was to give the flat a 'face-lift', to attract potential buyers for the flat and increase its value. During the TV programme I was presented with three different possibilities for 'styling' the flat. I chose the plan that is presented in Figure 13.3. It was to me the most appealing one in terms of the colour scheme and the changes suggested and seemed realistic in terms of the budget that I also had set for the makeover (not wanting to spend a lot, as I planned to move).

Not everything that was in the plan was realised exactly as the professional stylist had planned it, and partly the plan was realised with 'loan furniture', which then I could buy, if I wanted. The images in Figure 13.4 show that the stylist's plan for the living room and the kitchen was not realised quite as planned.

Compositionally the changes were not great—no walls were knocked down etc., but the Elements in the living room got somewhat shifted around and that did compositionally create a feeling of 'more space' in the area. These changes can conveniently be explained by considering some

Figure 13.3   The styling plan.

| The Living Room After-View | The Kitchen After-View |

Figure 13.4   The living room and the kitchen after-view.

of the changes in the *experiential* Elements: some experiential Elements were taken out of the composition of the two spaces totally and some were replaced by other Elements which functionally however were about the same, although not quite. The three-seater sofa, which I had placed facing the big windows, thus giving my guest a nice view of 'the trees and nature', was now placed where the two-seater sofa had been (the two-seater was put into the TV/guestroom). A new, relatively big armchair from Ikea was now put in the three-seater's position (but now only one person could enjoy the view). Next to it was placed a new item, a small, round table with a clear glass surface, with the Aalto-design vase on the top. The old arm chair remained where it was, but the small white Ikea table was removed. The small round birch table between the sofas was replaced by a long, white, low-level rectangular Ikea table, set between the three-seater sofa and the new Ikea armchair. The sofa and the arm chairs got new cushion covers. A new standing lamp complemented the SITTING arrangement and the cheap, 'temporary', Chinese paper lantern light was replaced by a standing light set behind the three-seater. The 'bar'-bookshelf was replaced by Lundia's latest product, a white bookshelf, and the 'music centre'-bookshelf had to give way to a white Lundia chest of drawers onto which my Iittala 'Archipelago'-design candle holders were put. This left a lot of open space above it, but the stylist set a new table Lundia lamp on it and found a picture within a white frame that suited the wall position well.

Further, in the kitchen, the rectangular birchwood kitchen table and chairs were replaced with a round white table and some Ikea chairs (in the styling plan, Figure 13.3, the old table is still in its place, but later the stylist put my original table and chairs into the balcony and the round table indoors, cf. dynamism in choice). The home woven carpets were replaced by broader, commercial carpets that covered most of the floor surface of the sofa-armchair group and the free floor space close to the column.

Probably the biggest personal experiential change for me was that the stylist (and her helpers) almost completely removed those Elements that somehow represented travels or my personal living. My Brazilian bird and my not-so-many stuffed animals (each with a story to tell) were packed into a storage box. My refrigerator magnets from all over the world, which held numerous reminder notes for me, were also removed. The oddly placed kitchen lamp in the middle of the kitchen ceiling had to go, too, but was not replaced by another. The CDs and books were stacked away behind the doors of the white Lundia shelf behind the new armchair.

What changed *interpersonally* both in the living room and the kitchen and partly throughout the flat were some slight, unifying changes in the colour scheme and some changes in the materials. The stylist liked the colours of my kitchen curtains (see Figure 13.2 and 13.4), the 'retro colouring' of various shades of light blue, green circles on white. She took this as the colour scheme throughout the styling. Moving from the kitchen curtains towards the living room, the Lundia lamp shade on the chest of drawers picked up the green as did the picture representation in the white frames; the green and white then continued in the curtains that had been there and the blue-green-white was then picked up again in the new cushion covers of the three-seater and the arm chair. The colours were then also repeated in the bedroom and my TV/guest-room (third bedroom) and my office-room (second bedroom) in cushions and curtains. The other colour scheme that became clarified within the living room and kitchen area was the prevalence of 'white'. Again moving from the kitchen, which as a whole had already been 'relatively white' (cupboards, tiles behind the kitchen workbench, fridge), this area got a strengthening of white on the surface of the white, round table. Yet, for contrast, the chairs kept some of the earlier 'brownish, wooden theme' in the kitchen, but definitely reduced the effect of 'wood', which I had followed with my choices of the kitchen table and the chairs and also with the other two pinewood Lundia bookshelves (the 'bar' and the 'music centre'), which now had been replaced by the white Lundia chest of drawers and the new white Lundia bookshelf with glass doors. The 'whiteness' was further increased by the replacement of the small, round, birch-wood table with a large, white-top rectangular sofa table and the white large carpets. Also interpersonally significant was the texture of the new carpets; their size and their 'fluffiness' gave the flat 'a touch of luxury'. 'Upgrading' was also realised in the glass table that was placed next to the new arm chair, and of course in the size of the arm chair itself, being soft and big, just enormously comfortable to 'sink in'.

DISCUSSION

In The Before View of the Living Room–Kitchen Area, it was suggested that the metafunctional hotspots of my layperson's styling was the integration of meanings as the STANDING and SITTING arrangements of the living room area, the BAR and the MUSIC-centre as the outer zones, supporting the STANDING and SITTING and the kitchen areas functioning as a hotspot of FOOD. How did the professional stylist see these layperson's metafunctional hotspots, and did her changes influence the hotspots?

The STANDING and SITTING hotspots were unified materially through the fluffy, big white carpets, and since there now was more room in the SITTING arrangement (after removing excess elements), the moving back and forth between STANDING and SITTING did actually become easier. The big white table gave a shared nibbles/glasses space for those using the SITTING area. All of the hotspot areas became unified with the colour of white, and around the STANDING and SITTING also with the green-white of the curtains, with the white, bluish, greenish colours in the sofa cushions and the green lamp shade on the top of the chest of drawers and the painting above it, culminating at the origin of the colours—the retro-coloured curtains in the kitchen. The white kitchen table top unified the FOOD hotspot in colour to the STANDING and SITTING hotspots. Its round shape may also be taken to ease the movement around it, if we think of the guests coming from the STANDING and SITTING, as the guest could go around the buffet table taking what they wanted—in the rectangular shape they were forced to start from one direction, usually from the kitchen workbench side, and end at the other, in the direction of the living room. So the STANDING-SITTING-FOOD hotspots seemed to have been kept and their functionality improved.

The previous BAR and the MUSIC-centre, however, went through such changes that they lost their functionally cohesive purposes. Both of course had been multi-purpose hotspots: the MUSIC-centre had hosted also finer cutlery, serviettes, tablemats, trays, some decorative items and some of my books that were not most frequently used. The drawer in the new white chest of drawers, which replaced the 'music centre', was supposed to contain racks to keep my CDs in order, but the racks were, however, never delivered during the styling process (cf. 'dynamism'). Without the racks, the drawer ended up hosting the cutlery etc. and the CDs of the previous 'music centre' found their place on the shelves behind the glass doors of the new, tall, white, Lundia bookshelf that replaced the old 'BAR' hotspot, and the books and souvenirs were put into boxes and moved to storage. According to the styling plan, a much lower, but broader Lundia bookshelf with glass doors should have stood at the place of the tall, white bookshelf. But the delivery from the shop brought two lower bookshelf systems which however where too broad to be placed on the 'ex-BAR' hotspot. They were placed into the TV/guest room instead and the videos (VHS/DVD) were brought to accompany the CDs in the tall bookshelf, which also ended up having some of my books (organised by the stylist in descending order according to the height of the book, rather than following my thematic/author organisation, the result being a 'mish-mash' organisation of the books).

In short then, the previous MUSIC-centre hotspot got reduced to SERV-ING-HELP-post (with cutlery etc., but one big drawer could not contain everything that had previously been in four drawers). The MUSIC-entertainment hotspot became totally dysfunctional. The stereo equipment was placed in the TV/guestroom (the quality of the music through the speakers perhaps being fine for that room but not for the living room), and when I wanted to play a CD, I had to get the CD from the living room and then go and put it on in the TV/guest-room and then return to my guests (and even when I was alone—so the amount of my listening to music decreased as the result of the non-functional flow of to-and-from music). The previous BAR-hotspot also became dysfunctional. The glasses were put into the kitchen, the wine and other spirits into various cupboards that had space. The telephone/fax machine got put into the office (where it rightly belongs).

Experientially the stylist's motivation seemed to be to clarify the living room–kitchen area (as well as the whole of the flat) experientially, as in her view I had too many furniture-Elements in the rooms, too many personal things on the bookshelves. Removing personal items when one intends to sell the flat is essential, according to the discussions with the stylist and the real agent, to give the flat full possibilities in the potential buyers' minds. The buyers have to see this potential in the flat, and if it is full of personal items then it is difficult for potential buyers to see themselves as dwellers in the flat. The flat living room–kitchen space indeed seemed more spacious. The unification of decorative Elements to certain design items, their colour as well as the colours in the curtain materials and the sofa cushion materials, the coherence of the interior decoration, plus the lush carpets gave the flat a touch of 'simple luxury' that was appealing. All in all, the compositional changes were not great but together with the experiential changes in Elements and the interpersonal changes in unifying the colours, they did improve the spatial organisation and thus certainly made the living room and kitchen area more open and appealing. Certainly the personal lesson that I learnt was the necessity and the process of 'dejunking' or 'depersonalising' for a reason; we do get attached to many things in our life histories that are possibly only appealing to us, but certain histories also have their place.

Because the US subprime loan crisis slowed down the housing market and I was planning a job/home exchange with a foreign academic, the flat was taken out of the market as soon as the sales contract with the real estate agent ended. And since I continued to live in the flat, very soon my few stuffed animals, for instance, with their stories to tell returned to their places on the top of the sofa, and I did reorganise some other of the stylist's changes, which I considered dysfunctional for me. For example, I reinstalled the BAR and reordered my books thematically, not according to their sizes. No doubt when I re-enter the flat into the market for sale, I shall have to 'dejunk' again and I have to remind myself of the lessons learnt from the stylist's way of thinking about how space, elements and materials realise their functions. But at the same time, I think that in my new home, I can also use the tools presented here, to create a new home with overall metafunctional unity and hotspots that make my life as well as my guests' visits pleasurable in the new future home.

CONCLUSION

This paper has discussed an individual flat as a piece of universe and as a home. When we analyse any such instantial unit as a flat/home 'here and now', we must also at the same time consider the various semiotisation processes that such a unit goes through when it is placed exactly where it stands and how exactly it came into being. We have seen how such a unit as a flat in a multi-storey building is situated as a part of the urban and social environment in a way that makes meanings socially (certain kind of people find the area appealing, affordable etc.). A flat is planned as a unit of a building, which, in turn, coheres in a certain way with the suburb in which it is placed, and within the building it is meant to cohere with the units that are planned to be its companions (although in a hierarchical way as bed-sitter, two-room flats etc.). We have seen how even during the planning and construction phase, a certain dynamic resemiotisation can take place—buildings and flats are not always built the way they were originally planned. Due to the constructional changes, the flat analysed here was resemiotised when the two smaller flats were joined together into a bigger one, and this process influenced both the whole of the building as well as the individual, joined flats.

Once buildings and flats are ready and the first inhabitants move in, the history begins, and this history involves various cycles of resemiotisation. Every time a new set of inhabitants moves into the flat they do their own interior decorations following certain experiential, interpersonal and compositional principles that influence building up the flat, the rooms and the elements in them as 'a home', as a representation of 'their world' and 'their discourses' (cf. the notion of 'semiotic spanning' Ventola 1999; Ventola and Charles 2002). The semiotic, spatial organisation of our surroundings influences our talk much more than we as laypersons think. We construe our daily lives in spaces that are designed for certain kind of activities and talk. Yet, we hardly ever think of how our actions and discourses link up with the rooms and the elements in the rooms. Professionals do.

In this paper, a transformation of a layperson's design of a home was set up against a professional stylist's construal for a home. It is clear that a professional interior decorator has been trained to look at a home 'from a distance', and through refurbishing it can realise new experiential, interpersonal and compositional meanings within a home (coherence etc.), whether for the client's own tastes and purposes or for selling a flat or a house. This paper has shown that the tools developed within systemic functionally oriented approach (here labelled as *multisemiotics/ multisystemiotics*—or perhaps *polysystemiotics?*[1]), can offer us useful tools for analysing the meanings that our contexts—whether homes or official buildings etc.— can carry. What still needs to be worked out and usefully combined with it is the study of discourses in these places, taking also into consideration the realised semiotisation choices of contexts and their influences on the discourses in these spaces, in a more sophisticated way than is currently done. But to reach those goals, we have to step out of our disciplinary boundaries and see how human interaction truly interactively works within its contexts. Linguists have learned to look at language in context, but any context, even a private flat, encodes meanings that get very intricately interwoven to discourses of these interactions. Learning this combined way of analysing discourses will have to be our ultimate goal when trying to make sense of the complex multisemiotic world in which we work and live.

NOTES

1. As suggested by Michael O'Toole (personal communication). The author is also grateful to him for commenting on the draft version of the paper.

REFERENCES

Alias, S. (2004) 'A semiotic study of Singapore's Orchard Road and Marriott Hotel.' In O'Halloran, K. L. ed. *Multimodal Discourse Analysis,* London, New York: Continuum: pp. 55–79.

Björkvall, A. (2009) 'Practical function and meaning: a case study of Ikea tables.' In Jewitt, C. ed. *Handbook of Multimodal Analysis,* London: Routledge: pp. 242–252.

Jones, C., and Ventola, E., eds. (2008) *From Language to Multimodality: New Developments in the Study of Ideational Meaning,* London: Equinox.

Karlsson, A. M. (2004) 'How to build a house from reading a drawing: professional and popular mediations of construction.' *Visual Communication* 3 (3): 251–279.

Kaskinen, P. (2008) 'My home is my castle.' *Helsinki Times*. Available online at <http://www.helsinkitimes.fi/htimes/index.php/housing/3096-my-home-is-my-castle-> (accessed 1 April 2000).

Martin, J. (1992) *English Text*, Amsterdam: Benjamins.

Martinec, R. (2005) 'Topics in multimodality.' In Hasan, R., Matthiessen, C. M. I. M. and Webster, J. eds. *Continuing Discourse on Language: A Functional Perspective*, London: Equinox: 157–181.

Matthiessen, C., and Halliday, M. A. K. (1997) 'Functional grammar: a first step into the theory.' Available online at <http://www.ling.mq.edu.au/nlp/resource/VirtuallLibrary/Publications/sfg_firststep/SFGintroNew.html> (accessed 1 April 2009)

O'Halloran, K. L., ed. (2004) *Multimodal Discourse Analysis: Systemic Functional Perspectives*, London: Continuum.

O'Toole, M. (1994) *The Language of Displayed Art*, 1st ed, London: Leicester University Press.

——— (2004) 'Opera Ludentes: A Systemic-Functional View of the Sydney Opera House.' In O'Halloran, K. L. ed. *Multimodal Discourse Analysis*, London, New York: Continuum: pp. 11–27.

——— (2010) *The Language of Displayed Art*, 2nd ed, London and New York: Routledge.

'Pistetalo' (2009) *Wikipedia*. Available online at <http://fi.wikipedia.org/wiki/Pistetalo> (accessed 26 June 2008).

'Ruskeasuo' (2009) *Wikipedia*. Available online at <http://fi.wikipedia.org/wiki/Ruskeasuo> (accessed 26 June 2008); for location of Ruskeasuo, see http://en.wikipedia.org/wiki/Ruskeasuo (accessed 16 March 2009).

Stenglin, M. K. (2008) 'Binding: a resource for exploring interpersonal meaning in 3D space.' *Social Semiotics*, 18(4), 425–447.

——— (2009) 'Space odyssey: towards a social semiotic model of three-dimensional space.' *Visual Communication*, vol. 8:1, pp. 35–64.

'Urban planning' (2009) *Wikipedia*. Available online at <http://en.wikipedia.org/wiki/Urban_planning> (accessed 26 June 2008).

Ventola, E. (1987) *The Structure of Social Interaction: A Systemic Approach to Semiotics of Service Encounters*, London: Pinter Publishers.

——— (1999) 'Semiotic Spanning at Conferences; Cohesion and Coherence in and across conference papers and their discussions.' In Bublitz, W., Lenk, U. and Ventola, E. eds. *Coherence in Spoken and Written Discourse. How to Create It and How to Describe It*, Amsterdam: Benjamins: pp. 101–125.

Ventola, E., and Charles, C. (2002) 'Multi-modal slide show.' In Ventola, E., Shalom, C. and Thompson, S. eds. *Conference Language*, Frankfurt am Main: Peter Lang: pp. 169–208.

Ventola, E., Charles, C., Kaltenbacher, M. eds. (2004) *Perspectives on Multimodality*, Amsterdam and Philadelphia: John Benjamins.

14 Art vs. Computer Animation
Integrity and Technology in *South Park*

Michael O'Toole

PREVIEWS

The opening to Episode 609 (July 2002), "Free Hat", of the TV comedy cartoon *South Park*[1] has four South Park kids sitting in the Bijou cinema watching previews for forthcoming films. The booming voice of the announcer proclaims:

> Coming this summer, it's the classic film that changed America, *E.T.: The Extraterrestrial*, the new, redone version for 2002. All the E.T. effects have been digitally upgraded. All the guns have been digitally changed to walkie-talkies. And the word "TERRORIST" has been changed to "HIPPIE".

> | | |
> |---|---|
> | *Stan asks:* | "Aw, dude, why would they do that?" |
> | *Cartman responds:* | "Yeah, hippies and terrorists are the same thing." |
> | *Kyle explains:* | "No, dude. They only changed "terrorist" to "hippie" to make E.T. more P.C. |
> | *Stan, satisfied:* | "That's gay." |

The preview resumes (Figure 14.1a):

> Coming this summer, it's the motion picture that changed America. *Saving Private Ryan*, the re-re-release, where the word "NAZI" has been changed to "PERSONS WITH POLITICAL DIFFERENCES" and all their guns have been replaced by walkie-talkies.

> *Stan is incensed:* "Why the hell do these directors keep updating their movies?"

When an even more extreme—and absurd—digital makeover of *Star Wars: The Empire Strikes Back* is announced, the boys walk out and demand their money back, without success. The following dialogue ensues:

| (a) Bombs and Walkie-Talkies in 'Private Ryan' | (b) Crowd Movement |

Figure 14.1   Previews and crowd scene.

> *Kyle:* Why don't they leave those movies alone? We liked them the way they were!
>
> *Tweek:* Don't you see what this means? All our favourite movies are going to be changed, and updated, until we can't even recognize them any more.
>
> *Stan:* Tweek is right. It isn't fair for those asshole directors to keep changing their movies and making them different. Movies are art, and art shouldn't be modified!
>
> *Kyle:* Yeah, what if they had modified the Roman Coliseum every year? It would just be another big douchey stadium now.

Stan and Kyle propose that they form a "Save Films From Their Own Directors" club and they nail a sign on a phone pole outside the South Park Elementary School gymnasium announcing a rally the next day to "Save Our Nation's Films". Cartman adds the words "FREE HAT" at the bottom of the sign on the grounds that "You have to offer fabulous prizes if you want people to show up for your stupid crap." The three regular members of the quartet, Stan, Cartman and Kyle, go off to get the gymnasium ready, while Tweek, the nervy newcomer (replacing Kenny, who is dead again) is ordered to go home and make fifty paper hats.

When they meet next day to see if anyone has turned up for the rally, they are amazed to find the room full: "Dude, there's like a thousand people in there!" But it turns out that the people have not come to save the nation's films from digital remastering, or to collect a free hat, but to free Hat, i.e. organise the release from prison of Hat McCollough, who had been convicted in 1982 of the serial murder of twenty-three babies.

The shots of the crowd in the gymnasium demanding the release of Hat are a nice example of the richer and more complex animation made possible by CGI (Computer Generated Imagery). Whereas the stop-start animation of earlier technologies involving paper models, including the first episodes of *South Park* in 1996, lacked fluidity and range of variation within the shot, CGI makes it possible for Trey Parker and Matt Stone to have a diversity of signs being waved: *"FREE HAT'*, *"FREADOM FOR HAT* NOW!*"* and "HAT DIDN'T DO IT", a range of movements in the crowd, and even individualised facial expressions (Figure 14.1b).

Much of the humour in this opening episode is purely visual, depending on the modal functioning of intertextuality (Nudge-nudge, viewer, what does this shot remind you of?):

1. The opening shot of four little figures in an almost deserted cinema: the many films about film-viewing: *Cinema Paradiso*, Buster Keaton's *Sherlock Jr.*, Woody Allen's *Purple Rose of Cairo* etc.
2. The words "Coming this summer", accompanying a pompous announcer's voice, "zoom" towards the viewer.
3. Animated versions of well-known shots from *E.T. the Extra-Terrestrial* (the kids flying across the sky with the moon in the background; the kids taking off from the road; the police moving in to stop the kids—but with walkie-talkies in hand instead of guns); from *Saving Private Ryan* (the landing at Normandy in all its bloody glory but with ridiculously animated soldier figures holding not guns, but walkie-talkies).
4. The roughly scrawled notice pinned to a phone pole ("Wanted" notices in any number of Westerns).
5. The "captive audience" in the gymnasium (political protest films) but with the boys' and our gradual discovery that it's the wrong audience.

And then, apart from these generic shots from film history, much of the intertextuality hinges on what we know of the characters and their town from the previous eighty-seven episodes of *South Park*. The four children: Stan and Kyle (who represent Matt Stone and Trey Parker themselves) are good friends and relatively "normal", motivators of the plot. They are also foils for the oddities like Cartman, a "know-it-all" bully with an unsettled family history, and Tweek, a frightened little neurotic, with a protective family who feed him too much coffee. All these four are depicted as circular blobs in distinctive costumes, though Cartman is too fat to walk, so he waddles; and Tweek is too nervy to take life as it comes, so he reacts to every crisis, small and big, with squeaks and absurdly jerky blinking with his triangles of eyelids. Even Tweek's father and the Bijou's ticket salesman are known to aficionados of *South Park* (*SP*) from their behaviour in earlier episodes.

The representational function is carried visually by the characters and their actions together with the developing plot lines concerning the boys' opposition to the digital remastering of films and the mounting campaign for the release of Hat McCulloch. Compositionally, Parker and Stone's animation allows for the alternation of symmetry (inside the almost empty cinema; inside the crowded gymnasium) with asymmetry (as the boys meld into a group and split as they disagree; as Tweek, "seeking his centre" during another crisis, dreams a hippie vision of harmony in his bedroom, fortified by yet another cup of coffee).

In the verbal mode, too, the interpersonal function is realised in the humour:

1. The hyperbolic claims of the film announcements: "the classic film that changed America"; "all the E.T. effects have been digitally upgraded"; "it's the motion picture that changed America"; "the entire cast has been digitally replaced by Ewoks".
2. The "crescendo effect" of the claims: "the new, redone version (of *E.T.*)" < the RE-RE-RELEASE (of *Saving Private Ryan*) < the classic RE-RE-RE-Release (of *Star Wars*).
3. The supposed PC (political correctness) of corporate changes of vocabulary: "TERRORIST" has been changed to "HIPPIE"; "the word "NAZI" has been changed to "PERSONS WITH POLITICAL DIFFERENCES"; the word "WOOKIE" has been changed to "HAIR CHALLENGED ANIMAL".
4. The boys' American youth idiom: "Oh, cool.", "Aw, dude", "That's gay", "Goddamnit, that pissed me off!", "You asshole!", "another big douchey stadium", "No, fatass", "stop with these faggotronics", "your stupid crap", "Dude, there's like a thousand people in there", "Then I'mo kick your ass, Tweek!"
5. This contrasts with the register of chairing a public meeting: "Okay, uh, we wanna thank you all for coming. We're really happy to see such enthusiasm for our cause." "Uh, one thing before I continue. Unfortunately, we don't have enough of the . . . free hats for everyone." "Yes, we apologise, but our friend Tweek here didn't make enough of them."
6. Then there is the contrast with the rowdy chanting of the slogan "Free Hat!"

NIGHTLINE

Later, as the boys count the sign-ups for their campaign (which the signatories assume is to free Hat), Tweek comes in with the news that Ted Koppel, the TV current affairs commentator, wants them to appear on his programme *Nightline*. The opening shot on air, like the earlier formal situations, is composed symmetrically: Koppel sits at his interview desk with the four boys in an inset over his left shoulder (Figure 14.2a).

His relationship with his guests, however, is anything but symmetrical:

Ted Koppel: A new movement is sweeping the country, led by four determined boys from South Park, Colorado. The organization was created to protect Hollywood's classic films from the hands of their directors. And also to free Hat McCullough. So, boys, I ask you the question that's on everyone's minds, why does your organization want to free Hat McCullough, the convicted, confessed serial murderer of twenty-three babies?

As with most media commentators these days, the secondary—but scandalous—issue takes precedence over the main one. Cartman is stumped by this unexpected line of questioning:

Cartman: *(blinks and gazes at camera)* I think that can best be answered by our official spokesman, Tweek. *[the camera moves from Cartman to Tweek]*

Tweek: Gaaarh!

Ted Koppel: Well, Hat McCullough admitted he killed those toddlers. Why do you want him free?

Tweek: *("TWEEK, ADVOCATE OF TODDLER MURDER" appears at the bottom of the screen)* Oh, Jesus, man! . . . N'ahah!

Ted Koppel: Just answer me this, Tweek: what do you see as "positive" about toddler murder!

Tweek: *(still with the subtitle)* Ahah. U-uh. It's easy?

Ted Koppel: Yes . . . *(looking sinister)* it is easy . . . Alright, then, on to your other cause, saving films from their directors. What got you boys interested in this, especially given your pro-toddler-murder status?

Koppel rounds off by attaching a complex nominalisation "pro-toddler-murder status" (which resists deconstruction) as a permanent label to everything the boys stand for. As his other guests, Steven Spielberg and George Lucas walk into the studio, they share in this labelling (Figure 14.2b):

(a) Studio and Location	(b) The Directors in Frame

Figure 14.2   Nightline.

> *Ted Koppel:* Gentlemen, these toddler-murder fans think you're insane
>   and shouldn't be allowed to alter your films. Your response?
> *Spielberg:* Well, first of all, both George and I are very firmly against
>   the murdering of toddlers.

Visually, the arrival of Spielberg and Lucas in the studio allows the *South Park* directors some interesting play with computer animation. Previously in the interview the boys were seen in a frame with some brick buildings with arched windows behind them—presumably a location shot from South Park—and the camera cut regularly between speakers, the dominant figure of Koppel in the TV studio, presumably in Hollywood, and the frame of the boys. But Spielberg and Lucas walk straight into the broadcast frame where the boys are, thus increasing their fear and subordinated status, as well as the unlikelihood of the encounter.

The computer generation also allows much more movement and characterisation than was ever possible with manual animation techniques. Throughout the interview Tweek is constantly quivering with fear and anxiety, while his companions only move when they speak. When Koppel, Spielberg and Lucas are speaking their heads and mouths move quite naturally. Although animated figures, they are also clearly recognisable from their common photographic or filmed images.

In the face of the boys' attack Spielberg maintains, "Changing *E.T.* was the best thing I ever did.", to which Kyle responds, "Dude, don't you see that it's not? It'd be like changing *Raiders of the Lost Ark*!" To the film's director, Steven Spielberg and its producer, George Lucas, this idea is a stroke of genius: "Why didn't we think of it before?!" (*a snatch of dramatic music from Raiders*).

CAPTURING THE LOST ARK

At a further meeting of their new club, Stan announces:

> Members, this is our darkest hour. We've just learned that George Lucas and Steven Spielberg now intend to update and change *Raiders of the Lost Ark*. There's only one way we can stop this important and historical piece of art from being harmed. Mr. Secretary? (*hands the mic to Cartman, who moves over to an easel*).

> *Cartman:* Thank you. (*turns a page on the easel to show a plan of George Lucas's Skywalker Ranch*) Our intelligence tells us that the original negative to *Raiders of the Lost Ark* is currently somewhere in George Lucas's house. We need to find and usurp that negative.
> *Man:* And if we get hold of the negative they can't change the movie?
> *Stan:* That is our understanding.

After this play with the procedures and language of public meetings, the camera moves into the visual register and creepy music of secret nocturnal break-ins, as the boys creep into Lucas's house in California, with a string of dark shots of his study and a torchlight on the videos on his shelves (including not only the updated versions of *Star Wars*, but "digitally enhanced" versions of his *First Day at School*, *Wedding Day*, *Kids' First Swimming Lesson* and *Weather*). They have just seized the original 1982 negative of *Raiders*, when Lucas comes in, demands the negative back and phones for the police. Kyle tries to reason with him (Figure 14.3a):

> *Kyle:*   It's not too late to do what's right. Give us the print. There's still some good in you, Mr. Lucas, We know there is. You yourself led the campaign against the colorization of films. You understand why films shouldn't be changed . . . When an artist creates, whatever they create belongs to society.
>
> *Lucas:*   Have I . . . become so old that I've forgotten what being an artist is all about?
>
> *Stan:*   Give the print to us so that we can protect it from Spielberg and anyone else who wants to alter it.

Enter Spielberg with three goons armed with walkie-talkies. The previous lyrical piano music reverts to *Raiders* sound track. Spielberg begins to behave like a Nazi (an ironic reference to his film *Schindler's List* and an anticipation of his later role in this story; Figure 14.3b):

> *Spielberg:* You haven't let these doe-eyed children affect your judgement, have you, George?! (*voice lowers*) Don't forget: you belong to me. (snatching the film from Lucas) Now take the children prisoner! . . . You troublemakers shall be my guests of honour at the premiere of the NEW Raiders of the Lost Ark! Your gay little club is over!

| (a) "Give me that print, George!" | (b) "Don't forget, you belong to me." |

Figure 14.3   Capturing the Lost Ark.

DIGITAL IRONY

While Spielberg's goons seize Kyle, Stan and Cartman, Tweek manages to escape and the film directors exit. At this point the most extended visual joke of the whole episode begins. A blank screen is filled with the zooming words "COMING THIS SUMMER" and the unctuous announcer's voice, as in the opening sequence in the Bijou cinema, proclaiming (over triumphal "preview music"; Figures 14.4a[2] and 14.4b):

> Coming this summer: (*title:* RE-RELEASE OF EPISODE 1 SOUTH PARK) It's the digitally-reenhanced re-release of the very first pilot episode of *South Park*! (*scenes from "Cartman Gets an Anal Probe"*) Yes, the classic, rough, hand-made first episode is getting a make-over for 2002. The simple, funny aliens are now super-badass and kewl! Flying saucer? No longer cheap construction paper, but a 4.0 megapixel non-drop digital masterpiece of technology! Yes, everything's new! New is better!

With the critics they had created—Stan, Kyle and Cartman—out of the way under Spielberg's control, the creators of *South Park*, Trey Parker and Matt Stone, turn the critique of digitalisation against themselves (Figure 14.4c):

> *Trey Parker:* When we first made *South Park*, we didn't *wanna* use construction paper. We just *had* to because it was cheap.
> *Matt Stone:* And now with new technology we can finally remaster *South Park*, make it look sharp, clean and focused.
> *Trey Parker:* Expensive. (*Both men nod their heads*)
> *Announcer:* Yes, all the charm of a simple little cartoon will melt before your eyes as it is replaced by newer and more standardized animation!

> [*A special-edition DVD of "CGAAP": new version for 2002 is shown. "ACT NOW" blinks on the screen over the DVD*]

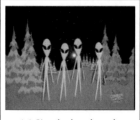  

(a) Simple, hand-made aliens	(b) Super-badass and kewl aliens"	(c) Focused... and Expensive

Figure 14.4   Digital irony.

Get this special enhanced version quick, because another enhanced version will likely be coming out for 2003!

This self-reflexive joke about the creators of *South Park* themselves abandoning the "charm" of their original style for the sharpness and standardisation of a remastered digitalised version is not only rhetorical, however. Parker and Stone resist the temptation of doing cartoon versions of themselves and, in contrast to the cartoon figures of the other film directors, Spielberg and Lucas, appear as "real-life" figures filmed in interview mode—something they hardly ever do throughout *South Park's* many episodes. They are "on trial" in the flesh before the jury of film history, guilty of remastering their own historic, and much-loved, creation.

Another ironic intertextual reference to *Raiders of the Lost Ark* enriches this sequence even further, since the archaeologist-hero, Indiana Jones, was motivated to find and protect the Lost Ark of the Covenant by his desire for historic preservation, while his rival, Belloq, is motivated entirely by greed.

IMPROVED HISTORY

Tweek, who has escaped capture by Spielberg's guards, now tries to enlist the support of the Free Hat Club to release his friends and prevent the premiere of the remastered *Raiders*. But the townsfolk are less interested in artistic integrity than in the release of the notorious serial baby-killer, Hat, so Tweek decides he must act alone. He is perfectly cast to enact that clichéd *topos* of Hollywood action films, the coward turned brave hero.

The episode that follows is an extended parody of the last major sequence in *Raiders*, in which Jones follows Belloq and the Ark and threatens to destroy it with an anti-tank missile launcher unless Belloq releases Marion, his heroine. He and Marion get tied up and have to watch the ceremonial opening of the Ark by Belloq and his Nazi helpers. However, Jones is aware of the danger of seeing the spirits released from the Ark, and he and Marion shut their eyes. As the lid is removed, the spirits within burst out and attack, the Nazis and their heads melt or explode.

As Spielberg, Lucas and their henchmen march through the desert with the new *Raiders* being carried in an Ark and Tweek's three friends as prisoners, Tweek appears on a hill overlooking a ravine, ambushing the procession with a bazooka—another narrative cliché of modern Wild West films. He threatens to blow up the Ark unless his friends are released. Spielberg confronts him:

> *Spielberg:* All your life has been the pursuit of seeing a great film! This new version of *Raiders* has digital effects beyond your wildest dreams! You want to see it screened just as much as I.

> *Kyle:*   Come on, Tweek! Blow it up!
> *Spielberg:* Son, we are simply passing through history. This . . . is imPROVED history. Do as you will.

Tweek hesitates, and three guards appear over the hill behind him. He lowers the bazooka.

DENOUEMENT

The "Free Hat" episode ends as it began—with a scene in a cinema. This time it is a makeshift open-air theatre somewhere in the desert, displaying the sign: "*RAIDERS OF THE LOST ARK. Premiere Tonight*" in flashing lights. In priest's robes and with an air of religious ritual, Spielberg and two assistants open the Ark and withdraw a film reel.

> *Spielberg:* This is the birth of the NEW version of *Raiders of the Lost Ark*! We shall screen it here, and then destroy all the old prints in celebration!

As the opening shots of the film run, the boys tightly shut their eyes in protest, but the "celebrity guests and other rich people", all dressed in evening dress, as for an Oscar Awards Night, make appreciative noises.

> *Spielberg:* It's beyoooootiful! [*A scene of Indiana Jones using a whip to swing across a chasm. Flaming arrows shoot past him. As he lands on the other side, natives approach. They look and chatter like Ewoks.*]
> *Viewer 1:* Wait a minute. This version is awful!
> *Viewer 2:* Yeah, they ruined it!
> *Viewer 3:* Oh my God, it's terrible!
> *Lucas:* (*suddenly scared stiff*) AaaaAAAAA!!

The three directors (now including Frances Ford Coppola) huddle in terror. On screen, Indiana Jones is reaching for a golden item. Rays of light burst like snakes from the screen and move out over the audience, shooting through the viewers' chests and killing them. Coppola, Lucas and Spielberg are overwhelmed by the energy from the rays. They become disfigured, and then their faces melt away. Spielberg's head explodes. The rays diffuse, and then gather back into the Ark. The spirits of all killed are gathered into the Ark as well. Finally, with a roll of thunder, the lid lands on the Ark.

The boys open their eyes. The ropes that bound them are gone and they are the only survivors. The next scene is in the daytime in South Park, which is celebrating the release from prison of Hat McCullough (still not cured of his hatred of babies . . .)

Figure 14.5 The spirits re-re-released.

The boys walk down the street away from the celebration.

Kyle: Do you think we did a good thing, Stan? I mean, no-one even seemed to notice.

Stan: Yeah well, sometimes the things we do don't matter right now. Sometimes they matter . . . later. We have to care more about later sometimes, you know? I think that's what separates us from the Steven Spielbergs and George Lucases of the world.

Cartman: That and youth. Those guys are old.

CONCLUSION

In addition to lampooning (verbally, visually and musically) Spielberg and Lucas for succumbing to the "Fascist" efficiency of computer animation, Parker and Stone (by now regularly using advanced computer animation techniques themselves) represent themselves in a live-action insert as "humane" in their remastered version of Episode 1 of "South Park".

As always with this series, intertextuality, parody and self-referentiality serve a modal function, bonding viewers with the absurd but honest politics of the child protagonists. Play with sub-frames and destruction of the space between screen and audience exploits the compositional potential of the digitalised audio-visual medium and enriches with purely visual jokes the humour of the story-line.

I want to claim that the story-line is both the challenge and the problem in writing a paper of this kind. When I have presented the arguments discussed here to a live conference audience, the story was largely carried by the clips embedded in my PowerPoint slides so that I was able to focus more specifically on the visual, audial and linguistic functions of individual scenes. Much of the multimodal work on cinematic/ televisual texts to date has, sensibly, been limited to the analysis of a single significant scene in a classic movie, or a single product being advertised, or a single news item. To begin to do justice to a twenty-five-minute episode from *South Park*, one has to tell enough of the story to clarify what is going on in individual scenes. This is quite laborious in running prose. But one also has to show the narrative or rhetorical functions of particular lines of dialogue or visual devices and to explain the intertextual nature of the jokes—visual, verbal and audial—in terms of the little world of South Park and its inhabitants and in terms of the larger world being satirised—in this case, the world of Hollywood directors and the fashion for (and economics of) remastering their most successful box-office hits—to say nothing of the intricate parodying of those hits.

We need to develop a narrative theory and a rhetoric as well as a grammar for the complex and moving multimodal texts of the TV and cinema. The work of the Russian Formalist theorists in the 1920s (several of whom laid the foundations for early film theory as well as literary poetics) introduced the important concepts of "the foregrounding of functions" and "the dominant" of a whole artistic work. These can help us to relate the micro-analysis of the grammar of the language, visual images and sound-track of specific scenes to the way they function in the text of the whole work.

To be really multimodal, I would like to finish with music (No, don't worry, not a song!). It was Walter Pater in his *Giorgione* who claimed that "all art constantly aspires towards the condition of music". I believe this to be true, and would like to claim some artistic status for "Free Hat". Not only is there a strong relationship (through a verbal pun and a political movement) between what one might call Theme 1 (the opposition to the digitalisation and re-release of film classics) and Theme 2 (the support for the release of Hat McCullough), but they intersect in the course of the whole episode in a rhythmic way, with particular characters (instruments) dominating one theme or another. What is more, the rhythm of the modalities of the cartoon (American-spoken dialogue, cartoon layouts, sound effects, music track) is what makes us keep watching and wanting to return. The whole of "Free Hat" charms the viewer with its musical structure and rhythms—and these remain with us after we have laughed at all the jokes.

ACKNOWLEDGMENTS

My son Janek O'Toole has given me invaluable help in selecting the *South Park* episode, in appreciating the characters and humour and in relating the satire to the work of Steven Spielberg and George Lucas. Janek's knowledge of the world of *South Park* and of recent film history is encyclopaedic, and I could not have presented this paper without his constant advice and encouragement.

NOTES

1. From "Free Hat", Episode 609 (i.e. the ninth episode in the sixth season) of the animated cartoon *South Park*. The creator/producers of the series are Trey Parker and Matt Stone. The director of this episode was Toni Nugnes.
2. Scenes from "Cartman Gets an Anal Probe", re-release of Episode 1 *South Park*. The creators of the series are Trey Parker and Matt Stone. The director of this episode was Trey Parker.

REFERENCES

O'Toole, M. (1994) *The Language of Displayed Art*, 1st ed, London: Leicester University Press.
―――― (2010) *The Language of Displayed Art*, 2nd ed, London and New York: Routledge.
Taylor, R., ed. (1982) 'The Poetics of Cinema'. *Russian Poetics in Translation*, Vol. 9 (the Russian original edited by Boris Eikhenbaum: *Poetika kino*, Leningrad: Kinopechat', 1927).

Contributors

JOHN A. BATEMAN

English and Linguistics Department
University of Bremen
Building GW2, A3480, Bibliothekstraße, Bremen, Germany 128359
Phone: +49–421–218–68120
Email: bateman@uni-bremen.de

John A. Bateman is a full Professor of Applied Linguistics in the English and Linguistics Departments of the University of Bremen, specializing in functional, computational and multimodal linguistics. His research interests include functional linguistic approaches to multilingual and multimodal document design, dialogue systems and discourse structure. He has been investigating the relation between language and social context for many years, focusing particularly on accounts of register, genre, functional variation, lexicogrammatical description and theory, multilingual and multimodal linguistic description, and computational instantiations of linguistic theory. He has published widely in all these areas, as well as authoring several introductory and survey articles on natural language generation and systemic-functional linguistics. His current interests centre on the application of functional linguistic and corpus methods to multimodal meaning making, analysing and critiquing multimodal documents of all kinds, the development of linguistically-motivated ontologies, and the construction of computational dialogue systems for robot-human communication.

RODNEY BERRY

Creativity and Cognition Studios
University of Technology, Sydney
1/11 Byron St., Sandy Bay, Tasmania, Australia 7005
Phone: +61–457–086–373 (mobile)
Email: rodberry@gmail.com

Born in Tasmania, Australia in 1963, **Rodney Berry** is a media artist and musician who has spent the last decade as a researcher at various institutions including ATR in Kyoto, National University of Singapore (NUS) and Nanyang Technological University (NTU) in Singapore. Currently, he is a PhD student with the Creativity and Cognition Studios at University of Technology, Sydney as well as an official 'geek-in-residence' at the Salamanca Arts Centre in Hobart, Tasmania. He has been a teacher of composition and sound design on top of his long career as an artist. His work has ranged from sculptural musical instruments and sound installations to computer-based interactive artworks. His interest in artificial life, technology and biology, virtual reality, augmented reality and tangible interfaces, has placed him with one foot in both the artistic community and the scientific community.

VOLKER J. EISENLAUER

Lehrstuhl für Englische Sprachwissenschaft
Universität Augsburg
Universitätsstr.10, Augsburg, Germany 86159
Phone: +49–821–598–5749
Email: volker.eisenlauer@phil.uni-augsburg.de

Volker J. Eisenlauer is an assistant lecturer at the department of English linguistics at the University of Augsburg. His areas of interest include Multimodal Discourse Analysis, Systemic Functional Linguistics and Hypertext Theory. Mr. Eisenlauer received his Master degree in Applied Linguistics from Macquarie University Sydney in 2002 and his M. A. in German Philology from the University of Augsburg in 2004. He is currently writing his Ph.D. thesis on Critical Literacy in Virtual Environments.

FENG DEZHENG

Multimodal Analysis Lab, Interactive & Digital Media Institute (IDMI)
Department of English Language and Literature, Faculty of Arts and
 Social Sciences
National University of Singapore
Blk AS5, 7 Arts Link, Singapore 117570
Phone: +65–8413–9917
Email: fengdezheng@nus.edu.sg

Feng Dezheng is a PhD Research Scholar at the Multimodal Analysis Lab, Interactive & Digital Media Institute, National University of Singapore. His research interests are in multimodality, Systemic Functional Theory and cognitive linguistics. He is especially interested in multimodal media discourse such as news or advertising, analyzing the meaning making of nonverbal resources, such as facial expression, within the SF framework and with theories from cognition, psychology and communication. Currently, he is working on the multimodal construction of emotion, social values and ideology in dynamic film discourse. He has published several papers on SFL, Appraisal Theory and discourse analysis.

ZANE GOEBEL

School of Social Sciences, Faculty of Humanities and Social Sciences
La Trobe University
Bundoora (Melbourne), Victoria, Australia 3086 Phone: +61–3-9479–1396
Email: z.goebel@latrobe.edu.au

Zane Goebel is Senior Lecturer in Indonesian Studies at the School of Social Sciences in the Faculty of Humanities and Social Sciences at La Trobe University, Melbourne. His research interests lie at the nexus of number of disciplines, including anthropology, sociology, education, linguistics, social psychology, history and cultural studies. In particular, he focuses on process of language ideology formation (i.e. Enregisterment), Social Identification, Narrative, Language Socialization, Identity, Migration and Codeswitching in urban, bureaucratic and school settings in Indonesia. His recent publications include: *Migration, Language Choice and Identity: Intercultural Talk in Indonesia* (in press, Cambridge University Press); Semiosis, interaction and ethnicity in urban Java. *Journal of Sociolinguistics* (In press 13/4); Language, Class and Ethnicity in Indonesia (*Bijdragen tot de Taal, Land- en Volkenkunde*); Enregisterment and Appropriation in Javanese-Indonesian Bilingual Talk (*Language in Society*); and Enregistering, Authorizing and Denaturalizing Identity in Indonesia (*Journal of Linguistic Anthropology*).

CAREY JEWITT

London Knowledge Lab and Centre of Multimodal Research, Institute of Education
University of London
20 Bedford Way, London WC1H 0AL
Phone: +44–20–7763–2112
Email: c.jewitt@ioe.ac.uk

Carey Jewitt is a Reader in Education and Technology at the London Knowledge Lab, and Research Director for the Centre of Multimodal Research, Institute of Education, in the University of London. Her research focuses on relationships between representation, technologies and teaching and learning and visual and multimodal research methods and theory. Carey is a co-editor of the journal *Visual Communication*. She has published a number of books on multimodal research and is editor of *The Routledge Handbook of Multimodal Analysis* (2009).

SUN SUN LIM

Communications and New Media Programme, Faculty of Arts and
  Social Sciences
National University of Singapore
Blk AS6, 11 Law Link, #03–11, Singapore 117589
Phone: +65–6516–1175
Email: cnmlss@nus.edu.sg

Sun Sun Lim, PhD (LSE) is Assistant Professor at the Communications and New Media Programme, National University of Singapore. She studies the social implications of technology domestication for young people and families, and new media literacies. She has conducted extensive fieldwork in Asia including in China, Japan, Singapore and South Korea. She has articles published and forthcoming in the *Journal of Computer Mediated Communication, New Media & Society, Communications of the ACM, Asian Journal of Communication* and *Science, Technology and Society*. She is a member of the Internet and Media Advisory Committee which advises Singapore's Media Development Authority on issues relating to new media literacy and media regulation.

CARMEN DANIELA MAIER

Aarhus School of Business, Department of Language and Business
  Communication
Aarhus University
Fuglesangs Allé 4, Aarhus, Denmark 8210
Phone: +45–89486274
E-mail address: cdm@asb.dk

Carmen Daniela Maier, PhD, is Associate Professor and member of the Knowledge Communication Research Group at Aarhus School of Business, Aarhus University, Denmark. She has recently co-edited the thematic section 'Knowledge Communication in a Multimodal Context' in *Hermes. Journal of Language and Communication Studies*. Among her latest publications are the articles 'Multimodal Analysis: An Integrative approach for Scientific Visualizing on the Web' in *Journal of Technical*

Writing and Communication and 'Visual Evaluation in Film Trailers' in *Visual Communication*. Her current research focuses on the multi-modal communication of knowledge and on the analysis of environmental discourses.

SITI NURHARNANI NAHAR

Communications and New Media Programme, Faculty of Arts and
 Social Sciences
National University of Singapore
Blk AS6, 11 Law Link, #03–15, Singapore 117589
Phone: +65–6516–3019 / +65–9876–1217
E-mail: cnmsnn@nus.edu.sg

Siti Nurharnani Nahar is a teaching assistant at the Communications and New Media programme, National University of Singapore. To date, she has taught various undergraduate courses—*Principles of Visual Communications, Media and Globalization, Advertising Strategies,* as well as *Theories of Communication and New Media.* Her research focuses on the impact of new media on young people. She is particularly interested in studies on health communications, credibility, multimodality and literacy. Prior to academia, she worked in the marketing and communications department in the private sector. During that period, she also served as panel member of the Film Consultative Panel (Singapore), which advises the Media Development Authority on issues relating to controversial films.

ELMIE NEKMAT

College of Communications and Information Sciences
University of Alabama
P.O. Box 870172, 478 Reese Phifer Hall
Tuscaloosa, Al 35487–0172
E-mail: mbnekmat@crimson.ua.edu

Elmie Nekmat is currently a PhD candidate in Advertising and Public Relations at the College of Communications and Information Sciences, University of Alabama. He had completed his B.Soc.Sci (Hons) and M.A. at the Communications and New Media programme, National University of Singapore. His research interests include youths' popular use and adoption of new media technologies, and their media literacy pertaining to these technologies. Further pertaining to his interests in youths in the networked society, Elmie was Singapore's youth delegate to the

Association of South East Asian Nations' (ASEAN) 2009 strategic seminar on using ICT to foster regional spirit amongst youth. He is currently working on research looking at the use and impact of social media in public communication practices by organizations.

KAY L. O'HALLORAN

Multimodal Analysis Lab, Interactive & Digital Media Institute (IDMI)
Department of English Language and Literature, Faculty of Arts and
  Social Sciences
National University of Singapore
Blk AS5, 7 Arts Link, Singapore 117570
Phone: +65–6516–3912
Email: kay.ohalloran@nus.edu.sg

Kay L. O'Halloran is Director of the Multimodal Analysis Lab, Interactive & Digital Media Institute (IDMI) and Associate Professor in the Department of English Language & Literature at the National University of Singapore. Kay O'Halloran is an internationally recognised scholar in multimodal research and she has given plenary addresses on multimodal approaches to mathematics and science and the use of digital technology for multimodal analysis at many international conferences. Her publications include *Multimodal Discourse Analysis* (2004) and *Mathematical Discourse: Language, Symbolism and Visual Images* (2006), in addition to numerous journal articles and book chapters. Kay O'Halloran is Principal Investigator for several large projects in the Multimodal Analysis Lab (see http://multimodal-analysis-lab.org/).

MICHAEL O'TOOLE

Communication Studies
Murdoch University, Western Australia
20A, Holmes St., Shelley, Perth Western Australia 6148
Phone: +61-8-9457-3381
Email: L.otoole@murdoch.edu.au

Lawrence Michael O'Toole (b.30.03.1934) is Emeritus Professor of Communication Studies, Murdoch University, Perth, Western Australia 6150 L.otoole@murdoch.edu.au. He was educated at Chichester High School and Oxford University, (1954–1957): M.A. in Russian Language and Literature. He taught Russian at Liverpool and Essex Universities and wrote and broadcast two Russian Language courses on the BBC

(1966–69). He was founder of the Neo-Formalist Circle (1971–2006) and founder editor (with Ann Shukman) of Russian Poetics in Translation (1973–82). He was a Fulbright Scholar at the University of Virginia and Claremont Graduate School (1977–78). Moving to the Chair of Communication Studies at Murdoch University in 1981, he taught systemic linguistics, stylistics, narratology and semiotics. His books include *The Gateway Russian Song Book* (1962), *Structure, Style and Interpretation in the Russian Short Story* (1982), *Functions of Style* (ed. with David Birch, 1988), *The Language of Displayed Art* (1994) and the CD ROM *Engaging With Art* (1999). Retired since 2000, he is still writing and giving conference papers on multimodality and the arts of painting, sculpture and architecture.

BRADLEY A. SMITH

2/2 Kempsey Close, Dee Why, New South Wales, Australia 2099
Phone: +61–2-99841894
E-mail: semiosmith@gmail.com

Bradley A. Smith is an independent researcher, external collaborator with and former Research Fellow at the Multimodal Analysis Laboratory at the National University of Singapore. He is responsible for the integration of the phonic semiotic resources—such as intonational resources, music and other aural aspects such as sound effects—into the software applications being developed by the lab team. Bradley completed his Bachelor of Arts degree at Macquarie University (Sydney Australia) where he graduated with 1st Class Honours in 2004. In 2008, he completed his PhD thesis, entitled Intonational Systems and Register: A Multidimensional Exploration.

THEO VAN LEEUWEN

Dean, Faculty of Arts and Social Sciences
University of Technology, Sydney
PO Box 123, Broadway New South Wales, Australia 2007
Phone: +61–2-9514–3930
Email: theo.vanleeuwen@uts.edu.au

Theo van Leeuwen is Professor of Media and Communication and Dean of the Faculty of Arts and Social Sciences at the University of Technology, Sydney. He has published widely in the areas of social semiotics, critical discourse analysis and multimodality. His books include *Reading Images—The Grammar of Visual Design* (with Gunther Kress), *Speech,*

Music, Sound, Introducing Social Semiotics, Global Media Discourse (with David Machin) and *Discourse and Practice—New Tools for Critical Discourse Analysis*. He is a founding editor of the international journal *Visual Communication*.

EIJA VENTOLA

Department of Communication, School of Economics
Aalto University
PO Box 21210 (Runeberginkatu 14–16), FI-00076 Aalto, Finland
Phone: +358-(0)40–3538208 (mobile)
Email: eija.ventola@aalto.fi

Eija Ventola has recently been appointed to a professorship in Business Communication at Aalto University, School of Economics (previously Helsinki School of Economics), Finland. Her major areas of research are business language, multimodal and -medial discourse analysis, intercultural communication and contrastive linguistics, functional linguistics, text linguistics, discourse analysis, academic discourse. She has written many internationally published articles in these areas, and she is a co-editor of such recent publications as Interpersonal Communication, Vol. 2 of *Handbooks of Applied Linguistics* (2008 Mouton de Gruyter), *From Language to Multimodality: New developments in the study of ideational meaning* (2008 Equinox) and *The World Told and the World Shown* (2009, Palgrave).

PETER WIGNELL

Head, Academic Skills Development Unit
Southern Cross University
Lismore, New South Wales, Australia 2480
Phone: +61-2-6626–9635
E-mail: peter.wignell@scu.edu.au

Peter Wignell is Head of the Academic Skills Development Unit at Southern Cross University. He was previously a Visiting Senior Fellow in the Department of English Language and Literature at the National University of Singapore. Peter has been teaching and researching in Systemic Functional Linguistics and in the applications of SFL to education since 1985. His principal field of research has been in the role of language in the construction of specialized language. More recently he has been researching multisemiotic texts, in particular the relationships between words and images in books for very young children.

LONCE WYSE

Arts and Creativity Lab, Interactive Digital Media Institute (IDMI)
Communications and New Media Programme
National University of Singapore
Blk AS6, #03–41, 11 Computing Drive, Singapore 117416
Phone: +65–6516–7277
Email: cnmwll@nus.edu.sg

Lonce Wyse (b. 1960) wrote his first electroacoustic work in 1974. He studied composition at Interlochen Arts Academy and Oberlin Conservatory, and received a BS in Math and Computer Science, and a Ph.D. in 1994 from Boston University in Cognitive and Neural Systems. He spent a year in Taiwan on a Fulbright Scholarship building computational models of pitch perception before settling in Singapore where he directed research in interactive sound modeling at the Institute for Infocomm Research. In 2006 he joined the National University of Singapore as an Associate Professor of Communications and New Media, and teaches courses on Sonic Arts and Sciences and on New Media Aesthetics. He also directs the Arts and Creativity Lab at the Interactive and Digital Media Institute, where current research includes networked ensembles, sound interaction, and listening strategies for Electroacoustic music.

Authors Index

Subject Index